SERMONS ON
OLD TESTAMENT CHARACTERS

Rev. CLOVIS G. CHAPPELL, D.D.

SERMONS ON OLD TESTAMENT CHARACTERS

BY

REV. CLOVIS G. CHAPPELL, D.D.

HARPER & BROTHERS PUBLISHERS

NEW YORK AND LONDON

CONTENTS

SERMONS ON
OLD TESTAMENT CHARACTERS

SERMONS ON OLD TESTAMENT CHARACTERS

I

THE VOLUNTEER—ISAIAH

Isaiah 6:8

"Then said I, here am I; send me."

This "then" is a backward looking word. It looks away from the effect to the cause. It looks away from the stream to the fountain far among the hills. "Then," declares the prophet, "life for me took on a new departure. Then a moral revolution was wrought within my soul. Then I entered the service of the Lord Almighty. Then I became a volunteer in the army of the King of kings."

I

To what event does this "then" point?

Suppose I should say: "Then the skies were touched with rosy fingers of light. Then the hilltops grew golden with glory. Then the dewdrops upon the grasses glittered like a million jewels. Then the awakened birds burst into song. Then the working world went with light and leaden feet to its toil." When would you think that this wonderful transformation took place? You could not help knowing that it took place when the day dawned. It took place when the radiant "morning came singing over the sea."

Again if I should say: "Then the winter-stripped trees put on their verdant foliage. Then the lawn grew beautiful with a carpet of green. Then the robin returned with its breast of sunshine and its song of joy. Then the violets lifted up their modest faces. Then the staid old apple tree decked itself more charmingly than a June bride. Then the south wind became as soft as the breath of an infant and as caressing as the hands of a mother. Then

'Every clod felt a stir of might,
An instinct within it that reaches and towers,
And groping blindly above it for light,
Climbed to a soul in the grasses and flowers.' "

Here again you could not but guess the event to which this "then" of my story is pointing. When did all this take place? It took place at the coming of springtime. No other cause could work such a gladsome transformation.

Now, this "then" on the lips of Isaiah points to an event that brought the dawning of a new day to him. It points to a vision that brought him out of winter into spiritual springtime. And what that event was is made very plain. Even if it were not, I am thinking that there would not be one of us that could not guess. "Isaiah, what was it that brought to you the dawning of a new day? How did you get out of dead winter into living spring?" This is his answer: "I saw the Lord." Isaiah's transformation was the result of a vision of the Lord Jesus Christ.

And, mark you, we cannot account for Isaiah apart

from this vision. We can no more do so than we can account for a similar transformation in a million other lives. There were many reasons against this gifted young man's ever becoming a prophet. One great hindrance was the fact that Isaiah was a man of high social position. He was at home in kings' palaces. And it was true then, as it is true still, that "not many mighty, not many noble are called." God longs for the rich and privileged just as much as He does for the poor and unprivileged. But how rare it is to find one of these willing to break from the golden fetters that bind him to become a free man in the service of God.

Isaiah was one of these few. He refused to allow either his wealth or his position to stand in the way of his volunteering for the service of the King. No doubt his conduct was a disappointment to many who hoped for great things for him in the political arena. No doubt his decision excited the ridicule and scorn of some who had not seen his vision and who had not come to share in his great dreams.

"Gilded galley slaves of mammon,
How my purse-proud brothers taunt me.
I might have been as well to do as they
Had I clutched like them my chances,
Learned their wisdom, crushed my fancies,
Starved my soul and gone to business every day."

II

How did Isaiah come to see this vision of Jesus Christ? (For John tells us that it was Jesus that Isaiah saw.)

Let it be understood at once that he did not come to this experience by mere accident, nor did he come to it because he was a child of good fortune. Jesus Christ is ready to make himself just as real to you and to me as He did to Isaiah. We may see Him if we will, just as truly as did Isaiah in the long ago. All of us do not come to this vision by the same road. But the road is not the matter of supreme importance. The matter of supreme importance is the vision itself, the coming face to face with Jesus Christ.

How, then, did Isaiah come to this vision? We have the answer from his own lips: "In the year that King Uzziah died I saw also the Lord sitting upon a throne, high and lifted up, and His train filled the temple." This does not simply set a date, as others have pointed out. It rather tells the occasion of Isaiah's vision. Up to this time Isaiah had had his gaze fixed upon Uzziah. This king had been his hero and his hope. He was the greatest king that had held the throne since Solomon. He had been mightily helped, the record tells us, till he was strong.

Now, as often happens, the success of Uzziah went to his head. He became intoxicated with it. He became inflated with pride. One day, under the spell of his pride, he went into the Temple and stretched forth his hands to a holy task that God had reserved for others. He was smitten with leprosy. The fatal disease dragged him from the palace to the pest house. It wrenched the scepter from his hand. It tore the crown from his brow. It flung him out into the grave. And now the throne is vacant and Isaiah's heart is broken and his hope all but dead.

Under the burden of this great sorrow, Isaiah went into the Temple. Goaded on by the agony of his great need, he turned his eyes away from the throne that had been left vacant by Uzziah tc the throne of heaven that is forever occupied by the King Eternal. It was then that he saw the Lord, high and lifted up. Not that the Lord had just recently taken that position. The Lord had been there all the time waiting to reveal himself. But Isaiah had not looked His way. He had to have his heart broken before he could be induced to look.

Such has been the experience of many. It is possible for us to win our way into the presence of Jesus in the days of our health and worldly prosperity. There is absolutely no time when we may not find Him if we are only willing to seek for Him. But the trouble with us is that often we are so satisfied with the secondary, with the passing, with the things of a day that we do not seek Him. Too often we require a bit of heartbreak to make us turn our eyes to our ever present Saviour. Thus it was in the year that your baby died, in the year that you lost your wealth, in the year that your health was shattered, in the year that you turned from a new made grave,—it was then that you saw the Lord.

I know a woman whose face is beautifully radiant and out of whose eyes looks "the peace of a great discovery." Her influence pervades the community in which she lives like a rare and rich perfume. Friends seek her in joy and in sorrow, and "deeds of week-day holiness fall from her as noiselessly as the snow." But she has not always been like this. I knew her when as a Christian she was the weakest of the weak. How did the change come about? One day a great sorrow came. One day a compelling need put its heavy hands upon her two shoulders and crushed her to her knees. It was in this hour that she saw the Lord, high and lifted up.

"There, little girl, don't cry!
They have broken your doll, I know;
And your teaset blue and your playhouse too
Are things of the long ago.
But childish griefs will soon pass by,
There, there, little girl, don't cry!

There, little girl, don't cry!
They have broken your slate, I know;
And the glad, wild ways of your schoolhood days
Are things of the long ago.
But life and love will soon come by,
There, there, little girl, don't cry!

There, little girl, don't cry!
They have broken your heart, I know;
And the rainbow gleams of your youthful dreams
Are the things of the long ago.
But heaven holds all for which you sigh,
There, there, little girl, don't cry!"

III

What was the outcome of this vision?

1. It brought to Isaiah a sense of sin. "I saw the Lord," we hear him say. And what follows? "Then said I, woe is me! for I am undone; because I am a man of unclean lips, and I dwell in the midst of a people of unclean lips: for mine eyes have seen the King, the Lord of hosts." A sense of God always brings a sense of sin. Job had profound faith in his own goodness. But all this vanished in the presence of God. "I have heard of Thee by the hearing of the ear. But now that mine eye seeth Thee, I abhor myself in dust and ashes." No man ever sees himself in the light of the divine countenance that he is not led to cry: "Unclean."

On the other hand, there is nothing more true than that where there is no sense of sin there is no sense of God. Here is a man going through a form of prayer. "God, I thank thee that I am not as other men. I fast twice in the week. I give tithes of all I possess." What is the secret of this self-congratulation? Is this Pharisee holy beyond his fellows? No. The reason that he is offering this pathetic travesty on prayer is that he has a good eye on himself and a bad eye on his brother, and no eye on God at all. He is as unconscious of God as a mole deeply burrowed in the earth is unconscious of the sun. We need no better proof that a man has no sense of God than just the fact that he has no sense of sin.

2. This vision led Isaiah to confess his sin. Not only did a sense of his awful uncleanness dawn upon him in the light of the divine countenance, but he was led to pour out his confession into the ear of Christ. He put his sin-soiled lips in the dust and confessed that he was unclean. He had absolutely no good word to say for himself. He did not tell the Lord how honest and upright and clean he had been in times past. He did not offer any excuses. He laid no claim to anything of moral worth. He sobbed out the confession of his spiritual bankruptcy: "I am a man of unclean lips and I dwell in the midst of a people with unclean lips."

3. The third result of this vision was cleansing. In presence of Christ, Isaiah saw his sin and confessed it. And what took place as he confessed? "Then flew one of the Seraphim unto me, having a live coal in his hand, which he had taken with the tongs from off the altar. And he laid it upon my mouth and said, Lo, this hath touched thy lips; and thine iniquity is taken away and thy sin purged." No sooner had this man

made his confession of uncleanness than there came to him cleansing at the hand of God. For it was true then, as it is true to-day, "if we confess our sins, He is faithful and just to forgive us our sins and to cleanse us from all unrighteousness."

4. The final result of this vision was that Isaiah found and accepted his task. To this man, conscious of the forgiving love of God, there came a call to service. "And I heard the voice of the Lord saying, Whom shall I send and who will go for us?" How this call came we do not know. It may have come through the still small voice of the Spirit speaking within his heart. It may have come through his consciousness of his peoples' need and of his conviction that he had discovered an adequate remedy for their need. But this at least we know: Isaiah was made certain that the God who had cleansed him was in need of him, was appealing to him for help.

To this appeal Isaiah did not turn a deaf ear. His heroic response comes to us to-night like a trumpet call to battle: "Then said I, here am I, send me." He made the matter personal. Without consulting flesh and blood he put himself unreservedly into the hands of his Lord. And how mightily did God use him. For more than fifty years he was the supreme spiritual voice of his nation. And even to-day he is God's spokesman to every one who has ears to hear.

To-night the scene is transferred from the far off temple in Jerusalem to this church in which we now worship. Times and outward conditions have greatly changed. But the same Christ is here and He is making the same appeal to us that He made to Isaiah. He is calling to His friends, calling through their love to Him, through their sense of gratitude, through the needs of a shattered and broken world: "Whom shall I send, and who will go for us?" We must make Isaiah's manly response or the world cannot be saved.

Though Christ is calling to those who already know Him, He is calling no less urgently to those who are strangers to Him. Think not that you have to pass through an experience like this of Isaiah before He will accept you. "He receiveth sinners." He invites all men to enlist under His banner. Come to Him without knowing Him, and He will reveal Himself to you. Come to Him with all your sins and He will cleanse you and trust you and use you for His glory. His appeal is to every man. Therefore, it is every man's privilege to say: "Here am I, send me."

II

THE LURE OF THE WILDERNESS—JEREMIAH

Jeremiah 9:2

"O that I had in the wilderness a lodging place of
wayfaring men; that I might leave my people and go
from them! for they be all adulterers, an assembly
of treacherous men."

This longing to leave his people expressed by Jeremiah is altogether human. Jeremiah is not the only
preacher that ever wanted to change his appointment.
He is not the only worker that ever wanted to throw
down his task and get away. Many of us have uttered
this same cry. This is what the Psalmist was saying
long ago: "Oh that I had wings like a dove, for then
would I fly away and be at rest." There are some
who begin to utter this longing in their very youth and
it grows more intense as they get deeper into the years
and life becomes more serious with its baptisms of tears
—tears over losses and tears over bitter disappointments.

I

Why did Jeremiah wish to get away?
1. He wished to escape an unpleasant task. He
loved the country. But the wilderness lured him at
present because it offered him a refuge from the tem-
pestuous life of the city. God had called Jeremiah to
be a prophet. In response to that call he had entered

bravely upon his task. But he had not done so willingly. When Isaiah was called he responded with
eagerness: "Here am I, send me." His work seems a
joy. He meets his conflicts with a noble zest. But not
so Jeremiah. He protests and shrinks and begs to be
excused. "Ah, Lord God! behold I cannot speak, for I
am a child."

But in spite of his shrinking and in spite of all pro-
testations of his unfitness, the task is forced upon him.
Therefore he is now in the limelight, though the glare
of it offends him. He is in the midst of turmoil and
conflict, though he is a lover of peace and quiet. He is
forced to fight and contend, though the whole business
is hateful to him. "Alas, my mother, that thou hast
borne me a man of contention and strife to the whole
world." He is traveling the prophet's road, but his feet
bleed at every step that he takes. Therefore, it is only
natural that he should want to leave his people and hie
away to the wilderness.

Not only was the task of being a prophet distasteful
to Jeremiah because of his peculiar temperament. His
natural dislike was greatly increased on account of the
kind of congregation to which he had to preach. His
work brought him into daily contact with men whose
association was entirely disagreeable. He was a clean,
high-souled and sensitive idealist. Therefore, it was
no little agony to be compelled to work constantly with
men for whom he could find no more complimentary
description than adulterers, traitors, slanderers, for-
sakers of God. It is not a matter of wonder, therefore,
that he should want to leave such an uncongenial congregation and flee into the wilderness.

It has never been my lot to serve but one church
that was thoroughly disagreeable. This congregation

was not so far gone as the congregation to which Jeremiah preached. But they were not altogether the type to win a pastor's heart. I recall with appreciation what my predecessor said to them in his farewell sermon. "This is," said he, "my last message. I wish to remark in closing that if everything is true about your former pastors that you have said about them, every one of them ought to be turned out of the Church. If everything is true of you that you have told me about one another, the last one of you ought to be hanged. We will receive the benediction." And he departed with some of the joy that I think Jeremiah would have felt could he have escaped to that longed for lodging place for wayfaring men.

Then Jeremiah's task was made the more difficult and distasteful to him because his ministry had to be almost altogether a ministry of denunciation and of doom. He would have been delighted to say the pleasing thing and the complimentary thing. He would have been most glad to be a preacher of hope and a prophet of optimism. But his unrepentant and sinful people made it impossible. He was far too sincere to cry "Peace! peace!" when he knew there was no peace. He saw far too clearly to be blind to the fact that punishment must inevitably follow sin. While others were declaring that God would save His people under any circumstances, he was forced to declare that unless they repented they should be driven into exile. "What else can I do?" he has God asking. He knows that no nation can be "saved materially unless it is redeemed spiritually."

2. Jeremiah wanted to get away from persecution. The type of preaching that he was forced to do did not tend to make him popular. It did not win the applause and appreciation of his people. On the con-

trary, it made him exceedingly unpopular. It brought to him bitter opposition and persecution. At times that persecution took the form of cold neglect. When his sermon was over folks did not come forward and congratulate him and tell him how they enjoyed it, as you tell your pastor. They chilled him by their neglect and froze him by their lack of sympathy. There is the sob of a sensitive and deeply wounded heart in the cry: "I sat alone because of the wrath of God." He was weighed down by the burden of a great loneliness.

But there were other times when the persecution he suffered took another form. Sometimes he was ridiculed. He complains that he is made a laughing stock all the day. And what a heavy burden that is! There are few things harder to bear than to have folks laugh at you, scorn you, pass you by in contempt as a mere fanatic. When his book of prophecies was put into the hands of the king, this pathetic substitute for royalty showed no slightest appreciation. On the contrary, he made plain his contempt for the old prophet by taking his penknife and cutting the roll to pieces and burning it in the fire.

Then there were times when yet sterner forms of persecution were used. One day he was stoned out of his native village as if he were a wild street dog. At other times we find him suffering the pain and shame of the stocks. On another day his back was bared to the smiters and he had to undergo the agony and humiliation of being publicly whipped. He became thoroughly acquainted with the inside of prisons. One time he comes before us with hands and feet stained with stenchful mud, for he has been starving at the bottom of an old well. And though he was rescued, this was not wrought by any friend of his. It was not the work of any member of his congregation. It was the work of a negro slave who was too humane to see the old man die by the inch. Therefore, we are not going to blame him if again and again he wished to leave his people and flee into the wilderness.

3. He wanted to leave because his ministry seemed an utter failure.

No man, I think, ever preached with more passionate earnestness than did Jeremiah. He warned men night and day with tears. But his warnings were unheeded. His report was not believed. No man ever had a more fruitless ministry in his own day than did this prophet. It is hard enough to keep climbing when you are approaching nearer and nearer the summit. It is hard enough to keep fighting when victory is coming closer and closer. But to keep climbing when the summit seems to retreat from you and to keep fighting when victory becomes more and more remote, that is difficult indeed.

And remember that the pain of Jeremiah's failure was not the result of the sense of his own inability to win. The agony that he suffered over it was not born of the humiliation that it brought to him. His failure was inseparably connected with the failure of his people. His inability to reach them and to win them to repentance meant, so far as his own day was concerned, that his ministry had gone for nothing. But what was far harder to bear, it meant the loss and utter ruin of the people he loved. To stay by, therefore, meant not only the pain of toiling at a fruitless task, but the yet greater pain of watching the approaching death of the nation that he loved better than he loved his own life. His yearning to be permitted to leave has in it something of the shrinking agony of heartbroken Hagar as

she cries: "Let me not witness the death of my child!"
He wanted to get away from a ministry whose failure
meant not only his personal inability to win, but the yet
more bitter heartache of watching his nation die.

II

Did Jeremiah leave?
No, he did not. He was eager to go, yet he stayed.
He yearned to run, yet he remained steadfast. He felt
the lure of the wilderness and yet he remained amidst
the turmoil and toil of the city. And this he did not
because of any physical compulsion. He might have
gone time and again, and his own people would have
been glad to have him go. But in spite of the hatred
of his people and his own shrinking from his task, he
stood in his place and remained true for more than
forty long, weary years.

III

Why did Jeremiah stay?
1. He remained steadfast from a sense of duty. The
same bonds held him that held Paul. "Behold, I go
bound in spirit unto Jerusalem not knowing the things
that shall befall me there save that the Holy Ghost wit-
nesseth in every city saying that bonds and afflictions
abide me." He stayed at his post because he felt that he
ought to stay. When he uttered this cry, he knew that
leaving for him was an impossibility. "Oh that I might
leave." But what is implied is "I cannot. I must
stay."
"I must." That is a word that is frequently found
in the vocabulary of moral giants. "Oh, that I might

go," he said, "but I must stay. This I must do simply
because it is my duty." Now there may not be so much
of gush and of glow in a declaration of this kind as we
would like. But surely you will agree that such a sense
of duty is sorely needed to-day. Entirely too many of
us let ourselves off with the doing of the easy or the
pleasant. We listen for the voice of a shallow emo-
tionalism. And failing to hear it, we give heed to the
voice of laziness and indifference. We face the work
we ought to do asking too often how we feel and too sel-
dom what is our duty. Jeremiah listened to the voice
of duty. Hence he did the thing he ought to do whether
he felt like it or not.

2. Jeremiah was bound to his post by the cords of a
mighty conviction. He was absolutely sure of the truth
of the message that God had given him to deliver. The
fact that men refused to give heed did not in any sense
lead him to doubt the truth of his message. There were
times when it made it hard for him to preach. There
were times when he even resolved to keep utter silence.
But this resolution was soon shattered because the Word
of God was as a burning fire shut up in his bones.
Silence became unendurable. Under the pressure of an
irresistible conviction he felt himself compelled to
speak. He was convinced, in spite of the fact that his
message was being rejected, that its acceptance was his
people's only hope.

There were many other prophets at that time, but
their messages differed widely from the message of
Jeremiah. They were prophets of an easy and senti-
mental optimism. They came with the popular cry of
"Peace! peace!" upon their lips. But Jeremiah saw a
different vision. He was as sure of God's love as the
other prophets, but he did not forget the fact that as

intensely as God loved His people, just so intensely did
He hate their sin. He said with terrible clearness that
if they did not repent, if they did not turn from their
idolatry and adultery, God would be compelled to fling
them out of His sight regardless of His love. He was
gripped by the conviction that there was no safety for
the individual nor for the nation without righteousness.
Therefore, it is not to be wondered at that he remained
to shriek his message into the ears of his people when he
saw them hugging to themselves the damning delusion
that God would save them even in their rebellion and in
their mad clinging to their iniquities. This conviction
that he had a message that offered his nation its one
hope of salvation caused him to stand by his post when
he fain would have fled to the restful and easeful life
of the wilderness.

That same conviction should steady us. Is it a fact
that we have all sinned and come short of the glory of
God? Is it a fact that there is no other name under
heaven given among men whereby we must be saved?
Is it a fact that He is able to save unto the uttermost
them that come unto God by Him? Do you know
these facts? Do you accept them as facts? Then you
must preach them. It is not a question of whether men
applaud or hiss you. It is not a question of whether they
throw mud at you or throw bouquets at you. We must
speak the truth as God gives us to see it. To refuse is
to spit in the face of conviction and throw away your
crown.

3. Then Jeremiah was held to his task by the cords
of love.

These Jews had in them much that pained and
grieved and disgusted and even angered this prophet.
But in spite of all their sins he loved them still. They

were still his people.   And though they fill him with
indignation and though he declares he is full of the fury
of the Lord against them, yet his heart is in their keeping and he cannot for the life of him turn away from
them.   Often his words scorch and blister and burn.
Often his cheeks are flushed and his eyes are fiery with
anger.   Yet his heart is always full of love.

And do not think it strange that this prophet can be
intensely angry and intensely loving at the same time.
Love and anger are not in the least inconsistent.
In fact, his anger was born of his love.   If he
had not loved he would not have raged.   If he had not
loved he would have gone complacently to the wilderness in perfect and broadminded good humor.   That
is the secret of much that passes for tolerance to-day.
It is merely utter indifference parading in the borrowed
garments of tolerance.

Personally, I believe that it would be a distinct gain
if some of us had more capacity for anger.   Now I do
not mean that particular type of anger that is the result of selfishness; that anger that you felt when you
were not the principal speaker or did not get invited
to the party.   I mean the anger that comes to a morally
sound man when right is trodden under the foot of
might, when justice is made the victim of injustice.
Jeremiah had a great capacity for anger.   His words
are hot and burning words to this day.   No man ever
rebuked more unsparingly, and the secret of it is that
no man ever loved more tenderly.   Therefore, though
he shrieks at his congregation in white-heat anger, he
stays with them until the very last because he is in the
grip of a love that will not let him go.

4.   Then Jeremiah remained at his post through the
power of God.

From what the Lord said to Jeremiah, it is evident
that he was not by nature a staunch and courageous
man. He was sensitive and timid and retiring. But
God promised him in the very beginning that He would
stand close for help. "Thou, therefore, gird up thy
loins, and arise, and speak unto them all that I command thee. Be not dismayed at their faces. . . . For,
behold, I have made thee this day a defensed city, and
an iron pillar, and brazen walls against the whole land.
. . . And they shall fight against thee; but they shall
not prevail against thee, for I am with thee, saith the
Lord, to deliver thee."

There is absolutely no accounting for the steadfastness of Jeremiah apart from this promise. As He in
later years changed fluctuating Simon, the son of Jona,
into a rock of Christlike character, so He turned Jeremiah into the opposite of what he was. This He did
not independent of the prophet. He was able to do so
because Jeremiah was a man constant and earnest in
prayer. He opened the windows of his soul toward
God and the Spirit of the Almighty came in and made
him strong. In all the Scriptures I know of no finer
example of the power of God to equip a man for the
performance of a task that in the energy of the flesh
was absolutely impossible. Surely this man learned
long before St. Paul of the sufficiency of the grace of
God.

IV

What was the outcome?

So far as his own generation was concerned, Jeremiah
lived and died almost an utter failure. When his nation was in ruins, the last handful of Jews that were

left consulted him as to whether they should stay in their own land or flee into Egypt. He took the matter before the Lord and obtained an answer. He told them upon divine authority to remain in their own land. But in spite of his warning they fled into Egypt and carried the protesting and broken-hearted prophet with them. In Egypt he spent his last tearful days. Here he went on denouncing the sin of his wayward people. Here he died, and here his ashes rest in a nameless grave. And his ministry continued a failure to the very end. Not one bit even of "sunset success" was granted to him.

But if he failed to be heard in his own generation, he has been heard by the subsequent centuries. His influence upon his own people has possibly been greater than that of any other of the prophets. But his influence has by no means been confined to his own nation. He has put his passionate hands upon all the continents. We feel the uplift of his Spirit-filled personality as we meet in God's house to-day. And I dare to believe that as this redeemed saint looks back upon life from the midst of that innumerable company that have washed their robes and made them white in the blood of the Lamb, he sees of the travail of his soul and is satisfied.

III

IN HIS PLACE—EZEKIEL

Ezekiel 3:15

"I sat where they sat."

I

God has called Ezekiel to be a prophet. He is to hear God's message and warn men from Him. His congregation is made up of a company of exiles. They are the fragments of a shattered nation. They are the remnants of broken homes. They are people who have suffered. They have seen the fading of great hopes. They have witnessed the blight of bright promises. They have lost their possessions. Many have lost their loved ones. Some have lost their God. Ezekiel was sent, therefore, to a congregation acquainted with grief, to a people whose eyes were blinded with tears.

For this difficult task the prophet needed a special preparation. He needed a peculiar training. To what school did God send him? To what seminary did he go to obtain his education for this high and trying task? He was not sent into retirement. The school of solitude is often good and helpful. But it was not the school in which Ezekiel was prepared for his task. He went and sat down among the people to whom he was to minister. "I sat where they sat." He looked out upon the world through their eyes. He bled through their wounds. He wept in their tears.

II

A like preparation is needed by ourselves.

1. We need it in our international relationships. How different our history would have been if we had learned this long ago! Had we done so, the supreme tragedies of human history would have been averted. Had we done so, our rivers would not have so often run red with blood. Our continents would not have again and again been billowed by graves. Had we done so, the flower of our youth would not have been offered upon the altar of sacrifice. Had we done so, we should not have squandered treasure untold to gain nothing in return except broken homes and broken hearts and blasted ideals. What a difference it would make in to-morrow if each nation should learn to put itself in the other nation's place! Then truly we would beat our swords into plowshares and our spears into pruning hooks and learn war no more.

2. What a revolution this would work in our industrial relationships! Suppose capital should put itself in the place of labor and labor put itself in the place of capital. Suppose the employer should sit in the seat of the employee and the employee in the seat of the employer. Then there would be a rivalry in serving and not in being served. Then there would be competition in helpfulness and not in being helped. Then there would be a struggle in the high task of giving and not simply in the mean task of getting.

3. Then how helpful this would be in our relationships one with another. How looks the world from the windows of the sick room? How does it look to him whose every breath is a breath of pain? How does it look to him who knows he will never be well

again? How does it look to the one who is imprisoned by disease and who knows he will never go out from the narrow precincts of the sick room until he passes out to the yet narrower house in the cemetery? How, I wonder, does life look to the hopeless sufferer, to him whose every day is spent in Gethsemane? We who are strong and well need sometime to put ourselves in the place of the sick.

We who are older need to sit in the seat of the youth. How does it seem to be young—

> "To feel the wild pulsations
> That we felt before the strife,
> When we heard our days before us
> And the tumult of our life?"

How seems it to be young? What is the thrill of its intoxicating madness? What is the ecstasy of climbing Fool's Hill? Some of us older ones have forgotten. Therefore, we are out of sympathy and out of touch with the youth of our homes and of our church. We need to sit in the place of the growing boy. We need to take the seat of that young girl,—

> "Standing with reluctant feet
> Where the brook and river meet,
> Womanhood and childhood fleet."

Then youth, if possible, needs to sit in the seat of the aged. How seems it to be old? How does life look when the elasticity has gone out of the step and the last feather of the raven's wing has fallen from the hair? Maybe you who are old can remember something of the wild beating of your heart when for the first time you put on your armor for the fight. Maybe you can remember the thrill of hearing the sound of the conflict

from beyond the hills when you were making your first stab at life. Maybe you can recall the wild beauty of the landscape seen through the sparkling eyes of youth. But how looks it through the eyes of old age? How looks it to him who has wept over many a grief and many a grave? How looks it to the man who is not buckling on his armor, but is putting it off from a body that has had many a thrust and bears many a scar? How looks the world through aged eyes? Oh, we do not know, many of us. If we did we might be kinder to these aged bodies that are about us.

The man of opportunity needs to sit in the seat of the unprivileged. The intellectually trained needs to look through the cobwebbed, smoke-begrimed, dirt-darkened windows of the ignorant. You sit quite comfortably among the cultured and refined. How fares it with you when you are called to sit among the crude and the unschooled? I saw a thoughtless young man of polish inflict a sore wound upon an unlettered man the other day. And the man so wounded was old enough to be his grandfather. This young man did not mean to be cruel. He simply did not have heart enough and imagination enough to put himself in the other man's place.

We need to sit in the place of those who are socially unprivileged. I believe we sorely need at times to put ourselves in the place of the black man that is among us. He has not had our opportunities. He is fresh from the night of barbarism. It is a Christian rule that to whom little is given, of him shall little be required, and to whom much is given, of him shall much be required. But we require more of this unprivileged man than we do of the privileged. We punish his crimes

with a severity with which we do not punish the crimes
of him who has had a far better opportunity. And it
is my firm conviction that the frown of the Christ, who
ever took the part of the weak, is utterly against such
conduct.

Then it would help to try to get a glimpse of the world
through the eyes of the outcast. What is the outlook
of the prodigal? How does life look to the man who is
amidst the stench and the filth and the black hopelessness of the swine pen? How looks life to him who has
squandered his birthright, who has disinherited himself? How does he feel who has become a moral bank-
rupt? What is the outlook of him who not only despises
himself, but knows himself to be despised by others?
How does it feel to be weighted with the damning conviction,—"No man cares for my soul?"

Do you, sweet and pure and protected mothers and
daughters, have any conception of how life looks to her
who has thrown herself away? What does the world
look like seen through the bloodshot and tear-dimmed
eyes of her who is but a soiled rag of womanhood?
What is the feeling of her who has nothing better to say
for herself than—

> "Once I was pure as the snow, but I fell,
> Fell like the snow, but from heaven to hell,
> Fell to be trampled as filth of the street,
> Fell to be scoffed at, spit on and beat.
> Pleading, cursing, begging to die,
> Selling my soul to whoever would buy,
> Dealing in sin for a morsel of bread,
> Hating the living and fearing the dead.
> My God! can it be I have fallen so low?
> And yet I was once like the beautiful snow."

4. If we in the home should learn to put ourselves in each other's place, what a benediction this would bring to our domestic life! If the husband, for instance, would sometimes sit where his wife sits. If he would get her viewpoint, if he could realize the thousand petty worries and annoyances of home-keeping and child nurture! If he could only realize how she misses the little nameless acts of courtesy and of love by which he won her! If he could only see how hungry she is for those small attentions—the bouquet of flowers, the box of candy—these numerous little niceties that made her his in the bright morning of their love. If he could only know the bleak tragedy of the night that he brings when he finds more pleasure anywhere else than he finds in his own home! How the husband needs to sit where his wife sits!

Then the wife needs to sit where the husband sits. She needs to see the world through his eyes. If she might sit sometimes through the irritating grind of a day at the office! If she might realize his business worries, his constant battle to keep the wolf from the door! Yes, and if she could also realize his hunger for attention, for a little petting now and then. If she could only sit where this big overgrown baby sits! If these two, the husband and the wife, could only put themselves each in the other's place, how many heartaches would be avoided! How many abodes of domestic tragedy would be changed into homes of happiness and peace!

Then we who are parents need to sit where our children sit. We cannot be as patient and understanding as we should be without this. We need as fathers to realize that we were not always staid and settled and perfect, as no doubt we are to-day. We need to recall

that there was a time when we knew everything just as
our growing sons do. We need to remember that once
we liked loud suits and ties that spoke for themselves
just the same as our boys. And mothers need to remember that they sometimes giggled and flirted, even
as do their daughters.

Then, what is far harder, we sons and daughters
need, if possible, to put ourselves in the place of father
and mother. It is not easy for us to do this. But many
a broken heart and many a bitter tear would be saved
if we only would. If we could only realize how we hold
the happiness of father and mother in our keeping!
How we might gladden them if we only would! And
what capacity we have to shame them, disappoint them,
to wet their faces with hot tears! I have seen enough
joy and pride in the faces of a father and mother whose
lad had made good to raise the temperature of heaven.
Then I have seen enough bitterness and disappointment
and heartache to change a heaven into hell. Try to
think sometimes how you would like for your own boy
to behave toward you, how you would like for your own
daughter to treat you, and you will be more kind to
those who love you best and whose every thought is for
your highest happiness and usefulness.

III

What would be the good of our thus putting ourselves
in another's place?

1. Such sympathy would lead to a larger knowledge.
We never really know people until we are able so to
enter into sympathy with them as to sit where they sit
and to look on the world through their eyes. We cannot know them truly without this. We can know the

profile of their faces. We can know the tones of their voices. But we cannot know the real man. It is only by thus entering into sympathy with another that we can come to know him as he really is.

2. Not only would such sympathy lead to a larger knowledge, but the knowledge thus acquired would lead to a larger love. To know folks is to love them. Now I know on the spur of the moment that you are ready to differ from me. In your mind you are saying, "The reason I do not like John Smith is because I know him so well." No, you are mistaken. The reason you do not like him is because you know him so little. If you knew him well, knew the real heart of him, you would doubtless love him well.

In proof, let me ask you this question: Who are the people that you like the least? They are the people you do not know. There still exists some bit of prejudice between the North and the South. But where is this prejudice strongest? Not on the border where the Northerner and the Southerner are brought into constant contact. It is strongest among those who know nothing about each other. It is easy for a man who lives in Georgia to hate a man who lives in Boston. And it is easy for a man who lives in Boston to have a perfect contempt for the man who lives in Georgia. Their contempt is born of their ignorance. "I hate him," said Charles Lamb of a certain individual. "Why," was the reply, "I did not think you even knew him." "I don't," was the answer. "That is the reason I hate him."

On the other hand, who are the folks that you love the best? Answer: They are the folks that you know the best. I remember a time when I did not care a thing for my wife. You know when that was? It was when I did not know her. When I got acquainted with her that made all the difference in the world. The folks that we know are the folks that we love. We do not fall in love with pictures. We fall in love with those who by fellowship reveal to us their real selves. And when we really know them, love becomes natural.

If you want further proof, I point to Jesus Christ. He knew men as no other ever did. He knew them to the uttermost. Others saw Simon Peter's blunders; they heard his oaths; they looked upon his cowardice, and, seeing only the outside, they thought little of him. Jesus saw not only his blunders, heard not only his oaths, He looked upon his heart. He saw his defeat. He also saw his hard, pathetic fight before he went down. He heard his oaths of denial. He also heard his sobs because of his denial. And knowing Peter fully, He loved him freely.

3. Then the outcome of this fuller love born of a deeper knowledge is a larger helpfulness. Love is always eager to help. It will do the big thing if it can. If it cannot, it will do the little thing. It will give a fortune if it has it within its power. If not, it will dare cast in two mites. But serve it will, and help it will somehow, in some way. For the passion of love is not getting, but giving. It is not leaning, it is lifting.

IV

Now this big question: How was Ezekiel able to sit in the other man's seat? That is no easy matter. It is not easy for us. It was not easy for him. How was he able to accomplish the high task? Answer: He did it through the power of God. We have the secret from his own lips: "The hand of the Lord was upon me." He did not succeed in the energy of the flesh. He did not succeed by taking his selfishness in his own hard hands and strangling it. He succeeded through the help of God.

And that same help is available for you and me. If we are partakers of the divine nature, if Jesus Christ is in us the hope of glory, then He will do through us what He has been doing all through the centuries. He is always sitting where we sit. That is what He was doing when, though rich, for our sakes He became poor. That was the vision that Isaiah had of Him. "He was wounded for our transgressions; He was bruised for our iniquities. The chastisement of our peace was upon Him, and with His stripes we are healed. All we like sheep have gone astray. We have turned every one to his own way. But the Lord hath made to light on Him the iniquity of us all." If He took our place, we ought to take the place of each other. "If He laid down His life for us, we ought to lay down our lives for the brethren."

IV

THE MAYOR'S WIFE—LOT'S WIFE

Genesis 19: 26

"But his wife looked back from behind him, and she became a pillar of salt."

This is a queer old story. A woman, wife of the one time Mayor of Sodom, is fleeing from the doomed city. She looks back. She becomes frozen in her tracks. Death grips her. She becomes little more than a crude piece of statuary staring with sightless eyes back toward the city that is being swept from off the earth. A strange story, I repeat. One that the modern man is apt to dismiss with a smile as an old folk story with absolutely no meaning for our present age.

But Jesus read this story and formed an altogether different estimate. He read in it a message that was at once timely and timeless. He heard those death-frozen lips preaching a sermon that was needed by the men of His own day, and that is needed no less by us who live in the active present. So he said to us and to all men: "Remember Lot's wife." It is safe to say, therefore, that the time we shall give to the consideration of the Mayor's wife will not be wasted time.

I

Who was this woman?
1. She belonged to an excellent family. She was

39

part of that little company of pioneers that left Ur of
the Chaldees to create a new epoch in the world's civili-
zation. She was a member of that family to which the
world owes more than to any other family that has ever
lived. She was a part of that select group that has
given to the world its greatest prophets and some of its
sweetest singers. She was kinfolk with him through
whom God was to send to the world its Saviour. She
was kin to Abraham.

2. Being a part of this select family, it is reasonable
to believe that she shared the faith of this family.
When the tent was pitched and the altar was builded,
she was there. When prayers were said, she doubtless
bended the knee along with her Uncle Abraham and
with her husband, Lot. She was doubtless a woman enriched by the knowledge of God. In all probability
she was a woman of faith and prayer.

There came a time when, along with her husband, she
made a worldly choice. One day a separation between
Abraham and Lot was necessary. Lot pitched his tent
toward Sodom. In all probability neither he nor his
wife set out with the intention of moving into Sodom.
They only went in that direction. But into Sodom they
came. There they prospered in fame and fortune and
Lot became Mayor.

Not only did Mrs. Lot move with her husband into
Sodom, but, worse still, she allowed Sodom to move into
her. Sodom was a wicked city. Its disgusting rottenness was a stench in the nostrils of decency. Yet the
Mayor's wife fell in love with it. She inbreathed its
moral miasma not with loathing but with delight. It
laid its defiling and besoiling touch upon her very soul.
In spite of the pure religion in which she had been

taught, she was brought under the evil spell of the gay life of Sodom.

3. But even then she was not left alone. Doubtless she was the object of earnest prayer and solicitude on the part of her pious kinsman who lived in the uplands. Certainly she was the object of the keen solicitude of God Himself. Therefore, when the ruin of Sodom was impending, when ghastly death was rattling the latch of her door, God sent His messengers to warn her and her family. Certainly this woman cannot claim that she did not have a fair chance. She was faithfully warned. She was told with a most passionate earnestness of the doom that threatened the city. She was made to understand also that there was a way of escape—a way that would bring her to safety. Thus in many respects this woman was a woman of fine opportunities.

II

But in spite of all her opportunities, she failed. In spite of all warnings, she perished as did the most benighted and rotted soul in Sodom. How was it that she was overtaken by a ruin of which she had been so faithfully warned?

She did not fail because of her unbelief. When the messengers came with the declaration that the sin of Sodom was going to bring about its ruin, the Mayor's wife believed them. When they told her that sin would surely find the sinner out, she did not sneer. She did not laugh in the faces of the messengers and reply: "You are trying to frighten me into being religious." When they told her that what men sowed they would reap, she believed it, though to her it may have sounded a bit harsh and cruel.

Now her belief in these heaven-sent messengers put her in an exceedingly small minority. The vast multitudes of Sodom scoffed at this message. Even those of her immediate family found such preaching utterly ridiculous. When Lot knocked on the door of the house of his sons-in-law and said: "Flee for your life," his warning was little more than a stale joke. We can hear the amused twitter of those sons-in-law across the centuries. "He seemed to them as one that mocked."

And it is by no means certain that a messenger coming with a like message would receive an altogether different reception to-day. A discerning woman said to me this week: "The modern ministry is overemphasizing the love of God and is having too little to say of the justice of God." I replied: "I do not think we are overemphasizing the love of God. We cannot do that. But I do acknowledge that we have too little to say about the certainty of the fact that sin means suffering. We fail to give proper emphasis to that needed truth that the law of moral retribution can no more be ignored than can the law of gravitation."

To our fathers hell was a fearful fact. To us it is little more than a joke. It is a tame "cuss" word. When we want to swear a mouth-filling oath we get something stronger. But if we are just slightly irritated, we call hell into play. We tell our friends to go there. If the auto won't crank, we tell it to go there. If the nail we are driving escapes us, we consign it to the same place. To the vast majority of us hell is only a very tame and half lady-like swear-word. For a man to declare his belief in hell is, in the minds of many, to stamp himself a relic of the past.

But it is well to bear in mind that unbelief in a fact does not change that fact into fiction. There are many

reasons why I cannot but believe in some kind of hell.
And when my friends ask in astonishment, "Do you
believe that a loving Heavenly Father will send any
child of His to hell?" I answer: "Certainly not. But
even He cannot prevent His child from going there if
that child rebelliously sets himself against Him."
There are thousands in this city who are already suffering the pangs of hell. This they are doing in spite
of the fact that God loves every one of them with an
everlasting love.

Now it seems reasonable to me that if sin means hell
here in spite of the love of God, it is going to mean
it elsewhere. If sin involves suffering in the here and
now, I am not going to avoid that suffering by crossing over the Mississippi River. Nor will I avoid it by
crossing the continent. Nor will I avoid it by
crossing to the other side of the world. Nor will I
avoid it by crossing to the other side of death. To
count on the love of God to save you from hell by and
by when that same love is showing itself utterly ineffec-
tive in the here and now is to trust in a delusive and
barren hope. This one thing I have learned for an
absolute certainty, that sin kindles the flames of hell
on this side of death. For this reason, if for no other,
I feel absolutely sure that its effect is the same on the
other side. Therefore, I share with the Mayor's wife
in the belief that sin brings doom,—the very doom of
hell.

Not only did the Mayor's wife believe the stern message that was brought, but she responded to it. It is
true that there was no eagerness in her response. She
was utterly lacking in enthusiasm. She with her husband lingered. Life was waiting for her in the heights.
Death was pressing close upon her heels. Yet she lin-

gered.   Safety waited without the city.   Doom waited
within the city.   But still she lingered.   She seemed
bent on clinging to Sodom just as long as possible.   She
seemed bent on staying away from the highlands just
as long as possible.   Truly she was a great lingerer.

And surely many of us ought to be able to enter into
a sympathetic understanding of this woman.   We too
have lingered.   We have lingered, some of us, until our
best years have slipped into the past.   We have lingered until we have come near the sunset and the
evening star.   We have lingered until our children have
grown up in Christless homes and gone out to Christless lives.   Some of us have lingered, I fear, until the
world's grip upon us has grown tighter than hoops of
steel, until the voices of the heights have come to seem
very far away.

But in spite of the fact that this woman lingered, at
last she set her face toward the heights.   Not eagerly,
not enthusiastically, I repeat, but she did make the
start.   And that is something.   That is more than some
of us have done.   I wonder if I am talking to a man who
never took an earnest and purposeful step toward God
in all his life.   I wonder if I am talking to a single man
who has heard the Gospel message over and over again
and yet who has never made even the response that
was made by this woman.   She did move.   She did bend
her steps toward the heights.   She did set herself to
win salvation.   Have you with your greater light and
your far greater opportunity done as much?

But what happened to her that she did not win?   The
story says that she looked back.   That seems a light
offense.   What was wrong in her looking back?   The
wrong was not so much in the backward look as in what
this backward look indicated.   Years ago on the streets

of our village a gentleman rose to his feet after hearing a joke and went away laughing. A keen old physician looked after him and said: "If that man knew how near dead he is he would not be laughing in that fashion. He is suffering from a fatal disease. I can tell by the way he walks." Now the danger was not in the walk, but in what the walk revealed. So the sin of this woman was not so much in her backward look as in what her backward look indicated.

III

What did this backward look indicate?

It indicated a divided heart. It indicated an undecided will. The reason the Mayor's wife looked back was because she was still in love with Sodom even though her steps were turned away from it. She was little in love with the heights even though she was making her way in their direction. Life was calling to her from the hills. Also the voices of Sodom were calling from the lowlands. She was attentive in a measure to both voices. She felt the lure of both. She felt especially the lure of Sodom. Hence, with a divided mind, an undecided will, she looked back.

IV

What did this divided heart do for her?

1. It robbed her of her joy. Since death and disaster are so soon to be homing in the streets of Sodom, you would have thought that she would have gone out with great gladness. You would have expected that she would have hurried out with nimble feet, with a song on her lips and with deep joy in her heart be-

cause of her great deliverance. But what she was leaving more than counteracted the joy in what she was attaining. Being divided in her allegiance there was an utter want of joy in her heart. Fingering the mud with one hand and reaching for the stars with the other, she found nothing but wretchedness.

Divided hearts are always unhappy. No half-hearted Christian is ever a joyous Christian. How many people we meet who have no gladness in their religion! How many find the pilgrim's road a dull and drab and joyless road! How many find the yoke of the Lord anything but easy! And what is the secret? This: a divided heart. They have never been able to turn loose the willows that overhang the bank and be swept out into the wide sea of God's love. They have never been willing to turn loose every sin and lay hold with their might upon Jesus Christ. Hence to the joy that might be theirs they remain utter strangers.

Did you ever stand upon the seashore and witness its restlessness? How constantly its billows are heaving! How ceaselessly it flings itself against its restraining shores! What is the matter with the sea? Why does it not lie down and be at peace? It is a victim of the divided mind. The voices of cloudland are calling to it. It is being played upon by the magnetism of the heights. But when it is half a mind to respond to the call of the higher voices, the muddy old world puts its arms round it and whispers, "Stay with me." And it never quite decides to give up the world, nor is it ever quite able to stop its ears to the voices that call from the heights. Thus it is always tossing, thus it is forever a stranger to rest and peace.

2. The fact that the Mayor's wife had a divided

heart retarded her progress. The story says, "She looked back from behind." It does not take one who is undecided long to fall behind. Do you remember Elijah's question on Mt. Carmel? "How long halt ye between two opinions?" An undecided man is a crippled man. Indecision squanders our powers. It cripples us. And a man thus crippled cannot possibly keep pace with him who is not so afflicted. It is the man of decision, the man whose heart is united that makes progress, and only he.

When I was a boy my brother and I were one day passing through the fields together. We came to a little rivulet that on account of the spring rains had become a stream some twelve feet wide. We decided, however, that we had to cross this stream. And there was no way to cross it but to jump it. This we knew we could do if we set ourselves earnestly to it. I was to jump first. I went back from the stream to give myself a good running start and bent to the task. But just an instant before I was to make my spring my brother changed his mind and shouted, "Stop! stop! stop!" I half jumped and half did not jump. I became the victim of a divided mind. The result was that I landed right in the middle of the stream.

It is the decided man that wins and only he. A drop of water is a very weak and harmless thing. It falls from the heights so gently that it would hardly hurt a baby were it to hit him in the eye. But when I was in the Panama Canal Zone some years ago I saw them removing a mountain with nothing but some drops of water. These drops, however, instead of being scattered were centralized. They were saying, "This one thing I do." And when these raindrops, thus united, turned upon the mountain it took to its heels.

3. This indecision wrought her doom. As she went joylessly and half-heartedly toward the heights her steps became more and more slow. At last she stopped and looked longingly back to the city. The voice of her baser self said, "Go back." The voice of her better self said, "Go on." Inclination said, "Go back." Conscience said, "Climb to the heights." And there she hesitated till the smothering lava threw its arms round her and she became her own tomb. And when the smoke was lifted, she stood a crude piece of statuary. But the face of the statue was turned not toward the heights, but toward the ruined city of the plain.

Now you will misunderstand the story altogether if you think that the doom of the Mayor's wife consisted in the fact that she became a pillar of salt by the way. Her doom was not physical but spiritual. Her physical death was a mere incident. The tragedy of that backward looking bit of salt consists in the fact that it tells a story of a backward looking soul. The physical disaster that overwhelmed her did not make her turn back. It only preserved for us her photograph. It only took the picture for us of a human soul that, though wooed by the heights, could never get her consent to break from the sin and wickedness of the lowlands.

For instance. There were two figures found in Pompeii when it was unearthed years ago. One of them was a Roman sentinel. He was standing erect in his place at the gate of the city. His spear was in his ashen hand, his sword was at his side. His helmet was upon his head. There the ashes had embalmed him and kept him through the long years. Now this disaster that overtook the city of Pompeii did not put this Roman soldier at the place of duty and keep him there faithful and true. It only photographed him for us.

It only found him in the attitude of faithfulness and preserved him as it found him.

And there was another body found. It was that of a woman. Her feet were turned toward the city gate. Evidently she was fleeing with her might from the heavy doom that was overwhelming the city. But though her feet were toward the gate, her body was turned backward. Her hands were outstretched toward the ground. And just beyond her finger tips was a bag of pearls. Possibly she had dropped them. Possibly they had been dropped by another and she had seen them in passing. Anyway she could not shake off their spell and she turned to pick them up, and the lava came down and embalmed her. But this disaster did not place her in that attitude of grasping greed. It only photographed her so that the future generations might see. Thus death did for Lot's wife. It did not turn her face backward to the world. It only photographed that face for our beholding.

This, then, is the message from those dumb lips. (1) A divided heart is a wretched heart. To find joy in Christ you must be out and out for Christ. (2) A divided heart makes no real progress toward the heights. To be a useful and growing Christian you must be a whole-hearted Christian. (3) A divided heart in the end means death, moral death. If you require proof, "Remember Lot's wife." Therefore, I summon you to a thoroughgoing decision—"Choose ye this day whom ye will serve." In that direction is victory. In all others—defeat and failure.

V

A WOMAN'S WRONGS—HAGAR

Genesis 21: 17

"What aileth thee, Hagar?"

The scene of this story is a desert. As far as the eye can see the weird waste stretches. Above it the heat specters dance, and here and there the scorching sands drift in whirling eddies as the winds play with them. From out a hot and copper sky the sun shoots its arrows of fire. And there is not a tree in sight with an offer of friendly shade. The only visible protection is a few dwarfed and scraggy bushes whose shelter is little more than a meager mockery. In this pitiless furnace silence reigns—a silence deep and profound.

Suddenly that silence is broken. There is a low moan followed by the abandoned sobbing of a woman. She is weeping as only those weep whose hearts are broken. As we hurry forward, we find a lad lying under one of the scraggy bushes. His lips are cracked. His tongue is swollen. His eyes are bloodshot. He is weakly calling for water. Over there a bow-shot away sits a woman, his mother. Her back is turned upon her boy. She has not the heart to see him die. At her feet is a water bottle as dry as the sands of the desert. The only moisture in all the wide waste is the hot tears that flow down her swarthy cheeks.

Why is she sitting here? She is not waiting for help.

She is waiting for death. She has lost her way. Weary hour upon weary hour she has tramped in the trackless desert to no avail. Her water supply has given out. Her strength has failed. Her hope has died. And now, utterly spent, she sits upon the hot sands heedless of the fiery rays of the sun and gives herself to an abandon of grief as she waits for ghastly death.

Now it was to this woman, lost and hopeless and dying, that God spoke. It was this woman, sinful, but more sinned against than sinning, that was startled by a question from the Lord Almighty. He broke in upon her sobs to ask this question: "What aileth thee, Hagar?" This greatly wronged woman thought herself absolutely alone. She thought herself utterly abandoned and forgotten. But suddenly she finds herself companioned by One of whom she knows but little. She finds herself questioned by One at whose hands she had expected no consideration.

I

What is implied by this question? On the surface it seems a rather strange question for God to ask. It sounds as if there were no great heart in it. It seems a bit like mockery to ask such a question. "What aileth thee, Hagar?" The question might have been asked in such a tone as to fill the woman with rage. But be assured it was not so asked by our Lord. It was a question fragrant with budding hopes.

1. This question brought to Hagar the realization that God had not lost her. He knew where she was. She had lost herself. She had wandered here and there over those hot and trackless wastes till she had no idea where she was. She hardly knew east from west. She

did not know the way to any springs. She did not know the path back to Abraham's tents. She did not know any road that offered the least promise of help or safety. She was hopelessly lost.

Now it was to this poor, bewildered woman that God spoke. And His question indicated at least this: that He was watching over her. She had traveled far, but she had not traveled beyond His knowledge nor beyond His presence. Neither have you. You have not dodged Him. "Whither shall I go from Thy presence, or whither shall I flee from Thy spirit? If I ascend into heaven, Thou art there. If I make my bed in hell, behold, Thou art there. If I take the wings of the morning and dwell in the uttermost parts of the sea, there shall Thy hand lead me and Thy right hand shall hold me." Hagar had lost herself, but God had not lost Hagar.

2. This question not only implies that God knew where Hagar was, but that He knew her sorrows. He knew her wrongs. He knew that she was suffering and why she was suffering. "What aileth thee, Hagar?" That was God's way of saying: "My child, there is something wrong with you. You have more heartache than you know what to do with. You have a heavier burden than you are able to bear. You have a wound that is beyond your power to heal. You have a sickness for which you know no cure. There is something wrong. This you know and this I know."

3. Then this question implies that God wants her to tell Him her story. He was eager for this woman, smarting and burning under the lash of her wrongs, to tell Him all about it. He wanted her to tell Him all the sore vexations of her heart. He was yearning for her to take Him into her confidence and tell Him all

that was vexing her, all that was tormenting her, all that was making for the wrecking and marring of her hopes and her dreams.

And He is the same God to-day. How eager was Jesus to listen to the stories of needy souls that came to Him when He walked among men. When that timid woman slipped up in the crowd and touched His garments and was healed, He did not allow her to go away. He turned about and said:—"Who touched me?" He could not be satisfied till this woman came and fell down before Him and told Him all the truth.

"What aileth thee?" Have you a secret wound that you dare not reveal to any human eye? Have you a heart-breaking story that you cannot tell to your husband or to your wife or to your dearest earthly friend? Then tell it to Jesus. He will be infinitely interested. He will be infinitely patient and understanding. When nobody else can understand you, He can. When nobody else will listen to you with patience and with appreciation, He will. Bow your head and heart and tell Him.

> "I must tell Jesus all of my troubles,
> I cannot bear my burdens alone.
> I must tell Jesus and He will help me,
> Jesus can help me, Jesus alone."

4. Finally, this question implied that if Hagar would only tell her story, God was willing and able to help her. He is not asking you to make bare your wounds for nothing. He is not asking you to show Him all your heart out of morbid curiosity. His question means that if you will only come and tell Him, He will be willing to help. And not only is He willing, but He

is also able. There is no need that He cannot meet.
There is no bondage from which He cannot set us free.
"He is able to save unto the uttermost them that come
unto God by Him."

Many a burdened heart has come to me that I would
gladly have helped, but I could not. Many a wound
have I seen that I would willingly have healed, but it
was beyond my power. But there is nothing too hard
for God. There are no knots that He cannot untangle.
There are no tears that He cannot dry. There are no
burdens that He cannot help you to carry. There are
no stains that He cannot wash away. However dark
may be some of the pages that you have written into
your life's story, remember this: "The blood of Jesus
Christ, His Son, cleanseth us from all sin." Come to
Him and tell Him about it. Come with the assurance
that He will listen to you, and, having listened, He will
heal your hurts and bid you go in peace.

II

What response did Hagar make to this question?
Her answer is not printed. One has suggested that the
reason it is not given is because it would not bear the
printing. If ever a woman had a story to tell, this woman had. The words that fell from her lips must have
been hotter than the sands of the desert. I fancy I
can hear her across the far spaces of the years as she
pours out the burning torrent. Her hands are clenched,
her eyes flash like the fiery rays of the sun, and her
swarthy cheeks burn as she spits out the story of her
wrong.

"A few years ago," she begins, as she fights back her
sobs, "I became a servant in the family of Abraham.

Not long had I been there before I discovered that it was a peculiar family. They were not worshipers of the gods of my fathers. They spurned to bow before Isis and Osiris, the gods of Egypt. They claimed that their God was the one God. They claimed that He had kindled the sun and had lighted the distant stars. They claimed that He had 'dipped His hand into the chalice of eternity and made the oceans to drip and the rivers to flow.' And, little by little, I came to share their faith.

"Later I discovered that the husband and wife had one great dream; that they were upheld by one over-mastering hope. That hope was the expectation of an heir. Their God had promised them a son, and this son was to be the inheritor of all the promises that God had made to Abraham. He was to be no ordinary man. In him, they declared, all the nations of the earth were to be blessed.

"But year after year went by, and the child that was hoped for and prayed for and expected did not come. At last faith burned low. Then one day the husband and wife talked together. It was Sarah's own suggestion. She said:—'God is not going to make good His promise to me. You had better turn elsewhere for the fulfillment of your hopes, else we will die in the wilderness and our family will utterly perish. I will give to you to wife my maid, Hagar.'

"Was I to blame? Was I not a slave? Was it not my duty to do the bidding of my master? So when I held my own laddie to my heart I felt no shame. I felt only an abounding pride. I looked the lovelight into his eyes with wildest joy. I dreamed of the day when my boy should inherit the promises that God had given to the heir of Abraham. And the days were bright with a hope that I thought nothing could destroy.

"But one awful day God made good the promise that He had made to Abraham. The angel of suffering came to Sarah's tent and Isaac was born. From that hour I knew that my hopes were to be disappointed. From that hour I knew that my boy was destined to be robbed of his rights. I knew that both he and Isaac could not be heirs to their father. I was sure that a final break between the household of Abraham and myself was inevitable.

"Only two days ago that break came. Sarah demanded that I be cast out. She would not delay a moment longer. She would not brook my presence even in the slaves' quarters. I was to be bundled off at once. So with a handful of food and a bottle of water I was turned out into the wilderness. I was driven forth into this desert and left to die. And here I am, the victim of another's sin. Here I am, weary and spent, robbed of my hopes, robbed of my dreams, robbed of my life, robbed of my boy."

It is a story of tragic wrong. There is no shutting our eyes to that. God did not shut His eyes to that fact. And to add to the bitterness of Hagar's heart, I can hear her fairly shriek her accusation:—"And Abraham was a pious man. He was a member of the Church. He was a friend of God." And because this is true, Hagar is in danger not only of hating Abraham and his wife, who have done her a great wrong, but she is also in danger of hating Abraham's God, who has done her no wrong. To hate anybody is an awful calamity. To hate God is the supreme calamity.

III

What answer did God make to this pathetic story? He did not urge Hagar stubbornly to nurse her grief and keep alive her hate. He did not tell her to live for the one purpose of getting even with the man who had wronged her. The roadway of anger and of bitter rebellion never leads out of the desert. It only leads deeper into its horrid depths. Nursing your wrongs and your burning hate is never the path to an oasis. Hagar must leave God to deal with Abraham, as you must leave God to deal with the one who has wronged you.

"Fear not," God whispers to this tormented and harassed and broken woman. "You are not doomed and forgotten. Your lad is not to be destroyed and thrown away. I have heard the voice of the lad where he is. His pitiful cries for water have broken your heart. But remember, my heart is more tender than yours. If you have grieved, greater has been my grief. If you have suffered, greater has been my suffering. Fear not, therefore, for I am here to meet your needs."

Then the story tells us that the Lord opened Hagar's eyes so that she saw a fountain springing up in the desert. Why had Hagar not discovered that fountain before? It was not because the fountain was not there. It had been there all the while. When she was draining the last drop of water into the parched lips of her son, this fountain was hard by holding out its cup of refreshment. While she was drawing every breath in agony, it was offering its comfort. While she was fisticuffing with ghastly death, it was prattling hard by of life. The fountain was right at hand all the while.

And, heart, the Lord does not have to make special

provisions for your salvation. He has already made it. The fountain has already been opened for sin and uncleanness. Complete provision has already been made for your needs. When Jesus said on the Cross, "It is finished," He meant that a full and perfect and adequate salvation had been provided for all the needs of all the world. Your help, like that of Hagar, is at hand. For the Christ of the Cross is at hand.

Why had not Hagar seen the fountain before? It may be that her eyes were too blinded by her tears. It may be that they were made dim by hopelessness and black despair. It may be, as another has pointed out, that she was too busy contemplating her wrongs, looking at her terrible injuries and irreparable losses. Many have missed the fountain so. To fix our gaze on our sins, our failures, our difficulties, is the way of despair. We must look away from these to Him. "Look unto me and be ye saved all ye ends of the earth."

And what do you suppose Hagar did when she saw the fountain? I imagine she ceased to sob over her wrongs. She ceased to wait for a tormenting death. She stooped down and kissed the spring on the lips and found refreshment. She filled her empty water bottle and brought refreshment and salvation to her child. Then and there she claimed the provision that God had made for her. She made haste in the fear that a moment's delay might mean the loss of her boy.

Will you be thus wise? Are you thirsty? Are you hungry of heart? There is One here who claims to be the Bread of Life. There is One, far closer to you than the preacher, who is saying, "If any man thirst, let him come to me and drink. He that believeth on me, out of his inner life shall flow rivers of living water." God is able to supply all your needs. He is able to supply them so abundantly that out of your inner life shall flow streams of refreshing for others, for those who love you and for those who call you friend. "Ho, every one that thirsteth, come ye to the waters."

VI

A THRILLING DISCOVERY—JACOB

Genesis 28: 17

"This is the gate of heaven."

I

What a fascinating discovery! How rich in joyous thrills! How full of gladsome comfort! How like the sheltering arms of a mother to a tired and frightened child! How like the welcoming lights of home to a fear-dogged traveler who has lost his way in the dark! Think of it! Here is a man who fancies himself utterly alone, when suddenly he finds that he is companioned by angels. Here is one who, lying down amidst the silence of the wilds, suddenly hears that silence broken by his Father's voice. Here is one who, believing himself far from home, wakes all at once to the realization that he has his hand on the latchstring of the house of many mansions. No wonder he exclaims with mingled awe and gladness:—"This is the gate of heaven."

II

Who made this discovery?

The answer to this question is at once surprising and encouraging. It is surprising because you would naturally expect that one who was able to win his way past the things of time and sense till he came to find the gate of heaven must have been a very holy man. You would naturally expect that one who, while his feet were yet upon "this dusty spot that men call earth," got hold on the door knob of the heavenly home, must have been a man whose hands were altogether clean and whose heart had hardly been soiled by a single sin.

On the contrary, the man who made this discovery was in no sense a saint. He was not even a decently honest man. He was a trickster, a cheat, a shrewd supplanter. When we first meet him he is far less lovable than his brother, Esau. Yet Esau is little more than a fine animal. One might perchance suppose that Jacob had come to this lonely spot where he lays him down to sleep bent upon some high and holy quest. But such is not the case. He is not a seeker after God. He is here because his crimes have made it impossible for him to remain at home. He is a fugitive from justice. Yet, strange to say, this man who cannot stay in the tents of his father because he is too much of a crook, is the man who discovers the gate of heaven.

If this is surprising, it is also encouraging. It is encouraging for the simple reason that if heaven's gate is to be discovered only by those who have never sinned, then there would be no hope for such people as Jacob and ourselves. For if there is one thing that we all must know about ourselves, it is this:—"We have all sinned and come short of the glory of God." As we meet together we cannot but be conscious of many a failure and many a shortcoming, and many a positive sin. Therefore, if sinlessness were the requirement for this discovery, we should be without hope. But since a trickster like Jacob can win his way to the gate, then there is hope for us, regardless of the stains of yesterday and regardless of the sins of to-day. I have, therefore,

this good news: every one of us may come to say with
the solid conviction of Jacob: "This is the gate of
heaven."

III

How did Jacob come to make this discovery?

Let us face the fact at once that he did not make it
by mere accident. He did not happen upon this gate as
you might chance to find a piece of coin that some one
had dropped or a treasure that some one had lost. We
may make cheap and half worthless discoveries by mere
good fortune. But we do not discover the things of
supreme value in that way. When the woman with the
issue of blood touched Jesus, it was no accidental touch.
She was not a thronger. The healing that came to her
was not a gift of good fortune. It was a gift of Christ
in response to her faith.

Neither did Jacob make this discovery because he was
the peculiar favorite of heaven. God does not distrib-
ute His gifts on the basis of favoritism. It is hard for
us to realize this, though it is one of the commonplaces
of His Word. James and John had not learned this
or they would never have come to Jesus with such a request as, "Grant that we may sit the one on Thy right
hand and the other upon Thy left in Thy Kingdom."

But what said Jesus? "To sit upon my right hand
and upon my left is not mine to give, but it is for him
for whom it is prepared of my Father." That is, the
first place in the Kingdom of Heaven does not depend
upon God's favoritism. It depends upon the capacity
of the receiver. Suppose some gifted singer were singing in our city. I might go to him and say: "Grant
that I may get more out of your concert than any other

man." What would he have to answer? "Such privilege is not mine to give. The man will get the largest pleasure out of my singing who has the largest capacity for enjoying music. If you have no ear for music, you will get no joy at all, however eager I might be to please you. Your enjoying depends not solely upon me. It depends also upon yourself."

Suppose I were to go to the custodian of a great art gallery and say to him:—"I want you to see to it that I get more pleasure and inspiration out of the pictures in your keeping than any other man. He would have to answer that my request was beyond his power. He could open the door and let me into the gallery. He could permit me to see those canvases where the great masters have spilled their dreams. But capacity to enjoy, to appreciate, to appropriate would depend not upon him, but it would depend upon myself.

And of this I am increasingly confident. God is giving us every revelation of Himself that we will permit Him to give. He is bestowing upon us every single favor that we are willing to receive. He is granting us every bit of power that we are willing to use. He is giving us all the spiritual wealth that He can induce us to appropriate. The longing of His heart is to enrich us with the infinite wealth at His disposal. He is willing to give us of the very best. "For the eyes of the Lord run to and fro throughout the whole earth to shew Himself strong in the behalf of him whose heart is perfect toward Him." He is eager to bring us to this wonderful discovery made by Jacob. Therefore, if we fail, the fault is not His, but our own.

How, then, did Jacob come to make this discovery?

1. He came to it through a sense of his own need Jacob was not an altogether young man at this time.

But he is away from home for the first time. He feels horribly alone. Homesickness comes upon him like an avalanche. The very silence of the night terrifies him. The stars in the sky seem to mock him. They are so far away. But they do not seem more distant than all he has loved in other days. They do not seem more distant than the God in whom he has dimly and imperfectly believed. To-night in these wild solitudes he is very wretched and very sick of soul, and his heart, if not his lips, is crying out for help.

2. Then Jacob cannot shut his eyes to the fact that the heartbreaking loneliness and homesickness of this hour are the result of his own wrong-doing. When he first began his journey the sunshine was doubtless bright about him. It is possible that he blamed Esau then. It is possible that he blamed almost everybody but himself. But it is different now. The thought comes home to him with sickening conviction. The fact that he is a fugitive, alone, separated from loved ones and separated from God is the result, not of the wrong doing of another, but of himself. And I have an idea that deep down in his soul he whispered the confession of a later penitent:—"Against Thee, Thee only have I sinned and done this evil in Thy sight."

Now it was this loneliness and this repentance that made it possible for God to reveal Himself to him. They made it possible for God to make real to him the eternal and the unseen. When he had come to the end of himself, when he had got to the place where his soul was thirsting for God, when his sense of sin had made him sorrowful and ashamed, then it was that God spoke to him and enabled him to say, "This is the gate of heaven."

And it is to such that God is able to grant this thrilling discovery still. If you have no need, you will never make it. But if there is a need, if you are thirsting for God; if your losses, your broken hopes, your broken vows, drive you to bow at His feet, then this discovery is ahead of you. We do not all come to it by the same road. Sometimes we find it at the door of disappointment. Sometimes the sick room becomes transformed by the grace of God into the gate of heaven. Even sometimes the door behind which a loved one lies dead leads us to the discovery of the gateway to the Father's house.

IV

Now what is implied by this discovery?

1. To be able to say, "This is the gate of heaven," means that the spiritual and the unseen have become genuine realities to you. It means that God has been realized. It means that Christ is no longer a far-off figure of history, whose face is becoming dimmer with the passing of the years, but a reality to you in the here and now.

"But warm, sweet, tender even yet,
  A present help is He;
And faith has still its Olivet,
  And love its Galilee.

The healing of His seamless dress
Is by our beds of pain;
We touch Him in life's throng and press,
And we are whole again."

2. To be able to say, "This is the gate of heaven," means not only that we have a real sense of our unseen

Lord; it means also that heaven itself is a reality. We are absolutely sure of the life to come. We are certain that Jesus is not deceiving us when He tells us that He is preparing a place for us. We sing with new and glad conviction:—

> "There is a land of pure delight
> Where saints immortal reign,
> Infinite day excludes the night,
> And pleasures banish pain."

We are certain that there is a home of the soul; that there is a place where love shall find its own. We become as sure of the home unseen as we are of the home in which we dwell.

3. Not only do we become certain of the reality of heaven, but we become sure of its nearness. Jacob had been feeling horribly alone. He had felt that heaven was far away. That conviction was born of his sense of sin. That same conviction has somehow found its way even into the songs of the Church. "There is a happy land, far, far away." I wonder how the poet found that out. There is no hint of it in the Bible. The Bible always represents the spirit world as very near. No wonder that our hearts fail us if we are convinced that heaven, with all that it means, is far away, while our heartaches and our sins and our tears are so near. But what we may learn is that heaven is so close that we may say, "This is the gate of heaven."

4. This discovery not only brings the realization of the nearness of heaven, but also the possibility of communion between heaven and ourselves. If heaven has a gate, it is for the purpose of communion between God and ourselves. The gate is open for the incoming of

our prayers. It is open for the outcoming of His help. It is open also at the end of the journey for the incoming of ourselves. It is open to admit you and me. If we fail to enter, it will not be because the gate is fast shut in our faces, it will be because we refuse our privileges. It is open to every man, woman and child who is willing to enter.

It should not be hard for us to believe this. Do you remember Lochlin Campbell in "Beside the Bonnie Briar Bush?" A thorough-going Pharisee he was. But his daughter went away from home and broke his heart. And the father suffered and grieved. Goaded by his rugged Puritan conscience, he struck her name from the Bible. But he could not strike her name from his heart. And one night she came back home. As she fell against the door it flew open. And she found herself in her father's loving arms. Heaven's door is open to you. If you will only dare to come to Him, you will make that discovery for yourself.

v

What was the effect of this discovery on Jacob's after-life?

Let us say frankly he did not prove altogether true to his vision. There remained much in him that was of the earth earthy. It was not till some twenty years later that Jacob became a real prince. But, while this experience did not work a complete transformation, it did something for him.

1. This experience led Jacob to a vow of consecration. After this he declared that the Lord should be his God. And that vow carried with it not only the purpose on the part of Jacob to accept the Lord as his God.

It implied also that Jacob became God's servant; that from henceforth he did not belong to himself. He belonged to the Lord who had revealed Himself to him, and who had accepted him and given him comfort in his hour of loneliness and strength in his hour of weakness.

2. This experience gave Jacob a new attitude toward his property. Then and there he registered a solemn vow that henceforth he would be a tither. Since he belonged to God, all that he possessed was God's. And in acknowledgment of this ownership he declared his purpose to give God a tenth of all that came into his possession. Jacob was far from being the man he should be. There was a tremendous amount of clay among the gold. But with all his faults, he was far ahead of many a twentieth century Christian. There are many of us to-day that fancy ourselves of a rather matured faith who are miles behind this very imperfect saint in this respect.

3. This experience brought to Jacob the beginning of a new power born of a new faith in God. Any man who can say with conviction, "This is the gate of heaven," is for that reason a stronger man. You remember when Elijah had been taken home to heaven how a number of prophets who had not been privileged to see this marvelous home-going, and to whom the unseen was therefore in large measure the unreal, were weakened by this translation rather than strengthened. They went beating about the hills, saying, "Where is Elijah?" But Elisha, who had been privileged to see, no longer inquired for Elijah. He said, "Where is the Lord, God of Elijah?" And it was in this power that he wrought his wonders. The man who is able to say, "This is the gate of heaven," has a strength and

power to which the man without this experience is a stranger.

VI

Here, then, is an experience full of richness, full of helpfulness, full of joy. It was an experience that was possible even in the dim centuries before Jesus came. It is an experience that is far more possible now. For we are living in the age of the Spirit. We are living when the Holy Spirit is ready to take the things of Christ and show them unto us. We are living in a time when every man, regardless of his circumstances, regardless of his past, may come into a saving and satisfying sense of God. A broad stairway stretches right from your feet into the open doorway of the house of many mansions. In the Church, in the sick room, on the street, in the place of business, you may be enabled by the power of God to say, "This is the gate of heaven." May we claim our privileges, not only for the sake of our own needy lives, but for the sake of those about us whose needs are great as our own.

VII

THE FORKS OF THE ROAD—MOSES

Hebrews 11: 24-26

"By faith Moses, when he was come to years, refused to be called the son of Pharaoh's daughter;
choosing rather to suffer affliction with the people of
God, than to enjoy the pleasures of sin for a season;
esteeming the reproach of Christ greater riches than
the treasures in Egypt: for he had respect unto the
recompense of the reward."

I

Moses is at the forks of the road. A very revealing
place is this spot where the roads fork. Here every
man shows himself for what he is. One man comes to
the forks of the road and undertakes to stand perfectly
still. He is afraid to turn either to the right hand or to
the left lest he go wrong. Or he travels the road to the
left for a season, then retraces his steps and for another
season travels the road to the right. Such conduct indicates that he is afflicted with the fatal malady of indecision. When Moses comes to the forks of the road he
refuses the one and sets himself steadfastly to travel the
other. By so doing he shows himself a man of decision.

II

There were two elements in this decision of Moses.
as there are in all decisions.

70

1. There was a negative element. "Moses when he was come to years refused." That is, there was something to which Moses said "No." And, mark you, his "No" was a full-fledged, one hundred per cent negative. It was not tinctured with a single ounce of "Yes." So often when we say "No" it is lacking in positiveness. Likewise, when we say "Yes," there is a weakness about it that indicates an admixture of the negative. Moses, when he stood at the forks of the road, looked at both roads, and to one of them he said a positive, vigorous, out and out "No."

2. But Moses did more than say "No." He did something more than refuse to take a certain road. He also said "Yes." He refused to travel one way, not that he might stand still, but that he might travel another way. So often we content ourselves with a mere refusal. When we hear the call of Christ almost the first thought that comes into our mind is not that to which we are to say "Yes," but that to which we are to say "No." We think of the Christian life on its negative side rather than on its positive side. We think of what we are to quit being and doing rather than what we are to become and what we are to do.

Now, it is altogether right to remember that certain things must be given up in order for us to become followers of Jesus Christ. But we must also remember this: That no amount of negatives will make us Christians. No man ever becomes a Christian by virtue of what he does not do. No amount of "don'ts" summed up will equal a saint, as no amount of ciphers summed up will equal a unit. Therefore, it is the poorest possible plea, when we respond to Christ's call to become disciples by enumerating the wicked things that we do not do. It is necessary to be able to say "No." But to simply say "No" and stop there is to end in utter moral failure.

There is a handsome wax figure in one of the stores on Main Street. When I approached him and told him where he could get a case of bootleg liquor, he refused to be interested. When I told him where he could bet on a sure thing, he was also indifferent. When I sought to amuse him with a smutty story, he had the decency not to be amused. When I complimented his competitor on the opposite side of the street, he did not turn green with envy. To every temptation he said a very positive "No." But when encouraged by his refusals to do the wrong, I invited him to prayer meeting, he was as unresponsive as the average church member. And when I passed the collection plate, he did not even see it. Therefore, I cannot call this gentlemanly wax figure a Christian. He is as far from being a saint as death is far from life.

The truth of the matter is that Christ is calling on you to say "No" not simply because he wants you to practice self-denial as an end. He is calling on you to say "No" to the lower because that is absolutely necessary in order for you to say "Yes" to the highest. He is asking you to say "No" to the darkness because in no other way can you say "Yes" to the light. He is asking you to say "No" to the mud puddle in order that you may say "Yes" to the infinite sea. He is asking you to say "No" to the ant hill in order that you may say "Yes" to the majestic mountain. He is asking you to say "No" to sin in order that you may say "Yes" to righteousness. He is asking you to say "No" to uselessness in order that you may say "Yes" to usefulness. He is asking you to say "No" to the Devil in order that you may say "Yes" to Himself.

III

This decision of Moses was costly.

1. There was much to be given up.

(1) This decision involved the giving up of the highest social position in all the land of Egypt. It was to pass in one step from this high position, not to a lower rank, but to the very lowest. It was to cease to be the son of the Egyptian princess in order to become the son of a Hebrew slave. And, mark you, social position is not a thing that we despise. There are people that are willing to pay almost any price to win and retain a high social standing. I have seen mothers willing to give their pure and tender daughters to dance with men that they knew to be libertines just in order to get them into society. When, therefore, Moses said "No" to this high social position, he said "No" to something that makes a tremendous appeal to the average man and woman.

(2) When Moses made this decision, he said "No" to the pleasures of Egypt. The Egypt of that day was the New York of modern life. It was the playground of the world. Here every pleasure could be enjoyed, from the most fastidious and refined to the most bestial and vulgar. All these pleasures were within reach of the hand of Moses. And, therefore, when he said "No," he rejected all that could appeal to a man who was in love with worldly pleasure.

(3) His decision involved the giving up of the treasures of Egypt. The Egypt of that day was the granary of the world. Down from its unknown source every year came the Nile, giving to Egypt its fertility. To Egypt came the ships and caravans of many nations, carrying away her grain and leaving behind their silver and gold.

Much of this treasure went into the coffers of Pharaoh. When Moses, therefore, said "No" to the treasures of Egypt, he refused to grip and hold vast wealth that might have been his for the taking.

(4) For Moses to make this decision was to bring bitter disappointment to one who loved him, and to whom he was under very great obligations. I think we have never given sufficient credit to this Egyptian princess who was Moses' foster mother. The fact that she was a heathen did not prevent her from being a good woman. It did not rob her of a mother heart. When that strange craft afloat on the Nile was found, and when its lone occupant pelted this Egyptian princess with his weakness and cannonaded her with his tears, she had the grace and the tenderness to capitulate. She took this little waif to her heart and protected him. It was to her that he owed his life. It was to her that he owed the fact that he had been educated in the royal universities. It was by no means easy, therefore, for a big-souled man like Moses to disappoint one who had thus helped him and who tenderly loved him.

2. But the cost of this decision of Moses is not to be measured alone by what he gave up. What he chose in place of it all was also costly. When he refused all that Egypt had to offer, what did he accept in its stead? When he said "No" to the privileges that might have been his as the son of Pharaoh's daughter, to what did he say "Yes"?

(1) He chose suffering. "Moses, when he was come to years, refused to be called the son of Pharaoh's daughter, choosing rather to suffer affliction with the people of God." This is an arresting statement. Here is a man facing a road that he knows will lead him to suffering, to agony, to disappointment, to battle and

conflict and tears. Yet, with his eyes wide open, he makes the choice. He does not dream for a moment that when he identifies himself with a horde of slaves he is going to have an easy time. He does not fool himself into believing that the course upon which he has decided will be all sunshine and all laughter. He knows that there will be battles to fight. He knows that there will be heavy burdens to be borne. He knows that there will be many a misunderstanding and many a disappointment and many a heartache. Yet, with his eyes wide open, and alive to all that is involved, he chooses to suffer affliction with the people of God.

IV

How did Moses come to make this choice?

1. He had a clear eye for distinguishing right from wrong. How easy it is for us to persuade ourselves that the thing we want to do is the thing we ought to do! How easy it would have been for Moses to have accepted the career that was open to him as the son of Pharaoh's daughter! He might have reminded himself of the large service rendered by Joseph. Joseph had saved his people in the past not by descending, but by ascending. Joseph had become prime minister of Egypt. He himself might have promised a kindred salvation by keeping his position as the son of Pharaoh's daughter. But he refused to let his own interests blind him. He saw that to cling to his rights would be to sin. He refused to blind himself to the fact that it was not simply sinful to choose the lowest, it was also sinful to choose the second best. He realized that God was calling him to choose the highest and to fail to so choose was to sin.

2. He knew that the pleasures and gains of sin are

only temporary. Sin is only charming in the present or
in the immediate future. It has no charm in the past.
How fascinating is sin a moment before it is committed! How absolutely necessary it seems to our happiness! But when it slips into the past its pearly teeth
become ugly fangs, its shapely hands become unshapely
claws, its winsome tresses become writhing serpents.
The sin of the future often seems as fair as an angel
from heaven, but the sin of yesterday is as ugly as a
fiend from hell.

What a pity that we do not have this clear insight
possessed by Moses. He faced the fact that there were
pleasures in sin. The Bible everywhere confesses that
fact. Sin has its laughter and its song and its sunshine. Sin has its pleasures, but they do not last. Its
most brilliant career soon comes to an end. Its bright-
est day soon closes. Its sweetest draught is soon drunk.
Its fairest flowers are soon faded. Choose the way of sin
if you will, and though you may laugh, your laughter
will be but temporary. Though you may rejoice, your
joy will be as fleeting as a shadow. Then one day when
the laughter has all died and your roses are all withered
and your songs are all hushed, you will have a whole
eternity in which to curse yourself.

3. He had a keen eye for the things of real value.
So clearly did he see, that he esteemed the reproach of
Christ greater riches than the treasures of Egypt. It
took a man deeply schooled in permanent values to reach
that conclusion. The treasures of Egypt loomed large.
They seemed very genuine and very weighty and very
abiding. The reproach of Christ—how uninviting!
How lacking in winsomeness! Yet Moses decided that
the thing of real value was not the wealth of Egypt,

but the reproach of Christ. What a seeing eye did this man possess!

4. Then Moses looked away from everything else to the coming reward. He believed that the future belongs not to sin but to righteousness. He believed it is the heritage, not of the holders of the treasures of Egypt, but of those who share the reproach of Christ. He refused to allow temporary gain to blind him to the gain that is eternal. He looked away from everything else to the coming reward. He looked away from Egypt's splendor and power. He looked away from Egypt's molehills and ant heaps to the majestic mountains that loomed in the hazy distance. His faith gave him at once the far view and the true view. "He had respect unto the recompense of the reward."

v

And what was the outcome of this decision?

1. Moses received the reward of a Christlike character. Do you see that man coming down from the mountain with face that is strangely alight? Do you find your eyes dazzled in his presence as if you were looking upon a sunrise? Whose is the face that must needs have a veil to cover it before we can look upon it? It is the face of a man who refused the treasures of Egypt and chose the reproach of Christ. The splendor of his face has not come to him from long gazing upon silver and gold. Such a gaze hardens the face and darkens all its radiance. Whence, then, came this winsome light? It has come from looking upon God. Had Moses remained in Egypt he would have missed many a conflict and struggle. He would also have missed a face

lighted with the light that shines in the face of Jesus Christ.

2. Through this decision Moses was able to render a great service to his own nation and to the world. "Whose are those white tents in the valley?" I ask him one day. "They are the tents of God's chosen people, Israel," he answers. "Israel?" I reply in amazement. "I thought Israel was in bondage. I thought her people were slaves. I thought they were giving themselves solely to the task of brick making." "They were," he replies, "till I came. But by the grace of God I have led them from bondage to freedom."

But I am in doubt as to whether Moses' service in freeing his people has been greatly worth while. They are such a peevish and fretful and whining lot. They are forever lusting for the flesh pots of Egypt. They are constantly complaining to Moses because he has not left them to die in the land of bondage. I cannot convince myself that his task has been worth the doing. So I speak my mind:—"Pardon me, Moses. You have made a heroic fight. You have set your people free. But they are a cantankerous lot, and I fear your labor has been almost, if not quite, in vain."

But Moses does not seem to share my doubts. "Israel does not count for much now," he replies, "but remember that he is only a child. He has by no means arrived, but he is on the way. You may not believe it, but he will yet render the world a great service. One day he is going to write a Book, and that Book will do more than all other books to banish the world's wrongs and the world's night and to bring in a reign of righteousness. One day he is going to give to the world an Isaiah with his inspired eloquence, and a Jeremiah with his broken heart and his streaming tears. One day

he is going to give to the world a skylark named David
and a flaming missionary named Paul. One day there
is going forth from his little country the best of all good
news:—'Behold, I bring you glad tidings of great joy,
for there is born unto you this day a Saviour, which is
Christ the Lord.' Israel does not count for much yet.
But he is on the way toward bringing the whole world
into his debt."

3. Then, incidentally, this decision enabled Moses to
win heaven. The New Testament makes us sure of
this. Read the story of the Transfiguration. Christ
has come. He is struggling under the burden of his
coming Cross. He needs help such as those deeply
schooled in the mystery of suffering alone can give.
Therefore, two men, passed from earth long years ago,
came to talk with Him of His coming crucifixion. Who
are they? One of them is the man who esteemed the
reproach of Christ greater riches than the treasures of
Egypt. Whence does he come? The One to whom he
speaks, his own shining face, the whole story, answers
that question. He comes from heaven. He is fresh
from the house of many mansions. There he had been
for long centuries. And there he is at this hour, glad
with the joy of those who are forever with the Lord.

We must conclude, therefore, that the best day's work
that Moses ever did was when he made possible the
writing of this sentence:—"By faith Moses, when he was
come to years, refused to be called the son of Pharaoh's
daughter; choosing rather to suffer affliction with the
people of God than to enjoy the pleasures of sin for a
season; esteeming the reproach of Christ greater riches
than the treasures of Egypt: for he had respect unto the
recompense of the reward." He gave up the passing
and the temporal, but he won the wealth that endures.

He won Christlike character. He won abiding usefulness. He won an inheritance among that elect company who "have washed their robes and made them white in the blood of the Lamb."

VIII

THE ANGELIC DEVIL—BALAAM

Numbers 23: 10

"Let me die the death of the righteous and let my last end be like his."

This beautiful prayer was uttered by an ancient poet-preacher named Balaam. A startling study is the character of Balaam. I have dared to call him the Angelic Devil. It is not a perfect name. It sounds lurid. It savors of the sensational. My one apology for using it, however, is just this: I could think of no other name which seemed more appropriate for this strange prophet who was such a perplexing mixture of good and evil, light and darkness, star dust and mud.

It is Dr. Watkins, I think, who tells of a certain scientific creation known as the diabolical fad. Some scientists learned how to take certain insects in their early stages of development and graft them into each other. For instance, they grafted the spider with the butterfly. The result was a peculiarly hideous monstrosity. It was a creature that wanted at once to fly and to crawl, to seek the sunshine and to seek the black shadows. It wanted to feast off the flowers of spring. It wanted also to feast off a loathsome banquet of dead flies. Some such strange mixture is this man Balaam. He has traits of character so magnificent that we cannot but thrill with admiration. He has other traits that are so vile that we cannot but shudder. And yet he is altogether human. Do not forget that. He is close akin to ourselves.

I

Now look first at Balaam on his angelic side. How many fine and noble qualities he had!

1. He was an exceedingly brilliant man. He was an orator of great power. Probably the people of his day spoke of him as "Balaam, the silver-tongued," or "Balaam, the golden mouthed." Not only was he a great orator, but he was a poet also, and that of a high order. To be convinced of this, it is only necessary to read the twenty-second, twenty-third and twenty-fourth chapters of Numbers. The man who gave utterance to these bejeweled sentences was certainly no ordinary man. Balaam was greatly gifted. He had gifts, in fact, that fell little short of genius.

2. He had a lofty conception of righteousness. Not even did the Hebrew people themselves run past this great poet-preacher in this respect. Hear Balak's question: "Wherewith shall I come before the Lord, and bow myself before the high God? Shall I come before Him with burnt offerings, with calves of a year old? Will the Lord be pleased with thousands of rams, or with ten thousands of rivers of oil? Shall I give my first-born for my transgression, the fruit of my body for the sin of my soul?" And how majestic is Balaam's answer: "He hath shewed thee, O man, what is good; and what doth the Lord require of thee, but to do justly, and to love mercy, and to walk humbly with thy God." Truly this answer is worthy of the greatest writers of the New Testament.

3. He was a man of very genuine convictions. He had very definite and well defined ideas of duty. To almost all of these convictions he became untrue. But to one of them he remained in a certain literal sense true to the end. He told Balak at the very beginning that if he were to offer him his house full of silver and gold he would not go beyond the word of the Lord to speak less or more. To the letter of this vow he remained true, though he broke the spirit of it into fragments. But when we first meet him he is a man of real convictions.

4. He was possessed of an amazing knowledge of God. He knew how to pray. He knew how to find his way into the secret place of the Most High. God heard his prayers, revealed to him His secrets, spoke to him as friend with friend. So far as the record goes, there was no other man of his time, with the exception of Moses, who enjoyed such an intimacy with God as did Balaam. Prayer seems a habit with him. In our text he is on his knees praying with all sincerity, I think:— "Let me die the death of the righteous and let my last end be like his."

5. He seems sincerely eager for divine guidance. The first time he comes upon the stage he gives an exceedingly good account of himself. This is the story: A delegation composed of the elders of Moab and Midian has come to see him. The purpose of their mission is this: To tell him that a new nation, Israel, is camping upon their borders. That that nation is too great for them to overcome in battle. That, therefore, they beg that he will come and curse them. "For," say they, "whom thou curseth is cursed and whom thou blesseth is blessed."

Now when Balaam received this invitation, he did

that which was quite natural for a really religious man.
He said: "I do not know whether I can go with you or
not. I will pray over it. I will seek the guidance of
God." And he sought that guidance and found it.
Men always do when they seek with a single eye. If
you really want to know the right, you can know it.
God told Balaam he must not go, that Israel was
blessed, and to oppose them would be wrong. So
Balaam told the delegation frankly that he could not
assist them. Then he sent them home. And, in my
opinion, Balaam's conduct up to this point could hardly
be improved.

II

But in spite of all this, Balaam is not one of the
honored saints of the Bible. His name does not appear
among the heroes of faith. On the contrary, he is
sharply denounced. In fact, I do not think there is
another character in the Word of God that is condemned
in sharper language than is this man Balaam. Three
of the New Testament writers mention him,—Peter,
John and Jude. And they all speak of him in terms of
bitter condemnation. Their words fairly scorch and
burn after all these centuries. Judas is not even spoken
of in words so scathing. This is true because Balaam
became an utterly bad man. If you watch him in the
subsequent days of his career, you will see the devil
gaining the victory over the angel

III

His decline is revealed by four separate scenes.
1. Balaam's servant looked out one day and saw a

goodly company coming across the plain. This was another delegation to wait on Balaam. This time the committee was much larger than the first one that came. It was composed of much more prominent men, and they offered a far greater reward. They came saying for their king: "Let nothing hinder you from coming to Balak." "Let nothing"—not even conscience, nor right, nor duty, nor God.

It is here that Balaam has his big chance. What do we expect this princely preacher to say to these men? We expect to see him become a little more erect and his cheek to glow with an honest indignation, and his eagle eye to flash fire. We expect to hear him say: "I told you before that your enterprise was wrong. Do you think the fact that a larger committee has come to see me will make it right? Do you think the fact that you have offered me a larger reward will make a course of action right that was wrong with a smaller reward? If it is wrong to engage in a practice in which only a penny is involved, would it be right to engage in that same practice provided the sum of millions were involved? If it is wrong to do a thing that is unpopular, will the fact that it suddenly becomes popular make it right?

But, sad to say, Balaam made no such answer. Instead he said: "I will ask the Lord again." There is where he began to tamper with his conscience, and, one by one, to blow out the lights within his soul. When he asked God the first time he really wanted to know the right and wrong of the matter. But when he asks God the second time, he is asking not to know what is right, but for the privilege of doing what he knows to be wrong. He is very eager to go to Balak. He wants the promotion and the money. He is also very eager to stay on good terms with God at the same time. He is in a hard place. To quote F. W. Robertson, from whom I received much help in the preparation of this sermon, "He wants to please himself without displeasing God." So his prayer is simply begging God for an indulgence. It is asking to be allowed to do a known wrong.

Now Balaam prays and prays, till at last he convinces himself that the thing he once thought wrong is right. And the story says that God told him to go. God will not and cannot force Balaam, nor you, nor anybody else, to walk in the path of duty. Balaam on his knees has succeeded only in blinding himself. He has succeeded in that most subtle and dangerous form of lying —lying to oneself. So he rises from his knees resolved to go to Balak.

2. The next scene shows him on his journey. The story informs us that God was angry with him for going, and that the angel of the Lord stood in the way as an adversary against him. It is told in the baldest language. Some may smile over it as a crude myth, and yet it is profoundly true. The ass on which Balaam rides becomes unmanageable. She turns out of the road. Balaam gets angry and strikes her with his staff. She then rubs up against the wall and crushes his foot, and he strikes her again. She then lies flat down and Balaam goes into a towering rage and gives her another hard blow, and wishes for a sword that he may kill her. I know a little how to sympathize with Balaam. I have never ridden a donkey much, but I have had to do with her kinsfolk. Even dealing with mules is not always conducive to sweetness of temper.

But what is the meaning of all this? Why is this preacher so irritable? How is it that you sometimes go into a surprising rage over the merest trifle? How comes it that the slamming of a door or the dropping of a plate oftentimes turns you into an active volcano? How is it that at times you are as easily touched off as a powder magazine? You call it nerves. Maybe so. But many times those nerves have come about as a result of disloyalty to your conscience. There is civil war within. Your soul is like a sea billowed by a tempest. For no man ever goes wrong that he does not go against God, and no man ever goes against God except in wretchedness. "There is no peace, saith my God, to the wicked."

So Balaam loses his temper. He gets his foot crushed into the bargain. He is crippled by his wrong doing. Many of us are crippled from the same cause. I wonder if you have a crushed foot to-night. Oh, the reason I am not more fleet in the errands of my Lord is because my own sin has crippled me. Some of us have crushed feet, crushed hands, crushed hearts. This is true, not because God does not love us. It is true because we have turned away from God, and, as Balaam, "have loved the wages of unrighteousness."

Now Balaam proposes to go back, but the Lord tells him to go on. I do not know how to explain this strange angel of the Lord who at one time opposes the preacher, and at the same time urges him on, except to say that it is altogether true to life. When a man seeks honestly to do right he sees clearly, but when he begins to try to do right and wrong at the some time, he gets confused. "If thine eye be single, thy whole body shall be full of light. But if thine eye be evil, thy whole body will be full of darkness. And if the light which is in thee be darkness, how great is that darkness." As surely as you and I are here, the man that plays loose with his conscience will stultify and kill his conscience. The man that refuses to see straight will lose his capacity to see straight.

3. In the third scene Balaam has come to Balak. Seven altars are built. And seven rams and seven bullocks are offered for sacrifice. Balaam reaffirms the one rule that he will not violate, and that he never does violate. He declares that he is going to say what God tells him to say at all costs, and he does this. But while he does it, he is at the same time guilty of the most tragic and fatal dishonesty. He determines that he will speak the truth as he sees it, but at the same time he does his best to keep from seeing the truth. His very first glance at the camp of Israel shows to him that they are blessed. But he proceeds to go from one place to another trying to get a partial view of them in the hope of blinding himself so as to be able to do the bidding of the man who has hired him and thus to win his reward.

I know what some of you are ready to say. It is this:—"Nobody would be so big a fool as that. He would not speak what the Lord showed him and yet try to keep the Lord from showing him anything." Yes, but there you are wrong. There are millions of Balaams. There are scores of them, I dare say, in this house. Here is a man, for instance, who says he will become a Christian if somebody will explain certain problems of the Bible to him. But he never seeks to have them explained. He has no interest in their explanation. Told that the sun is rising in the east, he faces the west.

Or take this situation. A preacher of our denomination cannot marry a divorced couple except they have been divorced for the one scriptural reason—infidelity.

But a man comes to me one day, pays me a delightful fee in advance, and asks me to marry him. I proceed to marry him and ask no questions. You speak to me about it next day and tell me he was divorced. I am surprised and say I did not know it. I took pains not to ask a single question lest I should know it. I am not only breaking my vows of ordination, I have not only proven untrue to the teaching of my Master, but I have stuck my head in the sand like an ostrich and have refused to see the facts.

There was a man in Tennessee a few years ago who undertook to run a school after the type of the famous Webb School. The discipline at Webb School is strict. If a boy will not behave, he is sent home. This man wanted a reputation for strictness, but he wanted to get the money from the pockets even of the disobedient. He would declare emphatically that if he saw one of his pupils do a certain thing he would send him home. But a friend of mine who attended the school said of him that he was constantly dodging to keep from seeing his rules violated. He refused to know what he might have known. So Balaam boasted of his honesty in declaring the truth, but he tried hard not to see the truth.

4. The last scene is in the background. Balaam has kept his vow and has had to go away under the displeasure of Balak without the coveted reward. But he could not endure the loss. He came again. And I imagine they met by night, he and Balak, and talked in whispers. And he said, "I cannot curse Israel, I have promised not to,—but I can tell you how to make them curse themselves." And a little later there was a great feast in Moab. The men of Israel were invited. The women of Moab offered themselves at the king's command. And a plague came upon Israel because of their

sin, and men fell by the thousands. And he who refused to curse them by word of mouth, cursed them in
the most hideous and devilish way,—by the cunning art
of seduction.

By this means I dare say Balaam won his reward.
No doubt he thus obtained all the coveted gold that
Balak had promised. Doubtless, too, he was promoted
to the great honor that had been such a strong temptation. And, best of all, he had been able to win these
without giving too severe a wound to his dying conscience. In all probability he congratulated himself
upon the fact that he had won his way without devi-
ating one inch from the literal truth.

But while he had clung to the letter, he had thrown
the spirit overboard. "While he had kept a rule, he
had violated a principle." While he had spoken truth
with his lips, he was a most dastardly liar in his heart.
And here again, I remark, that Balaam has many sons
and daughters. You would not tell that secret entrusted
to you for anything. You promised that you would not.
But you allow your friend to guess. Then it is so easy
to let him know that he has guessed aright. Thus you
have the thrill of telling the secret and at the same time
keeping your word.

A real estate man of my acquaintance sold a house
some time ago. At the date of the sale the house was
not wired and there were no arrangements for lighting.
The buyer had it put in the contract that there should be
a drop light in each room. Now that agent took drop
lights and tacked one to the ceiling of each room. That
was all. The house was not even wired. Yet he
claimed that he had kept his agreement. And in a certain literal sense he had. But what a cheap liar he was!

And such lying is doubly dangerous because it passes itself off for truth, thus blinding its victim to his own rottenness.

IV

To what goal did this road bring Balaam? What became of this gifted genius who spoke for God? What was the end of him who prayed in all sincerity that he might die the death of the righteous? The record tells the story. He did not die the death of the righteous. He died the death of the wicked. He fell amidst the forces of the enemy with the sword of Israel thrust through his heart. And to-day he stands out before us a charred and blackened ruin, the most bitterly denounced man in the Bible. What was the matter? Did he not pray to die the death of the righteous? Yes, but he was not willing to live the life of the righteous. He loved the wages of unrighteousness. He loved them so well that he lost his all in a mad effort to win them. "Let him that thinketh he standeth take heed lest he fall."

IX

THE OX DRIVER—SHAMGAR

Judges 3: 31

"And after him was Shamgar, the son of Anath, who slew of the Philistines six hundred men with an oxgoad; and he also delivered Israel."

I

Israel at this time was in sore need of a deliverer. They were completely at the mercy of their old time enemies, the Philistines. Through persistent raids their conquerors had reduced them to almost utter want. If any Israelite succeeded in cultivating a crop of wheat, no sooner would he have it threshed than the Philistines would swoop down upon him like birds of prey and carry it all away. Or if any succeeded in raising a small flock or herd, these were driven off before they were ready for the slaughter. Thus the people were often in dire want. For this reason also they lived in constant fear. Their highways were growing up because the people dared not travel them.

In the wake of this calamity came quite naturally the yet heavier one of utter discouragement. The people saw no chance to fight back. Their conquerors had seen to it that they should remain completely at their mercy. To gain this end they had compelled them to give up all weapons of war. They had taken the further precaution of allowing no single blacksmith to remain in

Israel. Thus they were not only without weapons, but they were without any chance of making any. It is not to be wondered at, therefore, that the morale of the nation was broken. They were not only defeated, but they were hopeless in their defeat. They had no expectation of a better day. They had lost confidence in themselves. Worst of all, they had lost faith in God. The truth of the matter is that their disloyalty to Him was the very fountain source of all their trouble. It would be hard, therefore, to imagine a people in sorer straits than were the people of Israel when Shamgar came upon the scene.

II

But even to these utterly defeated people deliverance came. And I can well imagine that it came from a source from which they least expected it. The man who wrought this deliverance for them was not a man of position. He was not a man with any royal blood in his veins. He was not, so far as we know, a man of the schools. Doubtless he had never had one single day of military training. He was a man of the people. He was a farmer. Had he lived in our day we would have possibly called him a hayseed. He had never cut any great figure on the public stage. His greatest achievement thus far had been the breaking and driving of a yoke of oxen. Yet it was this ox driver that God chose to work deliverance in Israel.

III

Why did God choose him? He did not choose him because he was a man obscurely placed. He did not choose him because of his disadvantages. Nor did he choose him because he was a special favorite of heaven. He chose him because Shamgar possessed those qualities that made it possible for God to make use of him for this great service.

1. Shamgar was possessed of a noble discontent. Now much of our discontent is ignoble. Much of it is petty and unworthy. Sometimes it is born of an effort on our part to keep up socially, or in some other way, with our neighbors. Our little bungalow suited us well enough till our neighbor builded a more pretentious house. We were well pleased with our Ford till he began to ride in a Dodge. After this we felt discontented and disgusted with that which in other days had pleased us well enough.

Some of our discontent is born of mere restlessness. Many of us are like children. We demand that we be amused all the time. We want to go from one party to another, or from one movie to another, or from one pleasure and pastime to another. We want somebody to be "booing" at us and "cooing" at us and making us laugh. And if such things are not going on all the time, we become restless and wretched and bored. But this is not noble discontent. It is the discontent of a shallow heart and an empty head.

There is no littleness in the discontent of Shamgar. It made his soul within him sick that he himself was so cowed and whipped and humiliated. It filled him with inner rage to see his people thus enslaved. When he saw the wheat of his neighbor carried off, when he saw his own cattle driven away to become the food of his enemies, he could not take it complacently. He could not look upon it as an inevitable calamity that must be borne. The sight made him clinch his fists. It filled his soul with rage and hot rebellion.

Now because Shamgar was filled with a burning discontent against things as they were, there was hope for him. He was a million leagues ahead of the man who had compelled himself to a kind of cowardly contentment. It is bad to be whipped, but to be content to remain so is infinitely worse. It is bad to be in the prison house of your foes, but to lodge there till you no longer care for freedom, that is more tragic still. To be in the Far Country among the swine is a terrible calamity. But to come to the place where you are content to live there, where you feel at home among the stench and the filth of it all, that is the very climax of calamity. To be in the Church and yet count for nothing is extremely pathetic. To be a spiritual pigmy, a moral dwarf, that is tragic indeed. But to come to the place where you persuade yourself that that is God's best for you, that is the supreme tragedy.

That is an old story of the eagle that was hatched along with a family of chicks. His fellow chickens laughed at the awkward brownish bird. He looked very funny indeed as he tried to pick up the little grain of the barnyard with his great hooked beak. He seemed to those chickens strangely out of place. And, good to say, he seemed to himself yet more strangely out of place. He did not know exactly what he was made for. But he was sure he was not made for that. So he stood day after day the picture of discontent, the embodiment of wretchedness.

But one sunny morning there came a far off speck in the sky. Then there was a strange wild call from the heights. And this ungainly bird, this ridiculous chick, that had been the laughing stock of the barnyard, looked up as if he understood the cry. And the call came again and nearer. And then fire seemed suddenly to glow in the lack-luster eyes of the barnyard fowl. And the chicks stood away in wonder. And the bird spread his burnished brown wings and circled above the barnyard, and then he was away to the freedom of his mountain wilds. He was made for the cloudland and the upper air. Therefore, he could never be content scratching among the filth of the barnyard.

> "I envy not in any mood
> The prisoner void of noble range,
> The linnet born within the cage
> That never knew the summer wood.
> Or what may count itself as blessed,
> The heart that never plighted troth,
> But stagnates in the weeds of sloth
> Nor any want begotten rest.
> I hold it true whate'er befall,
> And feel it when I sorrow most,
> 'Tis better to have loved and lost
> Than never to have loved at all."

If you are away from God to-night, that is a calamity. If you are wasting your substance in riotous living, or if you are wasting your substance in very decent and respectable living, that is a terrible tragedy. But there is something far worse. That is to be satisfied to do so. To be content with the worst when you might have the best. Or, what more often happens, to be content with the second best when you might claim the best. What have you gained of abiding value to-day by rejecting Jesus Christ? What would you have lost of abiding worth if you had followed Him this day? You are being cheated every day. But, sadder still, I fear some of you are becoming content to be cheated. That is the road to a wasted life. Shamgar was full of a noble discontent. That was the first step toward his becoming a deliverer.

2. Shamgar was a man of faith. He could see the difficulties as well as the men among whom he lived. He could realize the strength of the Philistines as well as they. He could realize the weakness of the Israelites. He understood quite as well as they that there were no weapons with which to fight. He himself had doubtless never seen a sword except when it had flashed in the hands of a Philistine. But the difficulties were not all that Shamgar saw. He saw the forces that make for conquest. He knew something of the history of his people. He knew how God had made bare His arm for their deliverance from the bondage of Egypt. He knew how again and again God had come upon the scene to work in their behalf. In this awful and trying time, I have no doubt Shamgar turned with strong faith toward God. He recognized the fact that all the deliverances that God had ever wrought had been through human instrumentality. He believed in the willingness of God to use men. He even went further than that. He believed in God's willingness to use himself. It does not take a great faith for me to say, "I believe God uses men." But it does take a great faith for me to say, "I believe that God will use me." It is with this vital faith that Shamgar set about his task.

3. Shamgar dared to make a beginning. He ventured to fight when the enemy came upon him, in spite of the meanness of the weapon that he had in his hand. He had the courage to do battle regardless of the odds that were against him. I imagine I hear him saying to himself, "Right here and right now I am going to stake my all on an effort to win deliverance from my enemies. They may rob me and kill me. There is every chance

that they will. But that is what would likely happen if I refused to fight. Hence I am going to fight."

And this he did, in spite of the fact that he had excellent excuses for refusing to do so. Had he come home at the close of the day without the bread for which his children hungered, he could at least have given them some very plausible excuses for not having made good. He might have said, for instance: "I was outnumbered hundreds to one. You could not expect me to stand up against such odds as that. I did not have a chance."

If they had felt that his failure was not justified by this excuse, he had another. "My foes," he might have said, "were armed. They all had swords. I did not have a thing except an oxgoad. I had only that old stick that I use to prod my cattle. Surely you are not unreasonable enough to think that I ought to have stood against that crowd that was armed with swords when I was one lone man with nothing but an oxgoad." These would have been very plausible excuses. But Shamgar was not good at excusing himself. He was better at fighting.

So when the enemy came upon him, instead of running he stood his ground. You can hear that oxgoad crack upon their skulls as he wields it lustily. He is saying to himself, "I may go home to-night without a bit of bread, but I will at least carry some scars to show that I made an honest effort. I may not get home at all, but when those who love me come to seek me they will find that I did not die as a coward dies. I will die fighting. I will die using every resource that God put at my disposal." Shamgar had only an oxgoad, but he had that. So instead of waiting for a better weapon, and instead of saying what he would do if he were more fully equipped, he used what was in his hand.

IV

And what was the outcome? Shamgar won the fight. The man who throws himself with what he has on the side of God always wins. When the lad brings his five loaves and two fishes and turns them over to Jesus, he has done his part. If Christ does not feed the multitude then, it is His own fault and not the lad's. If Shamgar strikes with his might with the weapon that God has given him, and then goes down in defeat, nobody can blame Shamgar. If you put yourself, your talents, your abilities in God's hands this night and then miss your crown, you can cry: "Unjust! unjust!" till you shake the foundations from under heaven. All God needs, all God requires for the winning of the battle in your life is for you to put yourself in His hands.

And not only did Shamgar win deliverance for himself, but he won deliverance for his people. Not only was he himself blessed, but he became a blessing. He seems a crude instrument for God to use in such mighty fashion. His battered oxgoad seems a poor weapon for Shamgar to use. But after all it is not so much the instrument that counts. It is the hand that wields it, and the heart that backs the hand.

What does God's call mean to you at this hour? It is not to wait for an easier time or for an easier place in which to set yourself to the task of being a Christian. That time and that place will never come. Your one duty is to begin in the here and now to face your foes with the weapon that you have in your hands. If you will make a beginning, you then put yourself in touch with the might of our infinite Lord. When Jesus said to the paralyzed man, "Arise and walk," He was calling on him to do the one thing that he could not do. But as the man dared to undertake it, the impossible became possible. And if you will dare this night to put yourself in the hands of Jesus Christ, He will work a mighty deliverance for you personally. Not only so, but he will make you a power for the deliverance of others. Only dare to begin, and the very might of God is yours for the winning of your battle.

X

THE EASY MARK—ELI

I Samuel 3 : 13

"For I have told him that I will judge his house for ever for the iniquity that he knoweth; because his sons made themselves vile, and he restrained them not."

This message of God to Eli is a sentence of doom. It tells of a coming judgment, not only upon this man himself, but upon all his house. No culprit at the bar was ever more surely sentenced to death than is this man sentenced. Sharing in his condemnation, in his heavy doom, are those that he most tenderly loves. "For I have told him that I will judge his house for ever for the iniquity that he knoweth; because his sons made themselves vile and he restrained them not."

I

Who was the man thus sentenced?

We should naturally suppose that he was one of the great outstanding sinners of the Bible. But such was not the case. On the contrary, he was a very pious and aged priest. He was a man who for over forty years had been judge in Israel. More than forty years it had been his task to hear God's message and to be God's spokesman to men. He was amiable and inoffensive. There was not a man living, I dare say, who could point out one single wrong thing that he had ever done. He was as guiltless of any aggressive crime as a new born babe.

Not only was he a harmless and amiable and inoffensive man, but he was a man of very genuine virtues.

1. Though old in years he had a youthful heart. It speaks well for the lad Samuel that he could love this white-haired old man, Eli. But it speaks no less well for Eli that he loved Samuel, and love him he did with a passionate devotion. It is beautiful to see these two together. It is fine to see Maytime and December thus drawn into bonds of tender friendship. It is good to see springtime thus in fellowship with winter. It is beautiful thus to see the sunrise and the sunset walking arm in arm. The deep love of Eli for Samuel shows that this old priest still had a heart that was at once kind and youthful.

2. Eli was generous. For long years he had been God's priest. It had been his task to hear God's message and speak that message to man. But now he sees himself being set aside. One who is easily young enough to be his grandson is taking his place. Samuel is an immeasurable distance behind him in point of that wisdom that is born of experience. Eli knows this quite well. Yet Samuel is being called to the place of honor and responsibility, and he himself is being deposed. Samuel is destined to increase, but he is going to decrease. But Eli does not rebel. He does not grow bitter. He does not give way to envy and say hard things about his successor. He is a man possessed of a beautiful generosity.

3. He is a man of fine spiritual insight. Young Samuel did not yet know the vocation to which God was calling him. There were voices speaking within

his heart, but Samuel did not know how to interpret these voices. But his old friend, Eli, knew. And Samuel was most fortunate in having him for his teacher. He it was that told young Samuel that the voices that he had thought only human were the calls of God. He it was that instructed him to say, "Speak, Lord, for thy servant heareth." For he knew, even in that far off day, that the man who was willing to do God's will would know. He knew that if in all our ways we should acknowledge Him, he would direct our path. He was a man of fine spiritual insight.

4. He was beautifully submissive to the will of God. When Samuel came to him with this stern and terrible message, a message that was fraught with deepest doom and bitterest heartache, how did he receive it? There is no word of complaint. There is no word of bitter criticism. There is absolutely nothing of rebellion. He simply bows his head and heart, and these words fall from his lips: "It is the Lord. Let Him do as seemeth Him good." Any man who can speak like that is certainly not a bad man. Any man who can so speak is certainly not far from the Kingdom of God. It would be hard to find a man more beautifully ready to suffer the will of God.

II

What then was wrong with Eli? Why was this stern sentence pronounced, not against his house simply, but against himself as well? Let me repeat, he was guilty of no crime. He had never robbed a widow's house and for a pretense made long prayers. He had not deliberately shut the door of the Kingdom of Heaven against men. He was not a drunkard nor a rake nor a libertine.

He had never stolen the blush from a maiden's cheek. He had never by any deliberate and outbreaking sin brought dishonor to himself nor to the high and holy office that he was called upon in the providence of God to fill. I feel confident that those who knew him could say in all truthfulness, "I never knew Eli to be guilty of doing a single wicked and ugly deed."

What then was wrong? We find the answer in the text: "For I have told him that I will judge his house for ever for the iniquity that he knoweth; because his sons made themselves vile, and he restrained them not." He is guilty because of what he failed to do. He himself was not guilty of positive and aggressive sin. His sons were. The evil doings of his sons were not hidden from his eye. He had thorough knowledge of their wickedness. He was thoroughly familiar with the fact that they were bringing shame upon themselves and shame upon the high office of the priesthood to which he had called them. Thus he became partner in their sin. Thus he became a sharer in their guilt and in their doom.

Why did he not restrain these wicked sons of his? Dr. Whyte says that it was because he was too busy; that with the duties of being at once priest and judge, he had no time for the ruling of his own house. But here I must be rash enough to differ from this great authority. Too great absorption in his work might have prevented his knowing of the wrong doing of his sons. That is usually the case. A man so busy is usually blissfully unconscious of what his own children are doing. But this was not the case with Eli. The text plainly says that he knew.

What, then, I repeat, was the sin of Eli? I am convinced that it was weakness. He was too soft. He was too easy. There was no staunchness in him. He was not willing to resist unto blood striving against sin. He was a loving father. But he was not loving enough to seem at times unloving. He was not kind enough to exercise a parental authority that might have seemed to his sons for the present unkind. Those Godless sons of his knew their father for an easy mark. And that knowledge made their choice of the downward way an easier choice. Thus it also helped to bring upon themselves and upon their father the heavy doom pronounced in this text.

III

Eli, then, preaches us a most startling sermon on the failure of pious softness.

1. It is a failure because it falls far short of Christlikeness. This is true even when it is most amiable and kind. There are many people who forget this. There are numbers who think that all that is necessary to be a Christian is simply to be affable and good natured and courteous. They seem to fancy that about the most Christlike thing one can do is to never get into anybody's way, never step on anybody's toes, never hurt anybody's feelings. Their whole duty is done by being suave and polite and thoroughly agreeable. They would never think of being so rude as to take a positive stand on a moral question lest by so doing they should wound the feelings of somebody else.

A Christian must be made of sterner stuff. To be Christlike is to be courteous, but it is to be much more. Our Lord was a fighter. He was the most courageous battler that ever set foot on this planet. He was the most relentless and uncompromising foe of evil that

our world has ever seen. I am aware that this is not
the impression that we get when we look upon the face
of Christ as portrayed by most of the artists. As a rule
they depict Him as a man capable of much patient suffering, but of little bold resistance. He is beautifully
tender, but he is not grandly strong. But such is not
the face that looks out upon us from the pages of the
New Testament. Here is a Christ who is both tender
and strong. He is patient to suffer the will of God.
He is also courageous to do the will of God.

For instance, Jesus went one day into a synagogue.
There were present some heartless religionists who were
bent on robbing a man with a withered hand of his
blessing. And what did Jesus do? He was not passive.
He was not merely agreeable and courteous. The story
says that He looked round about upon them with anger.
It was an anger that scorched and blistered and burned.
It was an anger that those men who felt it never forgot.
It was an anger that stamped itself deep on the memory of His disciples. John wrote about it fifty years
later. We can almost see the pallor of fear on his face
as he speaks of the wrath of the Lamb.

On another day Jesus went into the Temple. He
found that it was being desecrated. He found it being
changed into a den of thieves and robbers. Heartless
money-grubbers were there plying their trade. And
what was His reaction? Did he go aside and say how
sorry he was? Did He tell what He would do but for
fear He would hurt the feelings of those thievish dese-
craters? He did not. He seized a scourge of small
cords, and you can hear the lash of it upon their hard
faces across the far spaces of the years. No mild toler-
ator of evil was Jesus. He was a fighter. He resisted

unto blood striving against sin. And He calls on you and me to do the same thing.

2. Not only does mere amiable weakness fall short of Christianity, it is in great danger of becoming positive evil. Weakness and wickedness are not synonymous, but they are in great danger of becoming so. I know people that are too courteous, according to their idea of courtesy, to be Christian. I have a friend who is so polite that he would make Chesterfield look like a backwoodsman. As long as there is only one side to a question, he gets on beautifully. But whenever there comes a question that has two sides, he takes his position on the fence and begs the pardon of those on both sides for not getting off on their side.

Only this week I was talking to a man who is a member of the Church. He said with a great show of virtue that he had solemnly vowed that he was going to take but two drinks of liquor with anybody. He declared that he would not take more than one if he could help it. That is, he would take but one if he could get off at that without hurting the feelings of the man who had invited him. Why was he drinking? Not because he liked either the taste or the effect of the liquor. He declared that he did not. He was drinking purely to keep from being disagreeable. Thus he was lined up with the bootlegger, with the law-breaker, with the defier of the Constitution, and of common decency; with the violator of the laws of God and of man, just to keep from being disagreeable. Thus does weakness degenerate into wickedness.

3. Softness tends to make one a menace to others. To be an easy mark is not only to endanger yourself, but to endanger others as well. So far as we know Eli

never did a positive wrong in his life. Yet his whole pathway is littered with ruins. He toiled in the service of the Lord for almost a half century. But when the day was closed, he left behind him nothing but a hideous heap of wrecks.

(1) He wrecked his home. Those two boys of his lying dead on the battlefield,—how did they come to be there? They were there because they were dead in heart and dead in soul before they became dead in body. The secret of their deadness of soul was their sin. They themselves were guilty. But their sin clung also to the garments of their father. For the text implies that he might have prevented their sin if he had only had the sturdy, loving courage to do so. This is the charge made against him: "His sons made themselves vile and he restrained them not."

Mark you, the text offers no suggestion as to the method that Eli should have employed in order to have controlled his boys. It is not suggested that he should have resorted to the rod or should have lectured them soundly and sent them to bed. What is implied is that it was within his power to have controlled them by some method. It might not have been within his power when they were twenty-one years of age or even eighteen. If not, then it was within his power in their young and tender years. And since he might have controlled them, it was his solemn duty to do so. It was his duty to God and the church. It was his duty to the State. It was his duty to the boys themselves. In his failure he chose the path of least resistance for himself. But he chose the way of utter ruin for his sons. And it is true to this day that a child is better unborn than uncontrolled.

(2) Eli brought ruin not only upon his home, but also

upon his church. He allowed his sons to minister before the altar when he knew they were utterly corrupt. Thus he caused men to despise the church. Thus he drove them from its portals. Thus he robbed them of the uplift of its ministry. Thus he stole away their faith. What a pathetic story! He gave forty years to the ministry of the church, only to let his sons make a wreck of it in the end. And this he did because he did not have the force and the courage to restrain them.

(3) Not only did he wreck his home and his church, but he brought great hurt to his nation. As the people of Israel turned from the worship of Jehovah, through the corrupting influence of Eli's sons, they lost the courage and the stamina that fitted them to stand against their enemies. They went into battle without the strength and the uplift of the consciousness of the Divine Presence. Thus they went to defeat when they might have gone to victory. Yonder is a runner. He is coming with news from the front. Eli has waited with the utmost anxiety for that news. And what reply does he give to the old man's question? "Israel is fled before the Philistines, and there hath been also a great slaughter among the people, and thy two sons also, Hophni and Phinehas, are dead, and the ark of the Lord is taken." And the old man topples over backwards, breaking his neck, because his heart is already broken.

What a sermon, I repeat, does this pathetic old man with his home and his church and his nation toppling in ruins about him, preach on the tragedy of pious weakness! Could he speak, he might warn us against a like failure with these great words: "Finally, my brethren, be strong in the Lord and in the power of His might. Put on the whole armor of God that ye may be able to stand against the wiles of the Devil." For our task is not simply to avoid wrong, but to overcome it. We are not here to stand a siege, but to conduct an aggressive campaign. We face stern foes. We must not expect to win without a battle. We cannot destroy evil by politely letting it alone. We cannot kill an enraged tiger with a handful of confetti. We cannot drown a devil fish with a few drops of rose water. We cannot draw the fangs of a cobra with baby talk. Our task demands all our strength and courage, plus the help of God. "Therefore, put on the complete armor of God so that you may be able to stand your ground on the day of battle, and having fought to the end, to remain victors on the field."

XI

THE FIGHTING FARMER—GIDEON

Judges 6:14

"And the Lord looked upon him, and said, Go in this thy might, and thou shalt save Israel from the hand of the Midianites; have not I sent thee?"

This was God's message to a certain farmer named Gideon. Gideon was at that time beating out his wheat in a wine press. The dust was thick about him, but it was no thicker than his doubts. He was depressed and discouraged, but it was out of this doubting and despairful man that God made a deliverer. Gideon's name has come down to us as one of the heroes of faith. "And what shall I more say? for the time would fail me to tell of Gideon, and of Barak and of Samson and of Jephthah; of David also, and Samuel and of the prophets; who through faith subdued kingdoms, wrought righteousness, obtained promises, stopped the mouths of lions, quenched the violence of fire, escaped the edge of the sword, out of weakness were made strong, waxed valiant in fight, turned to flight the armies of the aliens."

I

Gideon a Doubter.

When we first meet Gideon he does not impress us in the least as being a man of faith. He seems a most

111

pessimistic doubter. He finds it impossible to reconcile the fact of a present and almighty God with the conditions that confront him. Very clear headed is Gideon. He is possessed of fine common sense. Therefore, as he faces the evil plight of himself and his people, he is driven to this conclusion: Either God is not the kind of God that he has been taught to believe He is, or, for some reason, He is no longer with and for His people.

The God of whom Gideon had learned from the history of his own people was a God of might. He was one who had been able to put His hand on a certain aged shepherd named Moses and set him to the seemingly impossible task of delivering Israel from bondage. This lone man with nothing but his rod in his hand and God in his heart had marched on Egypt and had conquered, and had led forth a horde of slaves. These slaves had crossed the Red Sea as by dry land. They had entered into their inheritance not by the might of their own armies, but by the might of God.

But those glad days were passed. Israel is now a shamed and a defeated people. In their land that God had given them to possess they were the playthings of their enemies. They were robbed and cheated and despoiled. They had been driven to earth. They hardly dared show their heads above ground. Gideon even now is threshing a bit of wheat in a wine press for fear of the enemy. He knows that at any moment they are likely to swoop down upon him and knock him on the head and carry away his little harvest. And God, so far as Gideon can see, is not concerning Himself in the least.

Suddenly a winsome stranger comes upon the scene. Gideon can hardly see his face for the dust, but he hears the words that he speaks: "The Lord is with thee, thou mighty man of valour." And what is Gideon's reaction to this cheering word? Does he burst forth into song? Does he break into a shout of joy? Does he spring from the wine press with the eagerness of one who is preparing to indulge in the gladness of battle? Not a bit of it.

Here is his answer: "If the Lord be with us, why then is all this befallen us? and where be all His miracles which our fathers told us of?" "Do not tell me," he implies, "that the Lord is with us. I do not believe a word of it. You are simply talking sheerest cant. You are trying to make me take a pious phrase as a substitute for a divine fact. If failure and defeat and slavery are marks of the Divine presence, then the Lord may be with us. But I have been taught that victory and freedom and abounding joy are indications of His nearness and of His help. If the Lord is with us, as you say, then He is not the Lord in whom I have been taught to believe. He must be a very puny and wit-less god, one who is of no more worth than the gods of the heathen."

Now it is impossible to blame Gideon for being per-plexed and full of doubt in his situation. He could see plainly enough that something was wrong. He refused to shut his eyes to the fact that there was little indica-tion at hand of a present and mighty God. Where he made his mistake was this: He failed to see that the fault was not with God, but was with himself and with his people. He was entirely correct in concluding that God was not showing His might as in other days. Where he went wrong was in failing to see that they were making it impossible for God to do what He was able and eager and willing to do. Instead of their waiting on God, God was having to wait on them. Gideon did not understand this, hence his doubt and perplexity.

Now, there are many to-day who are in the grip of the same kind of doubt that tormented and oppressed Gideon. As they look with open eyes upon our modern world, they are simply driven to this conclusion: either Christ cannot do what the New Testament claims He can do, or we are not giving Him a chance. And some of us are blundering just where Gideon blundered. We are laying the blame on our Lord instead of laying it on ourselves. The turmoil and the confusion that confront us on every hand do not proclaim the failure of God. They proclaim the failure of man to give God a chance.

Why are we standing to-day with almost the same possibilities of a world tragedy that we had in 1914, with the single exception of the fact that many of the nations are bled white? Why did we junk the League of Nations? It was not because the overwhelming majority of men everywhere did not believe in this great "adventure in brotherhood." It was not because we weighed this effort at world-peace in the balance of Christian principle and found it wanting. It was defeated by an appeal to fear, by an appeal to selfishness, by that devil's cry of "America first!" But this failure was not the failure of Christianity. It was the failure of ourselves to give Christianity a chance.

We are perplexed, many of us, by the slow progress of the Church. How far it is from being ideal! How lacking oftentimes in brotherliness, in winsomeness, in power! And yet it is intended to be a glorious Church without spot or blemish by any such thing,—glorious in its unspottedness, in its purity, glorious in its unfailing worth and in its unfading splendor. It is to be fair as the moon and bright as the sun and terrible as an army with banners,—an institution of which we can sing truly, "Like a mighty army moves the Church of God."

But when we look at actual conditions, we are grieved and disappointed. And we are led to wonder sometimes if Christ spoke actual truth when He said He would build His Church and that the gates of hell should not prevail against it. Again and again it seems that the forces within the gates of hell do prevail and are prevailing. And we wonder why it is so often conquered when it is intended to be a conqueror. Believe this. The fault is not with Jesus Christ, the fault is with the Church. So often He is not allowed to have His way among His own people. So often outside the very door of His own house He has to say: "Behold, I stand and knock."

The same perplexity meets us when we come to regard the individual. We are often disappointed in one another. More often we are disappointed in ourselves. A woman said to me some time ago, "I thought before I became a Christian and entered the Church that if ever I should become a Christian I would be the right sort of Christian. I would be willing to go anywhere and do anything to which my Lord should call me." And then she sighed disappointedly and said: "But I have found that I am very much like the rest of them." And what she implied was, "I have found that after all the business of being a Christian is a very dull and drab and commonplace affair. I have found that though Christ promises much, He really does very little."

And here again let me persuade your own heart that the fault is not with our Lord. He is indeed able to do exceeding abundantly above all that we ask or think.

He is able to make us conquerors. He is able to make all grace abound unto us. He is able to make us winsome with something of His own winsomeness and tender with something of his own tenderness. Not only is He able, but He is unspeakably eager. He yearns that we be at our best. He yearns to give us the best. For "He that spared not His own son, but offered Him up for us all, how shall He not also with Him freely give us all things?"

II

Gideon Became Certain.

If Gideon was a doubter to begin with, he did not remain so. He came into possession of a bracing certainty. He came to be a stalwart man of faith. How was God able to bring him into this roomy place?

1. Gideon was eager to believe. Gideon did not count his doubts as assets. He took no pride in them whatever. He did not boastfully talk them in the conviction that doubt is an unfailing mark of the broad-browed thinker. Possibly he knew that brilliant men are often doubters, and that stupid and third-rate intellects doubt also. Had Gideon been proud of his doubts, he would have doubtless clung to them unto the end of the chapter.

Now many of us are not so wise as Gideon. We count our doubts as our assets. If you are an earnest man, your doubts may be a gateway to a larger faith, but if you are the opposite, they may be the gateway to hell. The wife who doubts her husband is not enriched thereby, neither is the husband who doubts his wife. Certainly no man is to be congratulated simply because he doubts God. And those who pride themselves on their doubts do so either because of their intellectual egotism or because they seek through their doubts a release from moral obligation.   And to so seek such release is to mark yourself a fool.   "The fool hath said in his heart there is no God."   His trouble was not intellectual but moral.   The fact of God imposed restraints to which he did not desire to submit.   It brought obligations that he was unwilling to meet. Therefore, he took his doubt and used it as an eraser to rub God out of his universe.

2.   Gideon did not allow his doubt to interfere with his duty.   Most of Gideon's fellows had lost heart. They said: "God has cast us off.   He has forgotten us. He has left us to our enemies.   Therefore, we might as well give over our efforts and let things drift.   What is the use of raising a flock if the Midianites drive it away as soon as it is ready for the slaughter?   What is the use of sowing wheat and harvesting the same only to feed our enemies?   What is the use in keeping up the fight under these discouraging and hope-killing circumstances?"   So they left off the struggle.   But not Gideon.   He kept to his task, and when God spoke to him He had to make His voice sound above the sound of his flying flail.

Then, too, Gideon stood ready at the call of God to renounce the forbidden.   As God dealt with Gideon He led him to see that the allegiance of himself and of his own family was a divided allegiance.   Though servants of Jehovah, they had an altar to Baal.   Gideon was wise enough to see that this altar must go, the grove of Baal must be cut down.   And that very night Gideon's ax rang in the grove, and when the hour for morning worship came, Baal was a shattered ruin, and the altar of God stood in its place.

What was the outcome? Gideon came into possession of a thorough-going certainty. God dispelled his
doubts not by answering all his questions, not by giving him an explanation of all his problems. He brought
him into certainty by a revelation of Himself. We
read: "The spirit of the Lord came upon Gideon." And
Gideon became sure. So also may we. This I say with
absolute conviction. I have a right to say it on the authority of Jesus Christ, my Lord. Here is His word:
"If any man is willing to do His will he shall know."
Not "If he is a man of a certain intellectual or moral
bias," not "If he is a man of a certain moral attainment," but "If any man is willing to do His will," he
shall pass out of the mists of doubt and perplexity into
the bright sunshine of a joyous assurance. Christ chal-
lenges every doubter in the wide world, saying, "You
need not doubt any longer. You may be as sure of me
as you are of your own existence. All that is necessary
for this is your own personal surrender. 'Act as if I
were and you will find that I am.'"

The truth of this is also attested by the experience of
countless men and women. One of the greatest preachers that England ever produced was Frederick W. Robertson. His sermons are as live and vital to-day as
when they were preached. Even his pictured face is
full of inspiration. One business man said that he kept
his picture hanging in the office of his store, and that
when he was tempted to do a mean thing, he went and
looked at it and found help. But there were years during which this great preacher was bitterly tortured by
his doubts. How did he finally triumph? He refused
to let his doubts interfere with his duty. He continued
to do the right as God gave him to see it till he came to
know.

A few years ago I became acquainted with a man living near my church who was said to be a skeptic. I called on him one evening in his own home. He was a rather brilliant talker and disposed to argue. After more than an hour I saw that I was not getting anywhere with him, and I invited him to join with me in prayer. Then I went home feeling that my effort had been almost an utter failure.

Not many days later he came out to church. At the close of the sermon I went back to where he stood far under the balcony to speak to him. I said: "We have talked these matters over. Will you act upon them?" He said, turning to a post by which he was standing: "I would as soon confess my sins to this post as to confess them to Jesus Christ." "Well," I replied, "I will not argue that with you, but I want to ask you one question. Are you satisfied with life as you are living it?" He passed through a momentary struggle, and then said what we both knew was not true. "I am satisfied." "Well," I replied, "I have nothing more to say." And I went away and left him, and he went home seemingly as he came.

There came another day when he was out to the service again. When the invitation was given he came. And when he took my hand he said: "I have come to do what you suggest. I am surrendering to Christ." The service closed, and a number of friends shook hands with him. But he was afraid he would be misunderstood. So he came to me alone and said: "Do not think that I am a Christian. I am a stranger to Jesus Christ. But what I do say is this: that I have done what you told me to do. I have surrendered to Christ, but I do not know Him." "All right," I replied, "that is all I ask, for that is all that God asks." A few days later his wife told me the remainder of the story. On reaching home he said to her, "Can you pray?" "I will do my best," she replied. So they kneeled in prayer together. But she had hardly begun to pray when this man who had just declared himself a stranger to Christ took the lead of the prayer, and when he arose from his knees he had that light in his face that was never seen on land nor sea. The next time I met him his doubts had utterly vanished, and he was able to say, "I know whom I have believed."

III

The Outcome of Gideon's Certainty.

1. It was when Gideon became sure of the presence of God that he had courage to make a stand against the enemy. It was then that he dared to put the trumpet to his lips and to blow a blast that called the hosts of the Lord together. And the people responded, as they respond to this day to the man everywhere who speaks with an assurance born not of a mere tradition, but born of a personal experience with a personal Christ.

2. It was this certainty of the Divine Presence that gave Gideon the courage to sift the followers that came at his call. A man without faith continually bows down before numbers. His idol is likely to be the multiplication table. A man of faith realizes it is not so much numbers that count, but the people that are numbered. So Gideon selected from those who came at his call the men who were not afraid, and the men who put God first. And with this seemingly insignificant army he wrought deliverance for himself and for his people.

XII

A POPULAR HERO—SAMSON

Judges 16: 20

"And he said, I will go out as at other times before and shake myself. And he wist not that the Lord
had departed from him."

I

There is no doubt in my mind that Samson, one time
Judge in Israel, was an exceedingly popular man. He
had qualities that appealed with great power to the
people of the age in which he lived. In fact his are
qualities that make a strong appeal in every age. This
I say, confessing at the same time that, had I been
writing the eleventh chapter of the Hebrews, I would in
all probability have left Samson out.

1. He was gifted with a happy disposition. He enjoyed a joke. He was full of amusing pranks. He
had a ringing laugh in the presence of which the blues
somehow vanished. He had a sparkling eye and a
cheerful face, at the approach of which gloom had a
way of taking to its heels. So cheerful and jolly was he
that they could find no name so fitting as Samson, which
simply means sunny.

Now the individual who radiates good cheer may
have a great many faults and flaws. He may be lacking in a thousand particulars. Even then he will not
be without friends that admire him. Most of us are a

121

bit short on laughter. It is said that it takes only thirteen muscles of the face to laugh, while it takes sixty-
five to frown. Too many of us insist on overworking
these particular bodily organs. And the tragedy of this
kind of overwork is that it does nothing but harm.
"A cheerful heart doeth good like a medicine." People naturally gather round a cheerful man as candle
flies gather about a candle. If you want a sure road to
popularity, be an out and out optimist. It is quite certain that Samson owed much of his favor with the
people to the fact that he was so sunny and full of
laughter.

2. Samson was a man of fine physical courage. Now
physical courage is not the highest type of courage. It
is a courage that we possess in company with the bull-
dog. Yet we all admire it in spite of that fact. It is a
quality that is admired by every age and by every type
of character. The savage admires it, and so do the most
highly civilized. It is admired by the young and by
the old, by the ignorant and by the educated, by the
Oriental and by the Occidental. It is a virtue in fact
that commands universal admiration.

How the small boys of Samson's day must have honored him! How they must have regarded him with
an admiration that was close akin to worship! And
this was true not simply of the small boys, but of the
men and women as well. Had he not met enemy after
enemy with coolest courage? Was he ever known to
show the slightest tremor of fear? Was there ever a
hint of cowardice as he stood in the presence of his foes
regardless of how greatly he was outnumbered? People simply had to admire a man of his type. They
could not help it. Neither can we even at this distant
day.

And not only had this popular hero shown himself unafraid in the presence of men, but there was a story current that he one day had had quite a heated argument with a lion. Samson, you remember, was going courting. He was on his way to see his best girl. Suddenly a lion roared against him. Now the lion was young and Samson was young. The lion said: "This is my road." Samson said: "No, you are mistaken, it is mine." The lion repeated his original statement with emphasis. Samson replied: "My beloved is waiting for me just beyond you. Gangway, please!" And a few days later Samson passed along that same road with his hands full of honey. And later he had quite an amusing riddle about how out of the eater came forth meat and out of the strong came forth sweetness. Samson was a man of unusual courage.

3. Samson was an athlete. Thus he was the type of hero that of all others appealed to the half-savage age in which he lived. We claim to-day, of course, that we no longer put the measuring string round a man's muscle to determine his greatness. We put it round his head and especially round his heart. But that is only partially true. The higher type of hero does not occupy a much larger place in the popular esteem than the hero of the Samson type. His big advantage is that he holds our admiration longer. We soon forget the athlete. But he grips us hard during the days of his glory.

For instance, should the greatest American poet visit any ordinary city at the same time that Jack Dempsey was making his appearance in that city, I am not sure but that the overwhelming majority of the people would go to see the pugilist instead of the poet. Or if the President of the United States were speaking in

one stadium and Babe Ruth were batting in another
stadium a few blocks away, I am by no means sure that
a large and enthusiastic audience would not stay away
from hearing the President. When I was a student at
Harvard University, the man whose public appearance
created the most enthusiasm was not the president of
that great institution, but the captain of the football
team. If we so honor the athlete to-day, it is not at all
wonderful that Samson was regarded with the highest
admiration in the iron age in which he lived.

II

What was the secret of Samson's unusual strength?
He did not owe it to his excellent training. It was
not altogether a natural gift. His strength was a gift
from God. Of course that is in the profoundest sense
true of every gift that we possess. If you have ability
in any direction, you have not simply yourself to thank
for it. It came to you as a gift from God, and it came
to you to be used not for yourself, but for Him and for
your fellows. There is nothing you possess that you
have not received. Hence, you are a debtor to God and
to all mankind.

But God was able to give this man peculiar strength
because of his vow of consecration. Before Samson
was born his father and mother resolved that he should
be given to the Lord. When he himself had come to
years of discretion, he assumed on his own behalf the
vows they assumed for him. He became a Nazarite.
His consecration was by no means perfect. But it
made it possible for the Spirit of God to come in power
upon him as He could not have come without this vow.

This spiritual power is granted to men to-day on exactly the same conditions. "We are His witnesses to these things; and so is also the Holy Ghost, whom God hath given to them that obey Him." If we put ourselves in God's hands, He will fill us with His power and use us for His glory. That does not mean that He will give to all the same kind of power. "He divides," Paul tells us, "to every man severally as He will." To Samson He gave the type of power that was best suited to the iron age in which he lived. To you He will give the kind of power that you most need for the living of the life and the doing of the work to which He in His providence has called you.

III

Now there came a day when Samson proved untrue to his vow. How did he come to his fall?

1. In my opinion Samson had simply grown tired of being good. As Judge in Israel he had been quite decent for many years. At last the monotony of the life he was living began to tell on him. It got on to his nerves. He felt as if he must break away. He had an eagerness for laughter, a passionate hunger for pleasure. He felt, therefore, that he could endure his treadmill round of duties no longer. He must needs go on a lark.

And there is nothing peculiar about Samson's conduct in this respect. His desire to break away is a very normal desire. I think it is perfectly natural to almost all partially consecrated people. Have you never felt that you would just like to throw restraints and conventionalities aside and do something mean? Have you never had young people confess this desire to you? I was brought up on the farm. I noticed that when a mule was kept up in a stable for a day or two, if you let him out you had to watch out for the young colts and calves. He would kill them if he could. And we humans have a trace of this in ourselves. There are times when we feel the call of the wild. There are times when we feel that it would be a positive joy to do something downright wicked.

2. Then, there was a great deal of egotism in Samson. He was quite sure of himself. That is evidenced by the fact that he went for his holiday not among his own people, but among his enemies. He went down to Gaza. He was so magnificently strong! He had come off victor in so many contests, in so many battles, that he felt there was nothing to fear. In fact he had no doubt an undefined conviction that the danger to which he was exposing himself would add an extra tang to his pleasure. He was not in the least afraid of temptation. He rather welcomed it.

Now it is always a sad day when any servant of the Lord feels it necessary to go among enemies in order to have a good time. The Lord taught us to pray this prayer: "Lead us not into temptation." But Samson cast the prayer from him. He hunted for temptation. He found it and played with it and laughed in its face and said: "I can enjoy this sin, or I can let it alone. I am my own master." But there came a time when temptation turned the tables. It played with Samson and laughed at him. Samson broke his vow. Of course the loss of his hair was nothing. The loss of that for which the unshorn hair stood was everything. It signified his consecration to God.

IV

What were the results of this broken vow?

1. It cost Samson his strength. When his temptress greets him with the familiar cry: "The Philistines be upon thee, Samson," the hero rises with his old time courage and says, "I will go out as at other times before and shake myself." Heretofore all that was necessary in order for him to overcome his foes was to bestir himself. All he had to do was to bring those mighty muscles into play. But it is different now. The Lord has departed from him. And with His going Samson's strength becomes utter weakness.

God cannot give us power if we refuse to use it for Him. The father loved the prodigal son in the far country as much as he loved him at home. But he could not bless him there. Had he done so he would have encouraged him to remain in the swine pen. Our Father woos us in the far country, but He feeds us at His own table. Sin cuts us off from His help. It robs us of His power. It is purity that is strong, and that only.

> "My good blade carves the casques of men,
>   My quick lance thrusteth sure,
>   My strength is as the strength of ten,
>   Because my heart is pure."

2. This sin of the broken vow cost Samson his vision. The Philistines took him, the story says, and put out his eyes. When he broke with God, he broke with the light. When he went into sin he went into darkness. It is ever so. "Blessed are the pure in heart for they shall see God," and they only. There is nothing else

that so blinds us to God as sin. There is nothing else
that so completely hides from us His loving face.
However real God may be to you to-night, you can sin
against Him till He becomes as unreal as the dimmest
shadow of a dream. Sin means blindness, and that of
the most awful type, moral blindness.

3. This sin cost Samson his freedom. It bound him
with fetters of brass. It set him doing the work of a
slave. That is not what Samson expected. He thought
when he left Israel and set out to Gaza he was going to
find a larger life and a fuller freedom. That is the
promise that sin has made to its votaries all through the
centuries. But it is a promise that it has never kept.
Sin never means freedom. It means slavery.

The truth of the matter is, there is no freedom except in conformity to law. One day I see a magnificent
engine on the Southern Railroad. I speak to that engine and tell it how I admire its strength, its magnificent powers, its fleetness. Then I add: "But there is
one thing I cannot but condemn. That is your nar-
rowness. You allow yourself to be confined to a little
track less than five feet wide. A miserable little road
cart can go where you dare not go. When you get out
in the field why don't you assert yourself and claim
your freedom?" And that engine listens. And the
next day when it is going fifty miles an hour, it takes
my advice and turns out into the green fields. What
happens? The papers come out next day announcing
a tragic wreck on the Southern.

Pacing back and forth on the deck of a great trans-
atlantic steamer, I cannot fail to admire the grace and
beauty and comfort and power of this magnificent float-
ing palace. I speak to it of my high admiration. But
I tell the great vessel I cannot understand for the life

of me why, with her more than forty thousand ton displacement, she allows herself to be dominated and controlled by a little compass not larger than my two fists. "Throw the little tyrant overboard," I advise, "and do as you please." And the ship hears me, and overboard goes the compass. Is the ship free? It is not. It becomes a plaything of the winds and the waves. It is no longer mistress of the seas. It is a derelict, bound for no port, destined to cast anchor in no harbor.

Now, the same rule held for Samson. He also fails to find freedom in the violation of law. He must obey the law of his own being, which is the law of God. The wise man spoke a true word when he said: "Ye shall be holden with cords of your sin." The very moment you step aside from the path of righteousness, you begin to dress your soul in chains. Every sin you commit is a new thread in the cords that bind you. Samson went into the ways of wrong doing to find a larger liberty and a larger life. But he did not succeed. He only found fetters and a prison house and a slave's task. It is ever so. For "Whosoever committeth sin is the bond slave of sin."

Samson's fatal blunder, then, was that he alllowed himself to be duped into believing that the way of consecration to God was a way of impoverishment, while the way of rebellion was a way of enrichment. Yet in spite of the tragic experience of this man of the long ago, in spite of the tragic experiences of ourselves, we still listen to the same ghastly lie. Believe me! It is not God who makes men into weak, blind slaves. It is sin. If every man who has found that true in his own experience were to say "Amen" at this moment, it would boom like a cannonade and shake like an earthquake. Christ is not come to rob. He gives light and power. He sets at liberty those who are bound. If you want freedom in the highest sense, you will find it in obedience to Him. "If the Son shall make you free, ye shall be free indeed." All other courses end in slavery.

XIII

THE SELF-MADE FOOL—SAUL

I Samuel 26: 21

"I have played the fool."

This is the confession of King Saul. He is referring especially to one act, or to one series of acts in his life. He is condemning his conduct toward a young man that he once admired and loved, named David. But this same confession might have been used as a final summing up of Saul's life. It might serve as his autobiography. And that which deepens the pathos of this confession is the fact that this rôle was self-chosen. Saul was not sent into the world to play the part of a fool. God did not plan to deck him out with cap and bells. He was intended to play the part of a king. God planned that he should wear the garments of royalty. But he thwarted God's plan. He chose the rôle of fool. But he is not the type of fool that makes us laugh. He is a fool over whom we must weep if we can find any tears bitter enough.

I

When we first meet Saul there is much in him to admire.

1. He was a man of splendid physique. The record tells us that he was a choice young man. He stood head and shoulders above any man in Israel. He was

kingly in his appearance. He was princely in his bear-
ing. And, mark me, a sound body is a great asset in
winning the game of life. Many a man has won in spite
of the heavy handicap of physical weakness. But the
chances are certainly in favor of the man who has a
strong physical body.

There was a time when we put a far lower estimate
on the value of the body than we do to-day. I think I
have known folks who tended to admire a preacher all
the more if he was physically weak. They seemed to
think that a bad case of nerves or of indigestion added
to his piety. But we are realizing more and more that
the man or woman who gets the furthest, other things
being equal, must have a sound body through which to
work.

2. Then Saul was a modest man. This is evident
from his words to Samuel. When the prophet came
to anoint him king he told him frankly that he was of
the tribe of Benjamin and that Benjamin was the
smallest of the tribes of Israel; that his father's house
was the smallest of the families of Benjamin. Then,
too, he was not too big to work honestly at a lowly task.
He was in search of his father's asses, you remember,
when he found his kingdom. It is often the case that
in the faithful doing of the commonplace duty we find
ourselves called to the higher and the more conspicuous.

3. In the third place Saul had youth. He was in
the springtime of life. His best years were yet before
him. He was yet brushing the dewy flowers of life's
morning. He was at the age when choice can be most
easily made and most easily adhered to. He was at
that hour in which a right choice might bring to him
and to the world the largest results. He was a young
man.

"How beautiful is youth, how bright it gleams,
With its allusions, aspirations, dreams,
Book of beginnings, story without end,
Each maid a heroine, each man a friend."

4. Next, Saul had a great friend. When Charles Kingsley was asked for the secret of his own beautiful life, he answered: "I had a friend." This same great blessing was granted to Saul. It was his privilege to have Samuel for his friend and for his pastor. Samuel loved him with patient devotion. When Saul went wrong Samuel did all that human power could do to win him from his wrong. And to the very end of his life this faithful prophet never ceased to pray for him. He clung to him as a father might cling to a prodigal son.

5. He was chosen for a great task. He was chosen for this task not arbitrarily, but because he had more fitness for it at the time than any other man in sight. He was not simply the choice of Samuel, the prophet, nor of the people. He was God's choice. Not that he was in any sense perfect. He was far from it. But he was, I repeat, the best that God could find in all Israel at that time. So God set His seal upon him. The word says that the Spirit of God came upon him and that God gave him another heart.

II

What use did Saul make of his opportunities? What returns did he render for the big investment that God had made in him?

Answer: He played the fool. If we should ask in what specific way he played the fool, the answer would be readily given by all who are acquainted with his life. Saul sinned. He rebelled against God. He turned from following after the Lord who had lifted him out of his lowly place and put a crown on his head.

But, while that answer would be in a sense correct, it is not the truest answer. Saul did sin. He sinned deeply. But there have been countless others who have sinned in a far more ugly and hideous way than he whose lives yet ended in glory and in victory. Saul was never guilty of any sin half so detestable as the sin of his successor, who came to be a man after God's own heart. The tragedy of the life of Saul was not so much in the fact that he sinned as in the fact that he could never be brought to face his sin and to confess it and to hate it and to put it away.

For instance. God sent him one day with a command to destroy the Amalekites. He was to utterly destroy all their sheep and cattle, everything they had. Saul gathered his army in good faith and set out to the accomplishment of the task assigned. He defeated the Amalekites, but he took their king captive and saved the best of the sheep and the fattest of the cattle. And with these he returned home seemingly in perfect confidence that he had thoroughly fulfilled the command of his Lord.

But the Lord never counts a partial obedience as a whole-hearted obedience. Therefore, the word of the Lord came to Samuel saying: "Saul has turned from following after me." Not that Saul refused to do anything that the Lord commanded,—he only refused to do all. That is, he obeyed God in so far as it suited him, and beyond that he would not go. He killed the cattle that he did not want and kept the rest. He clung to the sins that appealed to him and threw the rest away. And such half-hearted obedience God counts as absolute rebellion.

When Samuel heard of Saul's failure, it broke his heart. "Saul has turned from following after me." Samuel never heard worse news than that. Every word is soaked in tears. Every syllable staggers under a weight of agony. There was no sleep for the old prophet that night. The record says that he cried unto God all night. What a privilege to have a man like that for your friend! What a privilege to have somebody, a father or mother or wife or pastor, who thinks enough of you to break his heart over your wrong doing! "Samuel cried unto the Lord all night." But he was not content even with this. Not only did he speak to the Lord about Saul's sin, but he resolved to speak to the king himself. That was fine. That was courageous.

So after a sleepless night we see this brave old preacher setting out to try to bring the rebellious king to repentance. All the way to Saul's tent I can imagine this prophet is praying. At last he arrives. But when the two men stand eye to eye, only one face is drawn with pain. Only one face is stained with tears, and that is the face of the preacher. Saul is seemingly as happy and care free as a little child. He greets his friend in a tone that is so pious that it fairly oozes unction. "Blessed be thou of the Lord," he cries. "I have performed the commands of the Lord." You see he has no disposition to acknowledge his sin. Seemingly he has no consciousness of wrong doing whatsoever. He lies as glibly as if he were morally color blind.

Then suddenly an embarrassing situation develops. The lie is scarcely out of his mouth when some of those fat sheep begin to bleat, and some of those prize cattle begin to low. Possibly Saul had the grace to blush. Possibly he was not too hardened to show a bit of confusion. But if he did he recovered himself quickly. He never lost his power of speech. He had an answer right on the tip of his tongue. "Oh, those cattle?" he said. "There are cattle there, it is true. They are not all dead, but that is no fault of mine."

When these cattle began to low Saul had a big chance. His sin became open and palpable. Had David been in his place, I feel confident that he would then and there have burst into tears and have asked the old prophet to pray for him. But not so Saul. Saul was just ready for more talk. He said, "I did not absolutely destroy all the sheep and cattle, but the reason I did not was the fault of the people. The people spared them. I am not to blame. They are to blame. A sin has been committed, but it is not mine, it is theirs."

Oh, this fatal excuse making! There is nothing that more surely shows an utter lack of repentance on the part of a man than the fact that he makes excuse for his sin. Just so long as you blame circumstances, just so long as you blame the Church, just so long as you blame anybody in the world but yourself, just that long will you remain unrepentant. Just that long, too, will you remain unforgiven. For if there is an excuse for sin, then you are not guilty. If you are not guilty, then you do not need pardon. If you are not guilty, you have no part in the redemption wrought through Christ. He is come to seek and to save that which is lost.

But the people, Saul, who was their leader? Were you not their king? Could you not control them? Had you commanded them to carry out the Lord's command, would they not have done so? Certainly they would. Saul knows, as Samuel knows, that the fault is all his own; that the guilt is all his; that he has nobody to blame but himself. But when he is driven from this hiding place, he still will not come clean and confess. He tries to put a religious face on his sin: "Yes, we spared the best of the sheep and oxen, it is true, but we did it for religious reasons. We brought them along to sacrifice to the Lord, your God."

And what answer does the prophet make? "Hath the Lord as great pleasure in sacrifice as in obeying the voice of the Lord?" You see what Saul is trying to do. He is trying to buy an indulgence. He wants to pay God for the privilege of sinning. He wants to do wrong and then get excused from it by giving to the Lord a few fat sheep and cattle. But the Lord rejected Saul's offer, as He rejects ours. There is nothing that will take the place of whole-hearted obedience. Driven thus from this last refuge, Saul makes confession. He says, "I have sinned."

Saul made that confession more often than any other man in all the Bible. It was on his lips again and again. From the number of times he uttered it, you might fancy that he was the most penitent of men. How often he is saying, "I have sinned, I have sinned!" But under what circumstances does he make these confessions? He makes them only when he is in some kind of difficulty. Whenever you hear Saul confessing after this fashion, you may know he is in some kind of trouble from which he wants immediate release. Here the prophet has told him that because of his sin God is going to take the kingdom from him. He does not want to lose the kingdom. Therefore he acknowledges his guilt. But never would he make such an acknowledgment except under pressure of some impending calamity.

And, mark you, Saul is not in a class to himself. How many of us never think seriously of Christ or of His salvation until we get into some kind of trouble! Our little baby is near death and we want help. We ourselves are nearing the crossing and we are afraid. A cyclone is on hand and we feel the need of a refuge. But the same winds that carry the clouds away carry away our penitence and our prayers. There are few folks so hopeless as those who never want Christ except when they are threatened by some kind of disaster.

III

What was the outcome of Saul's foolishness?

1. He became a Godless man. Hear that pathetic cry! "God hath departed from me and heareth me no more." We pity the man who has lost his sight or the man who has lost his hearing, or the man who has lost his health. We pity the man who has lost his loved ones. We even pity the man who has lost his money, who from a man of means has become poor. But what of the man who has lost his God? Certainly he has suffered the supreme loss. The most tragic figure on this side of the river of death, or on the other side, is the man who has no God. Saul became a man without God.

2. Saul became a wretched man. From this time on the light dies out of his skies. The flowers all wither in his garden. His springs all dry up. Gloom settles down upon him as deep as that woven out of the warp and woof of loneliness and despair. There is no laughter in his soul, no peace in his heart, no hope for the dawning of to-morrow. He has lost God, and, losing God, he is wretched.

3. He becomes fretful and feverish and suspicious. He lets himself fall into the hands of that torturing fiend called envy. One day when he returned from battle he was greeted with a song: "Saul has slain his thousands and David has slain his ten thousands." That song put an adder in his bosom. That song became a fire in his soul. And henceforth he suffers the pangs of hell because he has become a prey to envy.

4. Last of all he becomes a plaything of his evil forebodings. Once he had been a brave man. But now the sight of the army of the enemy fills him with terror. Like a hunted thing he turns here and there seeking some kind of help. He must have help, but he knows not where to find it. He cannot appeal to God, for he has never repented of his sin. During the days of his rebellion he has not learned how to pray. He feels that it is too late to learn the secret now. What is he to do? Where is he to go? In sheer desperation he turns to an old witch that has hidden herself away in a cave—a cave to which he himself had banished her in his better days.

Man is incurably religious. If he has not a true religion, he will have a false. There are times when everybody must pray. There are times when the strongest of us must needs seek help. There are times when the most self-sufficient must turn somewhere or to something in search of assistance. Saul had flung away God. He had flung away the truth. Therefore, goaded on by the demons of wretchedness and fear, he throws himself at the feet of a woman who is a miserable impostor.

From this scene he goes unhelped and unencouraged to his last fight. The battle goes against him. His faithful soldiers, his courageous sons fall about him. At last the fatal day is closing in utter disaster. Everything is lost. Then it is that I see a great kingly figure standing sweat-grimed and blood-stained, among the slain. He calls upon his armor bearer to thrust him through that he may not fall into the hands of his enemies. But that individual shrinks back with fear and horror. Then the poor lost king falls on his own sword. What does he mutter as he bites the dust in death? This, I imagine, "I have played the fool."

And, mark you, Saul did not go to his ruin alone. If he had played the fool on a hidden stage it would not have been so tragic. When I was a boy I used to help get timber in the forests in our great hills. Here and there we would saw trees that measured from four to five feet in diameter. Now and then a friend who was passing would stop and say: "It seems a pity to cut a great tree like that." But there was something even more tragic than the falling of this great giant of the forests. It was this: As it went crashing to its ruin it flung out its arms and carried other trees with it. Here it caught a graceful young poplar, there a tall slender hickory, and yonder a beech, over there an elm. It did not go to its death alone. Neither did Saul. Neither will you.

I cannot but think how differently his story might have ended. How Saul might have been a blessing to his children and a blessing to his nation; how after-generations might have been enriched by his life if he had only proven true to God. And what was his tragedy? Not so much the fact that he sinned, but the fact that he could never be brought to face and confess his sin and put it away. He refused to repent. Thus refusing, he flung away his here and he flung away his hereafter. Therefore, we can think of no better epitaph to be carved upon his tomb than this: "He played the fool."

XIV

THE WINGS OF A DOVE—DAVID

Psalm 55 : 6

"Oh that I had wings like a dove! for then would
I fly away and be at rest."

Here is a man who wants to run, or, to speak more
accurately, he wants to fly. Maybe he feels himself too
tired or too old or too utterly discouraged to run. So
he yearns for the wings of a dove that he may be quickly
up and away. Who is this man? Frankly, I do not
know. I take it that his name is David. This I say,
confessing at the same time that I can no more prove
that David uttered these words than you can prove that
he did not. Everything considered, however, this bit
of poetry seems to me to fit his sensitive and songful
lips better than those of any other man that I know.

One can easily imagine the scene. David is pacing
back and forth on his palace roof on the highest hill in
Jerusalem. From below comes the noise of turmoil and
confusion. Rebellion is abroad. And to add to the
king's heartache, this rebellion is being led by his own
son, Absalom. Hence his beloved city has suddenly become a restless and wretched place. But as he looks
away from the near, the distant scenes seem wonderfully quiet and full of peace. Far away the hills still
lift their heads in restful grandeur. Suddenly a dove
alights upon the roof and begins to coo to the sunset and

to the peaceful hills. With a fellow feeling for the bird, he approaches her. But she is a bit shy and whirrs away into the far vault of blue. Then he shades his eyes and looks after her until she becomes first a speck and then fades into utter nothingness. Then he wipes his eyes that have grown moist, partly from looking upon the brightness without, but more from looking upon the darkness within, and he says something through lips white with pain. What is he saying? Just this: "Oh that I had wings like a dove! for then would I fly away and be at rest."

I

A very human cry is this of the Psalmist. It is one that has sobbed its way through the centuries. All of us have uttered it in one form or another. It is a cry of the far distant past. But it belongs no less to the intimate present. This is what Jeremiah was saying when he cried: "Oh that I had in the wilderness a lodging place for wayfaring men, that I might leave my people and go from them." And Cowper was only paraphrasing Jeremiah when he cried: "Oh for a lodge in some vast wilderness . . . where rumor of disaster and deceit might never reach me more." Tennyson puts this same longing in the mouth of his disappointed lover in Locksley Hall:

"Oh, for some retreat
Deep in yonder shining Orient where my life began
  to beat,
There methinks would be enjoyment more than in this
  march of mind,
In the steamship, in the railway, in the thoughts that
  shake mankind."

And our own American poet expresses the same yearning in "The Bridge."

> "How often, oh, how often
> In the days that had gone by
> I had stood on the bridge at midnight
> And gazed on the wave and sky.
>
> How often, oh, how often
> I had wished that the ebbing tide
> Would bear me away on its bosom
> O'er the ocean, wild and wide.
>
> For my heart was hot and restless
> And my life was full of care,
> And the burden laid upon me
> Seemed greater than I could bear."

This longing for dove's wings is a part of my own experience. I shall never forget the first charge that I was sent to serve as a boy preacher. It was in a little new community in the West. There were problems connected with this charge that would have been very perplexing even for one of mature years and experience. The man whose place I took had gone miserably wrong. Two local preachers who were members of my church had also gone wrong. Quite naturally I found myself at the very beginning unwanted and in disrepute.

But at first I was not greatly dismayed. I looked with eager expectation to the coming of the Sabbath. I flattered myself that I had three good sermons, and I had made up my mind to preach the best of the three at my first opportunity. With the fine optimism of youth, I had great hopes that this sermon would put all the prejudice of my people to rout and give me a grip on their hearts. So on the following Sunday I went hopefully to church. There were very few present. My sermon did not seem to make any impression at all. One of my renegade brethren in the ministry invited me home to dinner with him, and I went because there was nowhere else to go. No sooner had I entered his home than he disappeared. I was shown a place at the table and dishes were set about me in hotel fashion, and I ate alone. You may believe that that dinner was a very brief affair.

When I arose from the table I looked about once more for my host. Not finding him, I seized my hat and hurried out of the house and out of the little village into the woods. Through this woods I went as one pursued. At last I came out upon a railroad track that ran east and west. I turned my steps toward the west. Here again and again I found myself unconsciously breaking into a run. Then I would stop and tell myself that I had made a tragic mistake. For by this time I had fully decided that I had never been called to preach, and that, let come what might, I never would preach. At last I paused to watch the sun as it slipped in behind a great summer cloud. And as I watched the sun thus hiding itself, I said: "I wish I could turn that big cloud on its hinges and slip in behind it and get away from all this." And I was saying just what David was saying, "Oh that I had wings like a dove! Then would I fly away and be at rest."

II

Now what was the matter with David? It was not that he was a mere weakling. It was not that he was a coward. It was not that he was a pigmy of a man.

On the contrary he was a big man, a many-sided man.

He was a great warrior. He had conducted many a victorious campaign. He was a great statesman. He had shown himself a king of real ability. He was a great poet. He had sung songs that will live as long as literature lives. At his best, he was a great saint. Then he had a marvelous capacity for winning the hearts of people. Jonathan wanted nothing bigger than to be second to David. Then one day he is hiding among the fastnesses of the hills. The enemy is about him. He is thirsty and he thinks wistfully of the well by the gate of Bethlehem. And he cries, more to himself, I imagine, than to others: "Oh that I had a drink from the old well." Three of his rough followers hear him. They slip out of their hiding places to return later, each with a drink of water from the longed-for well. And that water is so tinged with the sweat and blood of sacrifice that David is too big a man to drink it, but pours it out on the ground as a libation to their love and loyalty. Yet this great and greatly loved man longs for the wings of a dove that he may fly away and be at rest.

What, then, is the matter?

1. David was face to face with a task to which he felt himself unequal. Rebellion was abroad. His nation was being torn into fragments. The ship of state needed a strong man at the helm. But David felt unable to cope with the situation. There had been a time when his hand would have gripped the sword and he would have gone to the conflict in perfect confidence. But such was not the case to-day. He was no longer young. The weight of years was upon him. The fires of his early enthusiasms had burned low. He was no longer possessed of the fine madness of youth. There-

fore, in the face of the present crisis, he felt himself old and unfit.   Hence he wanted to fling down his weighty and unwelcome responsibility and fly away. Being so tired of wearing armor, he wanted to exchange it for the wings of a dove.

2. Then David wanted to fly from the torture of a broken heart.   The leader of this rebellion, remember, was Absalom, his loved and handsome boy.   He it was who was now teaching his doting father "how sharper than a serpent's tooth it is to have a thankless child." And David's pain was one for which he saw no slightest promise of cure save in flight.   Should he go out to battle against this unnatural son of his and be defeated, it might mean death for himself, and, therefore, so much added guilt for Absalom.   Should he go and win, his victory would be more bitter even than defeat. Therefore, it was only natural that this father, so piteously wronged and wounded, longed for the wings of a dove that he might fly away and be at rest.

3. Then David wanted to get away from a tormenting memory.   He found it impossible in these terrible days to keep that darkest sin of his life out of his mind. He tried to fix his attention on the fact that God had forgiven him.   But even as he did so that slimy and bloody deed seemed to reach a hand out of "the black coat sleeve of the past" to grip him with cruel fingers. A mocking voice seemed to say to him: "After all, you are to blame.   The Prophet warned you then that the sword would not depart from your house.   It has not departed.   It is here to-day, and you have none to thank for it but yourself."   And David wanted to fly from this tormenting memory.

4. Last of all David wanted to get away from an atmosphere that was poisoned by ingratitude and chilled

by lack of appreciation. His best friend had become unfaithful to him. "For it was not an enemy that reproached me, then I could have borne it. Neither was it he that hated me that did magnify himself against me, then I would have hid myself from him. But it was thou, a man mine equal, my guide and mine acquaintance. We took sweet counsel together, and walked unto the house of God in company. The words of his mouth were smoother than butter, but war was in his heart. His words were softer than oil, yet were they drawn swords." And so cruelly did David feel this wound that he seemed to himself utterly abandoned and forsaken. He felt that there was not a man in all the world to whom it mattered whether he rose or fell, lived or died.

III

And it is interesting to notice where this distressed and burdened man wants to go. "David, suppose you had wings like a dove, where would you go?" "Lo, then, would I wander far off and remain in the wilderness." And why the wilderness? That was his old home. That was where he used to live in the glad days of childhood. That was where he watched the sheep before he climbed so far up the hill that the atmosphere was full of chill. That was where he spent those carefree days before he wore a crown that now gave him the headache and the heartache. He wants to get back to his boyhood home.

> "Backward, flow backward, O tide of years;
> I am so weary of toils and of tears,
> Toils without recompense, tears all in vain,
> Take them and give me my childhood again.

Come let your brown hair just lightened with gold
Fall on your shoulders again as of old.
Let it fall over my forehead to-night,
Shielding my faint eyes away from the light.

And with its sunny-edged shadows once more
Haply will throng the sweet visions of yore.
Slumber's soft calm o'er my heavy lids creep.
Rock me to sleep, Mother, rock me to sleep.

IV

But David discovered before he had finished his song
that this very natural longing for the wings of a dove
was after all only a vain longing. He came to understand, as all of us understand sooner or later, I think,
that the attainment of rest does not depend upon flight,
but upon something else altogether. If rapidity of
flight brought rest, then ours would be the most restful
generation that the world has ever known. But we do
not find rest by passing from one side of the street to
the other or from one side of the world to the other.
Heartache is quite as swift-winged as we can hope to be.
Milton's devil made that discovery. "Infinite woe and
infinite despair, which way I fly is hell, myself and hell.
. . . The mind is its own peace and in itself can make
a heaven of hell, a hell of heaven."

Not only did the Psalmist discover that flight was no
remedy for his ills, but he found also that his one
remedy was in God. "Cast thy burden upon the Lord
and he shall sustain thee. He shall never suffer the
righteous to be moved." He came to understand that
what he needed was not a new physical atmosphere, but
a new spiritual atmosphere. He discovered that his

great need was not the support of the wings of a dove, but the undergirding of the Everlasting Arms.

Now this lesson that the Psalmist learned long ago is needed by ourselves. We are still tempted to believe that we can cure our ills by running away. But it is a vain belief. Our hope is not in flight, but in God. "And now, Lord, what wait I for, my hope is in Thee." Are you weary and burdened of heart? Are you heavy laden and in sore need of rest? Then here is your remedy: "Come unto me all ye that are weary and heavy laden and I will give you rest. Take my yoke upon you and learn of me; for I am meek and lowly in heart; and ye shall find rest unto your souls."

XV

THE LAUGHING FOOL—THE MOCKER

Proverbs 14:9

"Fools make a mock of sin."

I

What is it to make a mock of sin? It is to treat sin lightly, to regard it as a matter of no consequence. Ha! ha! Do you hear that laughter? Do you hear that merry jest? Do you hear that easy jibe of contempt? Do you see that man popping his fingers in mirthful scorn? What is the joke? At what is he laughing? Answer: Sin. He is making a mock of sin. And who is that man? Need you ask? That man is a fool. A cultured fool, perhaps. A rich fool clothed in purple and fine linen and faring sumptuously every day, possibly. A fool of the gutter, clad in rags and wallowing in dirt and feeding on filth, may chance. But at any rate a fool. For fools, and only fools, make a mock of sin.

II

There are many such mockers.

1. This is evidenced by many of the conversations in which we engage or which we may chance to overhear. Here, for instance, is a story of a bit of sordid conduct on the part of a young friend of ours. What

is our reaction when we hear it? Possibly we are
grieved. It may be we hear it with shame and heartache and humiliation. But probably we treat the matter very lightly. We say, "Oh, well, young men will be
young men." As if young manhood is never really
crowned until it is crowned with dirt. Or "It will
all come out in the wash." As if there were any ocean
large enough to wash away a moral stain. Or "It will
not matter a hundred years from now." As if soot
would be changed into snow by the mere passing of the
years.

We have a large fund of such phrases, and their
number and the frequency of their use proclaim the fact
that we treat sin lightly. By such expressions we endeavor to hide sin's hideousness from ourselves. It is
thus we try to conceal this vomiting volcano with words.
It is thus we endeavor to drown the stench of this moral
carrion under a floodtide of verbal perfume. Oh, we
have only to listen to the easy excuses for misconduct
and the cheap jests about wrong doing to realize that
one of the predominant dangers of the day is the habit
of making a mock of sin.

2. We recognize this tendency when we face the
lawlessness of our day. (1) There is the lawlessness
of the modern home. The disobedience of children to
parents is one of the commonest tragedies of the day.
But it is a tragedy that is treated as a very trivial
matter. Rebellion against all home authority, it would
appear, is a thing of no consequence at all. The other
day I saw an enraged child actually slap her mother in
the face, and the mother treated the matter as a joke.
How foolish! She forgot that she was sowing the seeds
of future rebellion in the heart of her child. She forgot that stern sentence of the Old Book—"The eye that

mocketh at his father and despiseth to obey his mother,
behold the ravens of the valley shall pluck it out and
the young eagles shall eat it."

(2) In like manner we regard the lawlessness of our
Nation. This lawlessness of our homes has given birth
to national lawlessness. Thus it has come to pass that
the American people are the most lawless civilized
people on the face of the earth. There seems absolutely
no law that we take with real seriousness. There is
hardly any form of crime in which we are not the
leaders. Our record for homicide is such as to startle
any thoughtful man. It is appalling, disgraceful and
horrible. It is costing us thousands of lives every year.
But it is not the only law we break. We make havoc
in a measure of all laws, knowing that the penalty is
sure of enforcement only against the helpless and the
poor.

Take, for example, our shameful violation of the
Eighteenth Amendment. We got rid of the legalized
liquor traffic at a terrible price. It cost us almost a
century of conflict. It cost us rivers of blood and
oceans of tears and millions of broken hearts. But at
last we kicked this murderous monster out of the front
door. But now, through our contempt for law, we are
allowing it to wriggle in at the back door. And who is
to blame? Not the negro bootlegger in "Black bottom."
Not the ignorant foreigner who has learned hatred for
all government through centuries of tyranny. Those
most to blame are the so-called good citizens who patron-
ize the bootlegger. Many of these are men in whose
veins flow the blood of ancestors who fought in the
Revolution. Such men are without excuse. And next to
these in point of guilt are ourselves. We are to blame
because we do not rise with the scourge of a hot and

holy indignation and drive such lawlessness from the land.

3. Then we see this tendency to treat sin lightly in the amusements of the day. How else can we account for the presence on so many screens of the sensual and obscene picture? I am not against all moving pictures. The moving picture theater, I am persuaded, is here to stay. It might be made the means of great good. But many of the pictures that we are allowing to be shown outrage all decency and make a joke of things that are fundamental to the soundness of human society. To call over the list of many popular pictures to-day is to proclaim with trumpet tongue the fact that the modern movie theater is making a mock of sin, and that we, the people, love to have it so.

4. The same tendency is seen in the modern dance. Everybody acquainted with the modern dance knows that its tendency is toward the immoral and indecent. This is true because privileges are readily taken and granted on the ball room floor that are not taken and granted anywhere else in decent society. When I was a boy I used to study by an old kerosene lamp. Not every candle fly that buzzed about that lamp got its wings burned. Not every fly that fluttered in from the dark lost its life in that fiery furnace. But every one that buzzed about the lamp flirted with danger, and many fell with scorched wings and writhing body into the arms of death. Not every one who dances becomes immoral or indecent. There are some who escape. But the tendency is downward and downward only.

5. We see this same tendency toward treating sin as a light matter in the conduct of many of us who are members of the Church. We proclaim it by our indifference. We proclaim it by our lack of earnestness. Out on Six-

teenth Street the other day the dirt caved in upon a colored man who was digging in a sewer. He was buried all but his head. I chanced to pass that way a very few minutes after the accident. I found there Red Cross nurses. I found representatives of the police department and the fire department. I found one or two ambulances. I found scores of people. In fact the whole city seemed to have bestirred itself in less than fifteen minutes for the rescue of one poor colored laborer. As I turned from the scene I could not but thank God for our growing sensitiveness to physical danger. Also I could not fail to see by contrast our appalling indifference to spiritual danger. Our lack of zeal in reaching those who are lost proclaims that even we who are professing Christians tend to make a mock of sin.

III

But the text says that the man who makes a mock of sin is a fool. Why does it make use of this harsh and ugly word? Answer: Because it is true.

1. The man who makes a mock of sin is a fool because of what sin is. What is sin? Fundamentally, sin is not a matter of outward act. It is an inward something. It is a perversion of the will. It is a disease of the heart. It is a rottenness of the inner life. It is crookedness of character. Now it is only natural that this crookedness of character should express itself in crookedness of conduct. It is inevitable that from this poison fountain should flow streams of polluted action. In the very nature of things this inner lawlessness expresses itself in lawless conduct.

This lawless conduct looks in two directions:

(1) There is wrong doing. "Sin," John tells us, "is

the transgression of the law." That is, sin in the heart expresses itself outwardly in the form of transgression. It leads to the doing of that which God has forbidden. It walks brazenly over the "Thou shalt not" of the Lord God Almighty. It does the thing that God says we ought not to do. And to do that forbidden thing is to sin. It is to sin against God. It is also to sin against yourself. For every law of God is made for your benefit. Every commandment of His is for your protection and for your highest interest. God has made no law in His own interest. Every one is for the interest of you and me.

(2) Then this lawlessness expresses itself not only in wrong doing, but in failure to do right. And all such failure is sin. "To him that knoweth to do good and doeth it not, to him it is sin." Sin, therefore, is the refusal to do what you know you ought to do. Sin is seeing the road in which you ought to walk and refusing to walk there. It is seeing the load that you ought to carry and refusing to carry it. It is seeing the fight in which you ought to engage and refusing to engage in it. It is seeing the need that you ought to meet and refusing to meet it. It is seeing the character that you ought to attain and refusing to set yourself to attain it. Now to treat lightly this lawlessness of heart that issues in lawlessness of conduct is not the part of a wise man. It is the part of a fool.

2. A man is a fool who makes a mock of sin because of what sin does. Sin is no trifling matter. It is a dangerous and deadly thing. To speak the plain truth, it is the one deadly and dangerous thing in God's universe. If you do not believe that, ask History. Ask the nations of the past that sin has dogged to their graves. Ask Babylon. And the swoop of the bat and the hoot

of the owl and the howl of the jackals, that home where the swinging garden once bloomed, will all tell you that sin is deadly. Ask Rome, whose eagles once spread their wings over the world, and she will tell you through her lost crown, through her Ciceros that are organ grinders, through her Cæsars that are fruit vendors, that sin is the most deadly and dangerous thing in the world.

If you do not believe the verdict of History, ask the individual. Ask David, as he breaks his heart over the one great sin of his life. Ask him as he sees that sin slip out beyond his control and make his son, Ammon, into a rapist, to make his loved daughter into a soiled and tarnished thing. Ask him, as he sees that sin make his idolized Absalom into a murderer and then into a shapeless bit of pulp at the bottom of a pit. Ask that neighbor of yours whose sin is finding him out in the debauchery of his own son. Ask your own soul as you find yourself bound Prometheus-like upon the snowy Caucasus of an evil past, while ever and anon the vulture of some youthful sin comes to tear at your bleeding heart.

If you do not believe sin is deadly and dangerous, ask God. Consult this Old Book. On its very first page stand burning words of awful warning against sin. Its every chapter is a record of God's battle with sin and His efforts to save men from its craft and its cruelty. We hear this fact in the thunders of Sinai. We hear it in the sobs of Gethsemane. We hear it in the agony of the Cross. If sin is not the most terrible and damnable something in the universe, then the Bible is the greatest jumble of nonsense that was ever gotten together. History, the individual, God Himself declare with one voice that sin is deadly and dangerous.

This is true because sin is the great divider. (1) It separates man from God. That is the history of sin upon the first page of human history. That is the history of sin in your life and mine. If you want the face of God to become as dim to you as the shadow of a dream, if you want Jesus Christ to be as unreal as any character in mythology, try sin. Sin is the supreme genius at blotting God out of our vision and out of our experience. Sin is the secret of the broken communion and of the unanswered prayers of some listening to me now. "His arm is not shortened that He cannot save, nor is His ear heavy that he cannot hear," but our sins have separated us from the light of His countenance and the joy of His presence.

(2) Not only does sin drive a dividing wedge between God and man, it also divides man from man. The one dividing force in this world is sin. Sin lies back of all our hatreds whether they be individual or national. Sin lies back of all our conflicts whether they be those between man and man or those between continent and continent. Back of every war that has crimsoned our rivers and billowed our world with graves has been this one cruel and ghastly cause—sin. The very day that sin is killed, that day the world will become a brotherhood.

(3) Not only does sin separate man from God and man from man, but it divides man from his better self. The most ghastly and horrible of all wars is civil war. Sin puts civil war within the soul. That is the climax of tragedy. The bitterest cry that was ever wrung from the lips of St. Paul was not when he was bound to the whipping post. It was not when he was stoned and left to die. It was when he was being tortured by a divided personality. It was when he was struggling to achieve

the good that he could not achieve. It was when he was
hating the thing that was gripping him and conquering
him. It was then that he uttered that wail that sounds
across the spaces of the years: "Oh, wretched man that
I am, who shall deliver me!"

(3) Then the man who treats sin lightly is a fool,
last of all, because in treating sin lightly he is likely
to treat lightly God's remedy for sin. If he counts the
malady from which he is suffering as a trivial matter,
then he is likely also to regard the need of a physician
as a trifling need. When the plague of serpents came
upon the ancient Israelites God provided a remedy.
But who, with the venom of death in their veins, availed
themselves of that remedy? Only those who took their
danger seriously. The others said, "Oh, it is a small
matter, a mere scratch," and, so saying, toppled into
their coffins.

Man, the danger from which you suffer is a real
danger. The disease that is gnawing at your vitals is a
deadly disease. And there is only one Physician that
can cure it. Therefore, you cannot afford to treat Him
lightly. For if you pass Him by you have passed by
your only hope. "There is none other name under heaven
given among men whereby we must be saved." He is
here just for the benefit of the sick. If you fancy yourself whole, His coming means nothing to you. "They
that are whole need not a physician, but they that are
sick."

Brethren, I count myself among the sick. I know
the tortures of this awful disease; for I have sinned.
I know, too, that within my own strength I cannot cure
this dreadful malady. I have tried, but I have met
nothing but failure. And that is your experience.
May God therefore grant us the wisdom to take seri-

ously this damnable disease. May we take it so seriously that we will come to Him who is able to save unto the uttermost. For "He was wounded for our transgressions, He was bruised for our iniquities. The chastisement of our peace was upon Him and with His stripes we are healed."

> "Just as I am without one plea
> But that Thy blood was shed for me,
> And that Thou bidst me come to Thee,
> O Lamb of God, I come, I come."

XVI

THE DRY BROOK—ELIJAH

I Kings 17:7

"And it came to pass after awhile that the brook dried up."

I

These were dark days in the land of Israel. Famine was abroad, and ghastly death was looking many eye to eye. The cause of this calamity, the author gives us to understand, was the sin of the people. It was sin that had cut off their water supply. It was sin that had withered their gardens. It was sin that had parched their fields. It was sin that had blighted their fruit trees. It was sin that had changed the land into a desert. Sin is ever the mother of desolation and of death.

Elijah had been sent of God to warn Ahab of this impending disaster. Having warned him, he went at the command of God into the wilderness. He made his abode by the brook Cherith. There God told him he would supply him with food to eat and with water to drink. It was a situation, I think, that was altogether congenial to the prophet. He was a man of the open spaces. He was a citizen of the out of doors. Therefore, he found life quite pleasant in these solitudes by the brookside.

A very companionable something was this brook. It sang of life and prattled of springs far up among the

hills. Better still, it whispered of the care of God and
of the provision made by a Father's love. When he
drank from this brook, therefore, he drank something
more than water. He drank in faith. He drank in the
firm conviction that God was interested in him, was
watching over him, was standing ready to supply all his
needs.

But one morning as he visited the brookside he was
struck by the fact that the little stream was less songful than it had been. Its prattle was more hushed and
subdued. There came to him the startling realization
that the waters of the brook were failing. It was a be-
wildering experience, but he could not shut his eyes
to the fact that the brook was slowly drying up. Then
there came a day when he made his way to its banks to
find it altogether dry. There was no song at all, but
only sand,—dry, parched, glittering sand, over which
the heat specters danced. But there was no drop of
water.

II

There is a sense in which this experience of the
prophet is not at all unique. There are few of us indeed that have not known at some time the tragedy of
the dry brook. We cannot but read in this story of
the prophet a bit of our own biography. What a beautiful brook yours was, clear, sweet and flower bordered!
The great trees bent above it and mirrored their loveli-
ness in its depths. Grass beautifully green grew upon
its banks. It was as songful as a mocking bird, as
talkative as a happy child. But it came to pass that the
brook dried up. And you cannot think of it to-day
without a stab of pain and a gush of tears.

What was your brook? Maybe it was a brook of worldly prosperity that vanished, leaving you with only scorching sands of poverty. Or it may have been the gushing stream of buoyant health that withered up under the blistering sun of disease till to-day every breath is an agony and every hour is torture. Or it may have been a brook of youthful ambitions and dreams. But your ambitions have been unrealized and your dreams have died under the burning breath of failure. Or perchance it was a brook of tender human love. But the loved one slipped away, and to-day there is a void that nothing in this world can fill. And you feel that the future must be little more than an unutterable longing for "the touch of a vanished hand and the sound of a voice that is still."

III

Why did the brook dry up? I wonder if there is any satisfying answer to this question. I wonder if the prophet found an answer that brought him consolation and healing of heart. I wonder if we who have passed through like experiences can find an answer that will bring a bit of help and healing to our hearts. Why did the brook dry up?

To begin with, let us be sure of this: the brook did not dry because God had forgotten His prophet. It did not dry up because God was so busy governing the universe and creating worlds that He allowed all thought of Elijah to be crowded out of His mind. You and I forget sometimes, but God never does. He is great enough to light suns and fashion stars, but He is also great enough to stoop to the humble task of clothing the lily. He is not too busy to sit by the sick bed of a sparrow and to be present at its funeral when it dies. And be assured of this; that whatever of seeming harm has come to you, or to this prophet, it did not come because of the forgetfulness of God.

Neither did this disaster take place because God had ceased to love His prophet. He loves us with an everlasting love. We may reject Him, we may wound Him, we may rebel against Him, we may rob Him of the privilege of blessing us, but we are absolutely powerless to kill His love. Cling to this fact more tenaciously than you cling to life itself, that God loves you. He loves you when your world is bright with sunny day. He loves you no less when it is black with starless night. He loves you when springtime is about you, gay with song and color. He loves you not one whit less when winter has come and your songs are silent as the lips of death. Elijah's brook did not dry because God had ceased to love him.

Neither did this brook run dry because Elijah had sinned. It did not run dry because Elijah had taken himself outside the circle of the divine will. I am not saying that brooks are never made dry for this reason. Sin is ever fruitful of moral famine and desolation. It is ever the mother of pain and anguish. There are many to-day whose lips are blistered by the burning sands of a dry brook, and their sorrow is made all the deeper by the conviction that the brook was dried up by the scorching breath of their own iniquity.

But, while we always suffer as the result of our sin, there is a pain that is not born of the sin of the one who suffers it. There are some who suffer because they are so wicked. But there are others who suffer because they are good. It took a long time for us to find this out. The wisest at one time thought that whenever any individual suffered, that in itself was proof positive that that individual had sinned. That is the reason that Job's three companions were so sure that their sorely smitten friend had gone wrong somewhere. But Job stood strong in his integrity and God vindicated his claim.

Why, then, did the brook dry up? It dried for the same reason that all other brooks in that drought-stricken area dried. There had been no rain. Back of this calamity, the prophet was convinced, lay the sin of Israel. Elijah, therefore, was suffering from a guilt not his own. He was sharing the pain and the tragedy of the sinning nation of which he was a part. Our lives are interwoven one with the other. We have the privilege of rejoicing with those that do rejoice, but the price we pay for this privilege is that we are compelled to weep with those that weep. Elijah's calamity, then, came to him at the hands of his sinning people.

IV

There are some profoundly important lessons, then, that we may learn from this tragedy of the dry brook.

1. God is not to be charged with this calamity. Even assuming that the drought was sent of God, it was the sin of the people that made it necessary for Him to send it. Whatever wrong, therefore, had come to Elijah through this experience, he could not justly charge that wrong to God. And what is true of the prophet is true of ourselves. Hold fast to this fact; that whatever evil has come to you, God is not the originator of it. "Shall not the Judge of all the earth do right." He shall. He does. To this solid conviction we may safely cling: God, our Father, has never inflicted one single wrong

upon any human soul since the morning stars sang together.

We need to hold firmly to this fact because there is a constant tendency to charge God with calamities for which He is in no sense responsible. "Why does not God stop the war ?" is a question that was asked again and again in those awful days of blood and tears. He did not stop the war for the same reason that He did not prevent it. And He did not prevent it for the simple reason that He could not. God made man free. He has given him the privilege of choosing the right. He has given him the power to take the path that leads ever upward and where the light lingers forevermore. But with this there must also go the privilege of wrong choice. If man is gifted with the possibility of climbing, he must also have the possibility of descending into the depths. Therefore, there are tragic calamities occurring every day that God simply cannot prevent and allow man to continue to be man.

Last week I was turning away from a new made grave. As I walked through the silent city of the dead, there was a certain tombstone that drew my attention. Or to speak more correctly, it was a certain word on that tombstone. That word fairly shrieked of tragedy and of bitterness, and, I half guessed, of frenzied rebellion. The word was "MURDERED." And I stopped to read. There was the name of a girl, then "Born 1901. Murdered 1917." And I wondered if these brokenhearted parents blamed God for that foul deed. I wonder if when the nurse went to sleep and your child died, you charged God with the calamity. I wonder if when that man lied to you, cheated you, robbed you, you blamed God and got angry with Him about it.

There is a story that years ago there was a charming

girl in the fresh bloom of womanhood. A man who was
an office bearer in the Church met her and made love to
her. He wooed her and won her and wrecked her.
From that day she became a hater of her kind. Sad-
dest of all, she shook her soiled fist in the face of the
Almighty and blamed Him. She was blind enough to
hate Him for a wrong that He hated with an intensity
infinitely beyond her own. Oh, heart, maybe you have
suffered, maybe you have been greatly wronged. If so,
in the name of justice, in the name of reason, in the
name of fair play, do not blame God. He is the eternal
foe of every form of evil. To blame Him, therefore,
is to be guilty of deepest injustice. To blame Him also
is to greatly wrong your own soul.

2. The second fact that we learn from the story is
that while God is not the author of evil, He is not helpless in the face of that evil. When the brook dried, Elijah did not have to die of thirst. Our God is infinitely
resourceful. He had other plans for him. Over yonder
at Zarephath was a widow at whose skirts a hungry
child was plucking. She was a woman who was not only
sorely in need of material bread, but more sorely in
need of the Bread of Life. God sent His prophet to find
sustenance there. She became a blessing to him and he
became a far greater blessing to her. There was a witness needed on Mount Carmel. God was eager to show
His wayward children that He could still answer by
fire, and Elijah must go from the brookside to accomplish this high task. Then Christ needed some suffering and understanding soul to talk with Him about the
Cross centuries later on the Mount of Transfiguration.
And Elijah needed the ministry of the dry brook, its
anguish and pain and perplexity, to fit him for this

high task that he was to share with Moses on the Mount! God did not dry Elijah's brook, but He overruled the calamity that had come through the sin of others to the enrichment of the life of the prophet and to the enrichment of the world.

Thus our mighty God has been working through all the centuries. That was a great wrong that the Jews did to Paul when they arrested him and had him put in prison. After remaining for two years in prison at Cæsarea, he was carried to Rome. God was not responsible for Paul's hardships. He was not responsible for his persecution. He was not to blame for his imprisonment in Rome. But if He was not to blame, neither was He defeated by the wicked designs of Paul's enemies. He turned the evil intended by foes into good. Thus Paul was able to write to friends one day: "The things that have happened unto me have fallen out rather to the furtherance of the Gospel."

That was a terrible calamity that came to the tinker preacher years ago in England. Bunyan was so eager to preach the saving Word to the people about him. But he was shut in jail. God did not put him there. But He changed his imprisonment into freedom. And He changed his limitations into illimitable opportunities for service. Shut in from speaking to his own day, he spoke to all days. He became an abiding minister, guiding souls from the City of Destruction to Mount Zion. He leads generation after generation to see the far views from the Delectable Mountains. He enables them from century to century to rejoice amidst the unfading beauties of the Land of Beulah.

3. This story tells us the conditions upon which God is able to change our evil into good and our losses into

gain. It was not a matter of necessity that the tragedy of the dry book became a blessing to Elijah. It might have been the ruin of him. It might have robbed him of his faith. It might have killed his usefulness. It might have caused him to die a rebellious madman upon its parched shores. Such things have happened again and again. I heard a man cry once this exceeding bitter cry: "I could curse God, if I knew there was a God, for letting Mary die."

How then did the prophet change his calamity into capital? Simply by remaining within the circle of the will of God. All things do not work together for good for everybody. There are times when all things seem to work together for our undoing and our utter destruction. But there is one for whom all things work together for good now and ever more, and that is the man that loves God. The man who loves God is defeated by no disaster. He is conquered by no calamity. There is absolutely nothing that can come to him that God cannot cause to work for his good. For such a man He can change every defeat into victory and every loss into gain. Therefore, if you are within the circle of His will, there is absolutely no harm that can come to you in time or eternity. Oh, what a wonderful God is ours!

"I know not what the future hath
    Of marvel or surprise.
I only know that life and death
    His mercy underlies.

And if my heart and flesh be weak
    To bear the untried pain,
A bruised reed He will not break,
    But strengthen and sustain.

And so beside the silent sea
I await the muffled oar,
Assured no harm can come to me
On ocean or on shore.

I know not where His islands lift
Their fronded palms in air,
I only know I cannot drift
Beyond His love and care."

SERMONS ON
NEW TESTAMENT CHARACTERS

Rev. CLOVIS G. CHAPPELL, D.D.

SERMONS ON
NEW TESTAMENT
CHARACTERS

BY

Rᴇᴠ. CLOVIS G. CHAPPELL, D.D.

Author of "The Village Tragedy," "Sermons on Biblical Characters," "More Sermons on Biblical Characters," "The Modern Dance," etc.

HARPER & BROTHERS PUBLISHERS
NEW YORK AND LONDON

CONTENTS

SERMONS ON
NEW TESTAMENT CHARACTERS

SERMONS ON NEW TESTAMENT CHARACTERS

I

THE LARGEST GIVER—THE POOR WIDOW

Mark 12 : 43

"Verily I say unto you, that this poor widow
hath cast more in, than all they which have
cast into the treasury."

I

The scene is the Temple of God in Jerusalem. The
collection is being taken. Christ is present and is
watching the proceedings with keen interest. He always does. He is profoundly concerned with what we
do with our money. He is ever attentive to our financial programmes. He is abidingly interested in our
conduct when the offering is taken. He watches with
deep concern what we do when we face the collection
plate.

Church people sometimes say: "I wish my pastor
would preach the Gospel and stop talking about money."
But it is impossible to preach the Gospel and not talk
about money. Christ had more to say about money
than He had to say about repentance, as vital as that
subject is. He had more to say about money than He

9

had to say about the new birth. He had more to say about money than He had to say about heaven. He had more to say about money than He had to say about hell. It is impossible, therefore, to preach the Gospel and not deal with this vital subject of money.

1. Christ is interested in the collection because money is power. Money is pent up force. It can be used for the defeating of the ends of justice. It can be used for the wrecking of character. It can be used for the retarding of the progress of the Kingdom of God. It can also be used for the promotion of that Kingdom. It can be used for the purifying of society and for the rebuilding of shattered and broken lives. Christ is therefore naturally profoundly interested in what we do with whatever financial power comes into our possession.

2. Christ is interested in the collection because what we do with our money is an index to our characters. The man who invests largely in the pursuit of pleasure is a pleasure seeker. The man who invests largely in books is a lover of literature. The man who invests largely in the Church of Jesus Christ is quite likely to be a Christian. Of course a man may give and give liberally and yet not be a saint. But it is utterly impossible to be a saint and be niggardly and stingy in our giving. What a man does with his money is a good indication of what he is.

For this reason every collection is a kind of judgment occasion. For this reason the plate that receives your offering becomes a throne before which your character is tested. You judge yourself. If the opportunity to give is an offence to you, if you are bored by it, if you are annoyed and even at times angered, you mark yourself not as an unselfish lover of Jesus Christ, but as a selfish lover of the world. If, on the other hand, you rejoice in the privilege of giving, you mark yourself as kindred to your Lord, whose supreme task is giving from eternity to eternity.

Not only do we judge ourselves in the presence of the collection plate, but Christ also judges us. He cannot help it. He sees what we give. If our gifts are mean and niggardly, He knows it. If they are sweet with the sacrificial breath of Calvary, He knows that. Therefore, when we face the collection plate, we either sadden our Lord or we gladden Him. We win His approval or His disapproval. We call forth either His commendation or His condemnation. We judge ourselves and are judged by our Lord by what we do with the wealth that He has put into our hands.

II

What did Jesus see as He sat over against the treasury?

1. He saw much that was commendable. He saw many rich men cast their gifts into the treasury. That was fine. There were rich men in that far-off day that were interested in the Church of God. They were interested enough to attend it. They were interested enough to support it by their means. And, thank God, there are such still. All the wealth is not in the hands of the Godless. There are rich men who are not too tired on Sunday morning to come to God's house. They do not all have to rest by going to the golf links and desecrating the Sabbath Day. Many of them are found in the Church and many of them give of their means to the support of the Church.

2. Not only were the rich men present with their

gifts that day, but they were liberal in their giving. "Many that were rich cast in much." These rich men did not give meanly. They did not say: "I will give my mite." Many a stingy man has read this story and has found in it only an excuse for increased stinginess. For a rich man to have given a mite would have been nothing less than a burning shame. These men did not throw in pennies when they might have thrown in dollars. They gave liberally. "Many that were rich cast in much." It was a magnificent offering that was made for the Lord's cause on that day.

3. But there was one giver who did not cast in much. "There came a certain poor widow." She was a woman who had suffered. She was a woman who had had her heart broken. She was a woman who had known the pinch of poverty. Not only had she known what it was to be miserably poor, but that was a present experience with her. She felt no uneasiness lest her home should be burglarised while she was at church. There was not the fraction of a penny in her humble little home. All she had in the world was in her hand. And that was so little that she was half ashamed to give it. And yet she could not withhold it. And so she cast into the treasury two mites, which make a farthing.

Had you been by when this money was counted at the close of the day, you would not have heard any praise for the great gift of this widow. It was only a fraction of a cent. It was hardly worth counting. But the many gifts of those who gave much bulked large. Any adding machine could have added them, but there was that in the gift of the widow that was beyond the power of the best adding machine. Christ alone could rightly estimate the full value of it. And when He had cast up the amount, He declared, "This poor widow hath cast more in than all they which have cast into the treasury."

III

What was there in this gift of the widow that made it more than all the gifts that the rich cast into the treasury? Certainly it was not more in amount.

1. It was more because it represented more fidelity on the part of the giver. It was so little that this widow could give. "What are two mites worth toward the carrying on of God's work in the world?" she might have asked. "What are they worth to Him who holds the wealth of the world in His hands? They will mean next to nothing to Him. They mean much to me. They are all I have." The human thing, therefore, for her to have done was simply to have done nothing. How many take that position! Their name is legion. But what lies back of such conduct? Unfaithfulness. And the one who is unfaithful in the least will also be unfaithful in much. It is not a question of how much good your gift will do to the cause of God. It is a question rather of your fidelity in the handling of that gift for your Lord, however small it may be.

A young fellow beat the street car conductor out of his car fare in our city the other day. What said he in excuse for his dishonesty? This: "The street car company is a large corporation. It has ample means. It certainly will not miss the seven cents that I failed to pay it. It does not need an amount so insignificant." But that is not the question. The street car company can get on without his seven cents, but he cannot get on well without being honest. The tragedy is not that the street car company will go broke without his money. It is rather that he will go morally broke by failing to be square. And it is not the fact that Jesus Christ cannot carry on His work in the world without our small gifts that constitutes the calamity of our failure to give. It is rather that we cannot otherwise hope to win His approval and enable Him to say: "Ye have been faithful over a few things, I will make you ruler over many things."

Fidelity in the use of our gifts and in the use of our means, however small, this is what wins the approval of our Lord. And this widow was bent on being faithful. She did not give simply because she felt like it. She gave because it was her duty to give. She gave because it was right. And, my brethren, we shall never give so as to meet the divine approval until we give from conviction. Some church members are liberal under the pastorate of one man and stingy under the pastorate of another. Such givers receive no commendation from Jesus Christ. He rather approves those that give from principle. He commends those who, whatever the situation is, are faithful in whatever talents He has put into their hands. It took a vast amount of fidelity to cause this widow to give this meagre gift, far more than was required of the rich to give their larger gifts.

2. This widow cast in more than all the rest in that her gift was more expensive to herself. There was more sacrifice in what she did. These rich men gave liberally, but they did not give sacrificially. They gave of their abundance. They gave of their superfluity. They did not have to deny themselves of a single pleasure because of what they gave. They did not have less to eat nor less to wear nor less comfortable homes in which to live. Their gifts were large, but they were not stained

by blood nor soaked in sweat. They only gave what they did not really need for themselves.

But the gift of the widow was costly. It cost her everything. When those two mites slipped from her lean fingers, she had absolutely nothing left. Her gift was, therefore, shot through with the spirit of the Cross. If there is no sacrifice in our service, if there is no sacrifice in our giving, then it is not Christian. Costless giving may help after a fashion, but it is not beautiful either in the eyes of God or of men. Christ puts His stamp of approval only on the giving that costs. His gifts cost Him something. Ours are to cost us something.

There is an old story of an artist who painted a picture that was touched by a lovely and fascinating crimson that no other artist was able to imitate. They studied this picture and sought for its secret in vain. But when the artist was dead and they were preparing him for burial, they noticed above his heart a half-healed wound. Then it was that they understood. As this artist had painted he had dipped his brush into his own heart's blood. That was the secret of the winsome crimson they could not imitate. That was the secret of the fascinating picture that had cast its spell upon them. They could not paint as he painted because they were unwilling to pay the price he paid. The picture that is beautiful is costly. And the giving that is beautiful is also costly.

3. This widow gave more than all the rest because there was more love in her giving. Her sacrifice would have gone for nothing had there been no love in it. "Though I bestow all my goods to feed the poor, and though I give my body to be burned, and have not love, it profiteth me nothing." The richest of gifts are but so

much refuse in the sight of God if there is a sordid motive behind them. On the other hand, the smallest gift is beautiful beyond all words if it is given for love's sake.

This widow gave because she loved. She was not seeking popular applause. She knew she would not find it. She was giving because her love would not allow her to withhold. For love, you know, is very active. It is very insistent upon doing something. It will do the big thing if it can. If it cannot, it will do the little thing. It will adorn a palace if it can. If it cannot, it will beautify and sweeten a cabin. It will serve in a big way if it is within its power. If not, it will serve in an obscure and hidden way. But of this you may be sure, love will give and give of its best. And that best will make the strongest possible appeal to the heart of Christ. It will also make the strongest appeal to the hearts of men.

Some years ago a saintly woman of my acquaintance told me of a visit she made to a sick girl away back in the heart of the hills. The girl's father was little more than an outcast. Her mother was dead. There she lay upon a bed that had no sheets. Her head was upon pillows that had no coverings. She seemed absolutely destitute of all knowledge of Christ. Into that needy home this women went and out of her own poverty she ministered, and to this benighted girl who was dying of consumption she preached Jesus. At her last visit the girl said: "I will not be living when you come again. Here is a keepsake I want to give you to remember me by." And she gave the woman who had led her to Christ a little pin that was not worth five cents anywhere. Yet it was the best she had. And that pin is a treasure to that saintly woman to-day. Love's tears had fallen upon it and had been transformed into diamonds. She values it because it is the best gift of a grateful and loving heart.

IV

Now, since this poor widow made the largest gift that was brought to the treasury that day, her story is one full of encouragement for ourselves.

1. It heartens us because it puts the very poorest of us on an equal footing with the richest. We who have the smallest gifts have exactly the same opportunity of winning God's approval as those who have the largest. Who will be the largest contributor to First Methodist Church this year? We do not know. It may be the one who has more wealth than any other man in the church. It may be the one who has the least. It will surely be the one who is most faithful and most sacrificing and most loving in the doing of what he can. The one who does that will rank with this poor widow. He will be graded as she was, one hundred per cent. The richest man in all the world cannot pass that mark. But the poorest in all the world can reach to it.

2. This story heartens us because it tells us the very smallest gifts, if they are our best, are not despised. Men may despise them. Sometimes they do. But this is true only when they fail to understand. Our Lord never fails to understand. Therefore, He never looks upon them with contempt. If two mites are our best, His heart glows with gladness just as much as if we had given millions. And if it be so that we have not even that much, He will receive with gladness whatever we give. "He that giveth a cup of cold water shall not lose his reward."

Therefore, since God does not despise our gifts, however small, let us see to it that nothing prevents us from offering them. Let us not be prevented from doing so by self-pity. Let not the pity of others prevent us. When we made the every member canvass a few weeks ago, some returned saying that they went into homes that were so poor that they hesitated to accept an offering. But let us not become pitiful beyond our Lord. He had no hesitancy in accepting the last mite from this poor widow. He will take the last penny you have and He will do it joyfully.

But this He will do not because He is grasping. He will do it because He knows that it is more blessed to give than to receive. He will do it because He knows our giving conditions our receiving. "Give, and it shall be given unto you." The sureness of your giving conditions the sureness of your receiving. A hand that is wide open to give will be wide open to receive. The hand that recklessly gives all will receive all. Therefore our Lord does not hesitate to take our very last mite because such giving does not impoverish us, but makes us rich forevermore. Let us therefore aspire to the place of the largest giver, for in so doing we will also win the place of the largest receiver.

II

THE EVANGELIST—PHILIP

The Acts 8 : 35

"Then Philip opened his mouth, and began at the same scripture, and preached unto him Jesus."

I

"Then Philip opened his mouth." That is fine. That is exceedingly hopeful. One of the tragedies of many who are in the Church to-day is that of the closed mouth. So many seem possessed with the demon of dumbness. We open our mouths to eat. We open our mouths to buy and sell. We open our mouths to gossip. We sometimes open our mouths to criticise. But too few of us open our mouths to preach Jesus.

"Then Philip opened his mouth." That indicates courage. It is only a few days since Philip has seen a very ugly murder that was committed because a certain friend of his insisted upon opening his mouth. If young Stephen of the clear head and shining face and Spirit-filled heart had only kept silent, he would not have been mobbed. If he had only known how to hold his tongue, he would not have been the victim of those cruel stones. If he had not insisted upon opening his mouth, his mangled body would not now be lying in its untimely grave up Jerusalem way. He was determined to open his mouth and proclaim the good tidings of great joy. Hence he died a martyr.

Philip was well aware of all these facts. Therefore, as he fled from Jerusalem, Prudence walked at his
side with her wise counsel and said: "Now, Philip, it is
all right to be a Christian; it is well enough to be a follower of Jesus Christ, but do not be too outspoken. Do
not insist on telling your story to others. Learn to keep
silent." But in spite of all these very sane admonitions,
it stands written in the text that "Philip opened his
mouth." It was a courageous thing to do. It is a thing
that many of us are afraid to do to this day. We are
not afraid to talk on many themes, but to open our
mouth to preach Jesus is something the very thought
of which fills us with a kind of terror.

"Then Philip opened his mouth." That speaks also
of spontaneity. Philip was not simply driving himself
to preach. He felt that he could not help speaking. His
testimony would have been that of some of his fellow-
disciples: "We cannot but speak the things that we have
seen and heard." There was good news in his heart that
was clamouring for utterance. There were Niagaras of
Gospel truth beating against the gateway of his lips and
demanding an outlet. So full was this man of his joyous theme that preaching Jesus was not so much a duty
as a privilege. "Then Philip opened his mouth, and
began at the same scripture, and preached unto him
Jesus."

II

Who was Philip?

He was not one of the apostles. He was not an or-
dained minister. Philip was a layman. He was a member of the Official Board of the First Church of Jerusalem. When the apostles decided that it was necessary

that seven men be elected to look after the temporal affairs of this infant church, Philip was one of the men chosen. He was not chosen for the work of the ministry primarily. He was chosen for the lowly task of serving tables. Yet we remember this man to-day not so much because he was a competent man of business as because he was a Spirit-filled and effective evangelist.

Philip conducted a successful revival in Samaria. He was used of God in preaching to the multitudes. But doubtless if you had talked to him near the end of his pilgrimage, he would have told you that the most useful part of his ministry had been his work with the individual. He would have said: "I have been able to render my largest service to my Master through my dealing with men face to face and heart to heart." If Philip had not so said, he would be an exception to the rule. For the most successful evangelists through all the years have won their greatest victories for the Kingdom through dealing with men one by one.

And this type of preaching is possible for every one of us. All of us cannot proclaim God's message from the pulpit. But there is not one but can preach Jesus to the individual. This is a high and holy privilege that is within reach of the least as well as of the greatest. There is absolutely no doubt but that Jesus Christ expects every follower of His to be a soul-winner. It may be that we do not expect so much of ourselves. Sad to say, a large part of the Church to-day leaves this supremely important task to the pastor and to a few faithful workers. But it is all wrong. Preaching Jesus to the individual is the privilege of every Christian.

Not only is this the privilege of every one who is

follower of Christ, it is also his solemn responsibility. Because we can preach Christ, therefore we ought to preach Him. And because we ought to preach, we are by no means guiltless if we refuse to do so. "Woe is me if I preach not the Gospel." That word befits the lips of every saint just as much as it befit the lips of Saint Paul. Because we can preach, we must preach. "Every branch in me that beareth not fruit, He taketh away." Even a fruitless fig tree met the curse of eternal barrenness. This was the case in spite of the fact that Christ had not invested His blood in the redemption of that fig tree. But He has invested it in the redemption of ourselves. We cannot, therefore, be fruitless and guiltless at the same time. Because we can preach, we must preach. Such was the conviction of Philip. He took the command of his Master to preach the Gospel to every creature seriously.

III

But how was it that the Lord was able to use him for this particular preaching mission ?

1. He could do so because Philip was obedient. He was open to Divine guidance. He had faith enough to obey God even when obedience looked foolish and ridiculous. Philip was engaged in a great revival in Samaria when the message came to him to leave this city with its populous streets and rejoicing multitudes. While the shouts of those being won to Christ were yet in his ears, he was ordered to set out for a desert country miles away. It looked like a very foolish thing to do. But Philip obeyed.

There are very few of us who are willing, with this evangelist and with Paul, to be fools for Christ's sake.

We are wofully afraid of making ourselves ridiculous.
Joshua was a man of the type of Philip. How the wise
must have laughed at him when they saw the absurd
tactics that he was using for the capturing of Jericho.
He was employing no battering ram. He was not shoot-
ing an arrow. He was not hurling a single spear. He
was just marching round the city blowing a ram's horn.
It certainly was a foolish and ridiculous thing to do,
at least in the eyes of men. But the significant part of
the story is that he captured the city. I have known
many a campaign conducted in a far more sane and
dignified fashion to fail of its objective altogether.
Blessed the man who has learned to obey God, for "Behold, to obey is better than sacrifice."

So Philip set out from Samaria and journeyed toward the south. He did not know exactly the purpose
of his journey, but he was sure that his Lord was not
sending him upon a fool's errand. Therefore, he trav-
elled with open eye and attentive ear. He was looking
for some way to be of service. There are those that
tell us how willing they are to be useful, but they never
find anything to do. But to those who are really willing, no day passes without its opportunity. Again and
again friends cross our path whom we might help if we
are only eager and watchful as was Philip.

After quite a long journey Philip reached the forks of
the road. He came into the highway that leads down
from Jerusalem to Gaza. It was a barren and unsightly country and seemed a most unlikely place for
God to send a man to preach. Philip wonders what it
all means, but he is not left long in doubt. Just up the
road yonder he sees a chariot coming surrounded by a
retinue of soldiers and servants. A great man is approaching. Of that much he is sure. And then the

Spirit spoke within his heart: "Go near and join thyself to this chariot."

Philip was doubtless astonished. It seemed a strange command. There were dozens of good reasons for his refusing to obey. Had we been by we would possibly have warned Philip after this fashion: "That man coming there is a perfect stranger to you. You never saw him before and will doubtless never see him again. Besides, he is a very prominent man. He is Secretary of the Treasury for the Kingdom of Ethiopia. He is a man of ability. He is a man of wealth and political power. Your Gospel is well enough for the poor. It is altogether a fit message for the down-and-out. But do not make yourself ridiculous by trying to preach to a man like this Ethiopian Statesman. His cup is already full. He will therefore not hear you. In trying to make him hear, you will only injure your cause and make yourself a laughing stock."

Now it is good to remember that this Gospel of ours is for the poor and for the unfortunate and for the outcast. But it is not for these only. It is also for the rich and for the powerful and for those who in the eyes of the world seem most favoured of fortune. It is for the down-and-out. It is also for the up-and-out and for all in between. Society has no greater tendency to become rotten at the bottom than it does at the top. I do not know but that we are in more danger of moral decay in America at the top than at the bottom. Our Gospel is therefore needed by all. "For all have sinned and come short of the glory of God."

That was true of this Ethiopian Statesman. In spite of his position, in spite of all that wealth had flung into his lap, he has more heart-hunger than he knows how to manage. His soul is thirsting for God, for the living

God. His Maker has so fashioned him that it is utterly impossible for him to find rest and peace and abiding satisfaction apart from Himself. He cannot be content with things. An Unseen Presence is with him as he rides that will not let him be content. The Spirit of God is there striving with him, wooing him, making him to loathe the thing that he is and to long for the better man that he may be. And that same spirit is speaking to our hearts to-day. We may stop our ears to His appeal, but He lovingly pursues us. He is present with us in our infancy before our mother's lips have kissed us. Through all our wandering ways He journeys with us, convicting us of sin, seeking patiently to lure us to those heights of holy fellowship that are within reach even of the weakest and of the worst.

What response did Philip make to the command of the Spirit? He obeyed. He refused to be frightened by the position of this Ethiopian. It is easier to preach to one who is at the rear of the procession than to one near the front. But our message is for all. So Philip listened only to the voice of his Lord. And we read of him this fine word: "Philip ran." Notice the eagerness of him, the earnestness, the whole-hearted enthusiasm. He ran. Oh, for more fleet-footed saints! We need them in the pulpit. We need them on the Official Board. We need them as Sunday School teachers. We need them throughout the entire membership of the Church. We are so slow. We go with such leaden feet about our tasks. Oh, that this sentence might be written about a growing number of us, "He ran."

Philip was enthusiastic and whole-hearted in his obedience. He ran fleet-footed on the errands of his Lord. And as he thus goes running toward the chariot, I dare say that he was praying earnestly that the Lord would give him an opening. He was planning how he might tactfully begin the conversation. And nothing requires greater tact than soul winning. Soon he is close enough to see that the great man is reading. That seems to make his task more difficult. Possibly he is reading some document of state and will refuse to be disturbed. But Philip does not hesitate. He presses bravely on.

2. Philip knew his Bible. Now the Evangelist is within hearing distance. This Ethiopian is reading aloud. And when Philip heard what he was reading, he had to hug his heart to keep it from leaping from his bosom. The words were entirely familiar to him. He had learned them in the Synagogue when he was a child. He had had them flooded with infinite light by the events of recent days. There was not another passage in all the Word of God that Philip would have been quite so glad to find this Ethiopian Statesman reading as the one he was reading, which was none other than the fifty-third chapter of Isaiah.

The stately words came to him on the desert air: "We all like sheep have gone astray; we have turned every one to his own way; and the Lord hath laid on Him the iniquity of us all. But He was wounded for our transgressions. He was bruised for our iniquities; the chastisement of our peace was upon Him; and with His stripes we are healed." "He was led as a lamb to the slaughter, and as a sheep before his shearers is dumb, so He openeth not His mouth." And Philip looked to see the light break upon the face of the Ethiopian, but there was no light there. There was only a frown of perplexity.

"Pardon me, but do you understand what you are reading?" And Philip's face was so radiant and so

eager that the great statesman felt at once that here
was one who knew. "No, I do not understand," he answered. "How can I except some man teach me."
Christ uses men for the salvation of other men. He
seems shut up to that method. If there is not "some
man" to teach, then the seeking soul will not be won.
A message must have a messenger. An evangel is of no
avail without an evangelist. "How can they hear without a preacher?"

3. He knew his Lord. Then this statesman who did
not understand invited Philip into his chariot. And I
can imagine that few men ever mounted a chariot more
rapidly or more eagerly than did this evangelist. And
they re-read this marvellous passage together. "He was
wounded for our transgressions. He was bruised for
our iniquities; the chastisement of our peace was upon
Him; and with His stripes we are healed." And the
Ethiopian is asking Philip a question. "Of whom is the
prophet speaking? Of himself or of some other?" In
other words: "Who is this that was wounded for our
transgressions. Who is this Lamb of God that taketh
away the sin of the world. Who is it that is able to
deal adequately with sin in your life and mine?"

Who indeed? Preacher, do you know? Sunday
School Teacher, do you know? Member of the Official
Board, do you know? Who is it that saves? Parents,
with your responsibility of training young lives for
God, do you know? When the blear-eyed outcast asks
this question, have you an answer? When the bright-
eyed, questioning child in your home asks it, can you
answer? Who is it that saves? Do you know? Not
as a theory, not as a tradition, but as a personal experience?

Philip knew. "And he began at the same scripture

and preached unto him Jesus." Would you not have liked to hear the sermon? We can imagine how it ran. "Of whom is the prophet speaking?" asked the Ethiopian. "He is not speaking of himself," the Evangelist replies, "he is speaking of Jesus. He is speaking of the One who was crucified in Jerusalem a few months ago. He is speaking of Him who conquered death and hell and the grave. He is speaking of One who is 'able to save unto the uttermost them that come unto God by Him.' He is our sin bea. er. 'With His stripes we are healed.' All you have to do is just to accept the healing that He brings to you; receive the salvation that He offers you."

And while Philip is yet speaking a light breaks upon the darkened face of the African Statesman. He enters upon the blessed experience that, thank God, is for all men in all times and in all climes. This man who was on his way from church with his heart yet hungry then and there found the Bread of Life. This man who, in spite of the magnificent ritual of the Temple, was yet burning with thirst, then and there "drank of the water of life freely." And we read this happy ending of the story: that he went on his way rejoicing. And not only did he rejoice, but it is safe to say that many another weary soul came to share his joy with him in the dark continent of Africa.

This scene brings to my mind a football game that I witnessed years ago. A husky fellow carrying the ball for the opposing team broke through our line. He dodged every antagonist. There is only one man now between him and the goal. If he makes this goal, the game is lost. And there is only one man to stop him, our wiry little quarterback. How small he looks! He seems not more than half the size of the man that is

carrying the ball.   Can the quarterback stop him? That
was the question that made our hearts almost stand still.
If he cannot, then the game is lost.

The big husky bore down upon him.   He made no
effort to dodge.   He knew that his seemingly insignificant antagonist would be too quick for him.   He rushed
into him head-on with the purpose of knocking him out.
Would the quarterback stand up to him? We knew that
if there was the least bit of yellow in him he would flinch
and lose.   But he never gave an inch.   And though I do
not know how it happened to this day, I do know this:
that even yet I can hear the terrific impact of the big
man's body against the ground where the little fellow
threw him.   And the day was saved because this one
man, our last chance, stood in his place and held true.

And this, I am persuaded, was the last chance of the
Ethiopian.   There was no man in Africa that knew
Jesus.   He was leaving the saints of the early Church
long distances behind him.   His one chance centres in
the Evangelist, Philip, and the Evangelist did not fail.
The battle was won and heaven was made glad, and the
heart of the saved and the heart of the preacher were
also made glad.   And now the scene changes from that
far off day to this, and from that bit of desert country
to this populous city.   And your road is running into
that of your friend, into that of your husband, into that
of your child.   It is your opportunity to preach.   It
is his opportunity to be saved.   What are you going to
do about it?

IV

Now, let me remind you, my brethren, that it was
not simply by accident that this needy statesman and

this Spirit-guided Evangelist met that day at the forks of the road. God's hand was in it. This Ethiopian had been to Jerusalem. There were quite a few Christians there. But they had missed him in some way. He had not been won by them. And now he is on his way home. Unless somebody heads him off; unless somebody hurries and gets between him and his destination, the chances are that he will never be reached. He will go home and die without ever coming into possession of the Life that is life indeed. He will go home with lips forever dumb that might have spoken a marvellous story to the glory of God and to the gladdening of many saddened lives.

I dare to believe also that it is not by mere chance that you and I have met at the forks of the road this morning in God's house. You have come a long and tedious journey. The preacher has also come a long way to meet you. He did not dream years ago when he entered the service of his Lord that his road would thus cross yours. But here we are this morning, you and I, at the forks of the road. I dare to believe that God has put me in the path of some of you to keep you from going away and missing the thrill of the knowledge of Jesus Christ. I dare to believe that He has thrown this message this Sabbath morning across your path to keep some of you from the tragedy of a wasted life.

And will you not also dare to believe, my brethren, that it is not merely by accident that your path has crossed that of your friend? Will you not believe that God has a blessed and holy purpose in bringing you into intimate fellowship with the members of your own household, with the pupils of your own class? You are travelling as Christ's evangelist. Your road has run into the road of a friend who is travelling away from

God.   The one big chance of that friend may be at your hands.   If you let him escape, he will never be reached. If you let your child slip by you unsaved, the chances are that he will spend his life in sin.   May God be able to write this about you, "He preached unto him Jesus."

III

THE DESERTER—DEMAS

II Timothy 4:10

"Demas hath forsaken me, having loved this
present world."

I

That is a disappointing sentence. It is the final
chapter in the story of this one time saint. Paul had
to write a word very much like this about John Mark
on one occasion. John Mark deserted Paul. But the
story of his desertion is not his final story. Mark came
back. "Take Mark and bring him with thee, for he is
profitable unto me for the ministry." That is the
last word we read about him. But Demas, so far as we
know, never came back. "Demas hath forsaken me."
He was gone when this pathetic sentence was penned,
and he remained gone to the end of the chapter.

"Demas hath forsaken me." What a tragic break-
down. But if this sentence tells of a disappointing
present, it also tells of a glorious past. It reminds us of
that good day in the life of Demas when he was the companion of Paul. It reminds us of that day when he was
the companion and fellow-worker of Paul's Lord.
Demas had shared the great hopes of this missionary
saint with whom he was associated. He participated in
his daring dreams. He had a part in his far and glori-

32

ous visions. Paul's purpose of world conquest was also in some measure the purpose of his friend, Demas.

Not only did this young man share in the daring dream of St. Paul, he also shared in his efforts toward the realisation of that dream. When Paul had gone forth to the preaching of the Gospel, Demas had walked at his side. When Paul had faced dangers, Demas had faced those dangers with him. When the foundation of a new church was laid, Demas was there. Demas had shared Paul's vision, and he had also shared Paul's task.

But that experience is of yesterday. That fascinating and heroic chapter is in the past. Demas is not found at the side of Paul any more. Demas no longer shares in Paul's dreams. He no longer labours at the high task that engaged his great-hearted friend. He has deserted his Master, Jesus Christ. And Paul writes with a sorrow that wets his face with tears. "Demas hath forsaken me."

II

What got the matter with Demas? Of what insidious disease did he sicken? Where began the little leak that set the waters to roaring about this pathetic wreck? Did Demas commit some crime that made it necessary for him to leave Rome? Did Demas get his hand into the coffers of the church and take that which was not his? Did Demas allow some ugly sin to grip him and squeeze the fine juices from his soul and fling him away into the Devil's garbage can?

No, Demas was guilty of no crime. He was besmirched by no disgraceful and ugly sin. The foe that wrought the ruin of Demas appears so innocent and harmless that we would scarcely regard it as a foe at all. What proved the undoing of Demas? The answer is in the text. "Demas hath forsaken me, having loved this present world."

So this text implies that if a man loves this present world he will cease to love God. It implies that the love of the world and the love of the Lord Jesus Christ cannot home in the same heart. And what is implied in this text is clearly taught elsewhere in the Word of God. John says: "Love not the world, neither the things that are in the world. If any man love the world, the love of the Father is not in him." He declares that the very moment the love of the world enters into our hearts, the love of God goes out. And James, if possible, makes it even more emphatic when he declares that the love of the world is enmity against God. That is, the lover of the world is not only not a lover of God, but he is God's personal enemy. And Paul wrote a letter one day that is bespattered with tears. He says: "I tell you even weeping that some of you are enemies of the cross of Christ." And that which made them enemies of the cross of Christ was that they minded earthly things. They were in love with the world.

Jesus Christ also spoke to the same purpose. He told Pilate frankly that His Kingdom was not of this world, that if His Kingdom were of this world, then would His servants fight. Those who were His children, those who were His subjects were not worldly. They were set free from the bondage of the love of the world. About the sharpest word that ever fell from His lips was that which He spoke to Peter when Peter urged Him to avoid the cross. "Be it far from thee, Lord," said this hot headed disciple when Jesus began to tell how He must suffer. But the Master was quick and cutting in His rebuke: "Get thee hence, Satan, for thou savourest not the things that be of God, but the things that be of men." That is, "You are not talking the language of the Godlike. You are talking the language of the world." So it is very evident that if the Bible is true we cannot love the world and be saints at the same time.

III

But what is this world that we are forbidden to love?
Surely it is not this physical universe of mountains and hills, of rivers and seas, of skies and stars. When God made these things He pronounced them very good. And if it should so happen that we admire them and even love them, I do not think for a moment that our Lord would object. Should we feel it in our hearts to exclaim:

> "O world, as God has made it, all is beauty,
> And knowing this is love, and love is duty,"

I do not think that we would be talking in language that is unchristian. Were we to see in "the meanest flower that blows thoughts that often lie too deep for tears," I do not think that we would for that reason be displeasing to our Lord. Were we to find "sermons in stones, books in running brooks and good in everything," we would not thereby stamp ourselves as pagan. If we were to cry with Wordsworth, "Heaven lies about us in our infancy," and then pass on to the even finer strain of Lowell:

> "Not only round our infancy
> Does heaven with all its splendour lie,

Daily with souls that cringe and plot,
We Sinais climb and know it not.
Over our manhood bend the skies,
Against our fallen and traitor lives
The great winds utter prophecy,
And to old age's drowsy blood
Still shouts the inspiring sea":

even here we would be talking the language of real
sainthood.   When we are forbidden to love the world,
then, it is not that we are forbidden to love and admire
this beautiful physical world that God has given us.

Nor are we forbidden to love the world of men.
"God so loved the world that He gave His only begotten
Son."   This love of God for the world was the love of
the men who live in the world.   The more we love folks,
the more we become like Christ.   Love is the big com-
modity that the world is short on:

"Do you know the world is dying
For a little bit of love?
Everywhere we hear them sighing
For a little bit of love.
For a love that rights the wrong,
Fills the heart with hope and song,
They have waited, oh, so long,
For a little bit of love."

No, we are certainly not forbidden to love the world of
men.   Let yourself go in this matter of loving folks.   A
broken-hearted mother said to me not long ago that she
was afraid she loved her first-born son too much.   He
was a fine, clean young fellow, and he was lying down-
stairs in his coffin at that moment.   When she said: "I
am afraid I loved him too much and God took him

away," I could but answer, "No, no, mother, you did not love him too much. You may have loved God too little. We all do that. But you did not love your laddie too much." The big tragedy of your life and mine is that we love so little.

IV

What then is the world that we are forbidden to love?
It is not a tangible and visible thing at all. To love the world, as another has pointed out, is to be brought into bondage to that something in the world that keeps the world from being Christ-like. What is it that keeps this every-day life that we are living in the here and now from being heavenly? It is this: there are so many of us that are selfish. There are so many of us that are putting forth our utmost endeavours to please ourselves. Self-pleasing is the spirit that dominates the world, and to love the world is to be brought under dominion of this spirit of self-pleasing. So that the text might read: "Demas forsook me, having desired to do as he pleased."

Now this desire to please ourselves does not always lead in the same direction. But it always leads away from God. The Prodigal Son was brought under the dominion of this spirit, and was thus led away into the Far Country. His elder brother remained very decently at home, but he was under the dominion of the same spirit, the spirit of selfishness. One man may live for his own ends and go to the gutter. His neighbour may live under the dominion of exactly the same motives and go to Congress. The significant matter is not the differing goals, but the common motive that is back of the arrival at both goals.

As Demas worked at Paul's side over in the great city

of Rome, he began to feel this love of the world tugging
at his heart. His friend, Paul, was always consulting
the higher Will. He was always subjecting himself to
the doing of Christ's will instead of his own. Demas
began to grow tired of it. There were people all about
him in Rome who were going their own way and seemingly making a great success of it. He could not shut
his eyes to this fact. He could not keep from asking
himself: "Why cannot I taste life as they are tasting it
and enjoy life as they seem to be enjoying it?"

It is night and these two saints are walking down the
streets of Rome on their way to church. About them are
the splendours of a city that has grown drunk upon the
vintage of the wide world. The atmosphere is perfumed
with pleasure and is vocal with the joyous laughter of
the gay. Soldiers are passing laden with the spoils of
war. Beauty is passing, offering her charms for the
taking. And Paul walks breast forward and seems
never to see the gay sights about him. But Demas sees.
And as he sees he begins to wonder if he had not better
"take the cash and let the credit go."

But the lights are growing dimmer and the streets
are narrower. At last they come to a place as weird
and dreary and repulsive as a tomb. It is a tomb—one
of the catacombs. And a few of the saints with faces
strangely alight are there for service. Demas sits down
among them, but there is not the joy in this meeting
with God's people that he once knew. In spite of himself he is out on the brilliantly lighted streets again.
Suddenly his mind is recalled from the gay scenes without to what Paul is saying: "The things that are seen
are temporal, but the things that are not seen are
eternal." "This great city of Rome that seems so abiding is only a passing show. A few more years and a bit

of wreckage and a stain of blood and a handful of bones will be all that will be left to tell that a caravan called Rome passed this way and camped for a night and then went into utter silence forever." And Demas said: "I wonder. Paul may be right, but I doubt it."

A few days later Demas' place is empty. He has fallen in love with the world. His heart has gone to the world and he has followed his heart. Desiring to please himself, he has left Paul and Paul's Christ and has journeyed to Thessalonica. He wants a life that is more colourful, more gay, less dull and drab and leaden. He is in love with the world. Therefore, he is going to take the way that he believes will most surely minister to his desire to laugh and revel and to enjoy. Paul may hold on to his life for Christ, but he is going to please himself for a while. And so he goes the way of the world.

You remember that rather strange condition that the father of Portia decided upon for the marriage of his daughter. Her picture was to be put in one of three caskets, and the suitor who chose the casket in which the likeness was found was to win her hand. One casket was of gold, the other of silver, the other of lead. The first had upon it this motto: "Who chooses me shall get what many men desire." The second, the silver, had this motto: "Who chooses me shall get as much as he deserves." The third, made of base lead, had this forbidding inscription: "Who chooses me must give and hazard all he hath."

You can readily see the difference in these inscriptions. The first two are practically alike: "Who chooses me shall get what many men desire." "Who chooses me shall get as much as he deserves." They both appeal to the man whose supreme passion is getting. But the

third says: "Who chooses me must give and hazard all
he hath." That appeals to one whose passion is giving.
And the picture was in the leaden casket. It was the
only way that this wise old father had of reaching a
hand from the grave and holding his daughter back
from the deep damnation of marrying a "getter."

v

Demas chose the golden casket. Demas became a
"getter." As such he left Paul and went to Thessalonica. What became of him after this we do not know.
For the sake of argument, however, we are going to as-
sume that loving the world, he won it. I imagine the
most palatial house in Thessalonica was the house in
which Demas lived. The finest carpets were the carpets
that were upon his floors, and the finest tapestry was
that that adorned his walls. And there were no feasts
in all the city like the feasts that were given by Demas,
the one-time friend and fellow-worker of St. Paul.

One night I attended one of these marvellous feasts,
and those that Demas had gathered about him were the
gayest of the gay. They belonged to the highest social
set of the city. And Demas entertained as one to the
manor born. But when the guests were all gone and
I went to congratulate him upon the great success of
his entertainment, I found him with care lines deep
in his face, and with an attitude so eloquent of heartache that I longed to cheer him up a bit. So I hastened to say, "Demas, I congratulate you upon your
vast wealth. But I wish you might meet a friend of
mine. I am sorry to say that he is in prison over in
Rome. His name is Paul. He is a great joy bringer."

And the soul of Demas stood up in his eyes and he

said: "Do you know Paul? I used to know him. The one oasis in this desert life of mine is the time I spent in his fellowship. The one bit of spring in this dreary and bleak winter was the time that I spent by his side. God forgive me for ever having left him. A thousand times while I have been money-grubbing here in Thessalonica I would have given every dirty dollar to have been at his side again as I was before the day of my shameful desertion."

And I turn away from this chilling atmosphere to look into a prison cell where Paul is being held. He is writing a letter. And as he writes a chilling breeze comes in through the prison window and fans the thin hair about his temples and I see him shiver. But he writes on. Again the breeze comes, but stronger and colder. And he feels behind him as if searching for a wrap, and then he smiles and says to himself: "Oh, my cloak. I remember now I left it at Troas with Carpus." And he writes: "Dear Timothy: 'The cloak that I left at Troas with Carpus, when thou comest, bring with thee. And do thy best to come before winter.'"

Poor aged Paul. I find it in my heart to pity him. But he pauses in his writing to look out a window. It is the window that looks into the past. It is a past of which he is not ashamed. There is many a sacrifice in it, many a conflict, many a persecution, many a sleepless night, many a tear. But the old hero looks upon it all with a smile, and then takes up his pen and writes: "I have fought the good fight; I have finished my course; I have kept the faith."

Here he pauses again and looks out through another window. It is the window that looks into the future. The scene that meets his gaze makes his face brighter still.   It is coronation day on the "other side," and among those who are being crowned he sees himself. And again he writes: "Henceforth there is laid up for me a crown of righteousness, which the Lord, the righteous judge, shall give me on that day.   And not to me only, but unto all them also that love his appearing." And as for me, I would like to take my stand anew this morning beside Paul, and, above all else, beside Paul's Christ.

WHITE FEATHERS—MARK

II Timothy 4 : 11

"Take Mark and bring him with thee: for he
is profitable unto me for the ministry."

I

Did you notice the name of the man for whom Paul
is calling? Paul, you know, is in the midst of trying
circumstances. He is in prison. He is surrounded by
dangers. Death is rattling the latch of his door. He
needs men about him who are to be trusted. Fair
weather friends are of no avail now. Parlour soldiers
count for less than nothing. He must have as his
helpers men of steady courage, men of hardy heroism,
men who stand ready to pay the last measure of devotion.

And when he looks about over his wide circle of
acquaintances for a man of this type, for whom does
he write? On whom does he call? Listen! "Take
Mark and bring him with thee: for he is profitable
unto me for the ministry." You read the sentence with
a gasp of amazement. Can it be that John Mark is
profitable? Can it be that the worthless has become
worthful? Has this useless young fellow become useful? Has this human liability changed into an asset?
For the last we heard of John Mark he was far

from being the type of man that we should call upon in a situation that demanded men of heroic mould.

About a dozen years ago when Paul and Barnabas were on the point of setting out on a second missionary journey, this man Mark offered his services, but Paul would not accept. He did not say then, "Mark is profitable unto me for the ministry." He said the opposite. Here is what we read: "Paul thought it not good to take him." Paul thought John Mark by his presence would add nothing at all. He did not think his joining the expedition would be of the least value. If you had asked him his opinion of this young man, Mark, he would have been obliged to tell you in all sincerity that he looked upon him as absolutely useless.

Not only did he regard him as useless, but as worse than useless. In a trying situation he would only be in the way. Instead of being an asset he would be a liability. Instead of being a help, he would be a hindrance. Paul loved Barnabas for many reasons. He loved him, in the first place, because Barnabas was genuinely lovable. Then Barnabas had befriended Paul at a time when friendship counted. When Paul went to Jerusalem the first time after his conversion, everybody suspected him. That is, everybody with one exception, and that one exception was Barnabas. Barnabas believed in him and stood by him.

Later when Barnabas went down to Antioch and saw how God was working in that great city, he sought some capable man as an assistant. The one to whom he turned was Paul. He introduced Paul to this vigorous church at Antioch. Then he and Paul had gone forth on their first missionary journey together. They had been brothers in a common enterprise. They had been the seers of a common vision, the dreamers of a common dream. They had preached together and prayed together and suffered together. They had been brought together in the bonds of a very intimate and tender fellowship.

There is no doubt that Paul loved Barnabas greatly. There is no doubt that this "son of consolation" was a tremendous help to Paul. But, as dearly as Paul loved Barnabas, and as helpful as he found him, he declared that he would rather go on his missionary journey alone than to go with Barnabas and John Mark. That is, he considered that John Mark would be a greater hindrance than Barnabas would be a help. He greatly desired the inspiring and bracing fellowship of Barnabas, but he had rather surrender that than be hampered and held back by that soft millstone, John Mark.

So it is very evident that at this time Paul had no admiration for Mark. He thought any missionary enterprise would be weakened rather than strengthened by his presence. He was firmly convinced that to have such a man as his assistant would mean a weight rather than wings. Yet some ten or twelve years later we find him speaking again of this man, and his tone is utterly changed. Instead of saying that Mark is useless, instead of declaring that he is not only useless but a positive hindrance, he writes about him this surprising and thrilling sentence: "Take Mark and bring him with thee: for he is profitable unto me for the ministry."

II

How did Paul come to change his opinion of Mark? How has he come to believe in the heroism of this

man whom he at one time considered so unheroic? How
has he come to believe in the usefulness of this man
whom yesterday he regarded as altogether worthless?
Answer: Paul had not changed. Mark had changed.
Mark had been remade. This bit of human waste had
become wealth.

It would be well to ask how Paul came to think so
meanly of Mark in the beginning. Certainly he did
not distrust him without reason. Paul had had experience with Mark. He knew him well. When Paul
and Barnabas had set out on their first missionary enterprise, this young man was selected as their assistant.
He had been greatly trusted; he had been signally honoured by his Lord and by his Church.

This missionary campaign launched by Barnabas and
Paul and Mark was the first that was enterprised by
the Christian Church. Many thousands of heroic souls
have gone forth on a like mission since then. They
have crossed all seas. They have penetrated all forests. They have preached in all nations. They have
laid their ashes on all shores. But at the vanguard of
this noble army of heroes walked these three men,
Barnabas and Paul and John Mark. Certainly John
Mark had been greatly trusted; certainly he had been
highly honoured.

What response did he make to this great confidence?
He proved utterly unworthy. He went over to the
Island of Cyprus with his two friends. From there
he sailed with them to the Continent and landed at
Perga. By this time the romance of the adventure
had altogether vanished. By this time he saw that the
delightful lark upon which he fancied himself entering when he left Antioch was a stern and exacting campaign. No sooner had he reached the city of Perga

than he made haste to turn his back on his friends and on their discomforts and their hardships and make his way to the restful home of his mother in Jerusalem.

So, you see, Mark was a quitter. God and His Church had honoured him with a task, but he threw it down. They had trusted him with a position of responsibility and he had turned his back upon it. He did very well when nothing was expected of him except to parade, but when the real fight came he threw down his weapons and fled. He was like that contemptible character in Shakespeare who said, "But for these vile guns, I would have been a soldier."

III

Why did Mark quit?

He did not do so because his two friends wanted him to quit. Paul and Barnabas did not drive him away from their presence. They did not wrong him and wound him and make his work an impossibility. He could not say when he got home, "I quit because of the unbrotherly treatment of those with whom I was sent to serve." Nor did he quit because he concluded that his presence was no longer needed. Mark knew the trying situation in which his two friends were labouring. He knew the odds against them as two lone men they faced the vast heathen millions. He knew that while the harvest indeed was plenteous, the labourers were pathetically few. He knew that he was needed. He knew that he could render a real service if he would only stand by. But in spite of this fact he left. But he did not leave because he was convinced he was not needed.

Why did he leave? We are not told explicitly. Of

this we are sure, however, that there was no justifiable excuse for his leaving. Had he had a good reason Paul would not have censured him as he did. And yet Paul did censure him most severely. Certain it is that he could give no reason for his conduct that would pass muster. In no way could he justify his having played the rôle of a quitter. And in this respect he is like those among ourselves who have quit. No man can justify himself for withdrawing from the fight and giving over the battle. No man can justify deliberate idleness. "To him that knoweth to do good and doeth it not, to him it is sin."

As we read between the lines, we are convinced of this: that Mark quit because he was afraid of the hardship, of the self-denial, of the dangers that confronted him. He had been raised in a home of wealth. Doubtless he had been considerably spoiled. He had possibly had too much petting. He was a bit soft. When he found that being a missionary meant downright hardship, that it meant privations, hard work and facing danger, he decided that the enterprise was too costly. He made up his mind that he would not pay the price. So he threw down his task and set out for home.

Thus he became John Mark, the Quitter. But he is not the only quitter. Their name is legion to this hour. Some of them are in the Church. When you became a member of the Church years ago you were full of enthusiasm. You were ready for any good work. For a while you made a business of your religion. You considered the services of the Church not as the responsibility of the pastor alone, but as a responsibility of yourself also. But little by little the fires died upon the altar of your soul. To-day, though you are still in the Church, you do not count. If everybody treated the prayer meeting as you treat it, there would not be another held to the end of time. If everybody treated the night service as you treat it, there would not be another church lighted for service until this old world became a cinder. Many of the quitters among us are those who have moved away from their old home churches into the city and have left their membership behind. Every city abounds in these. Our own denomination loses thousands of members in this fashion every year. I am told that in a single block in one of our large cities a religious census revealed the fact that there were thirteen hundred men and women who had once been actively engaged in various Protestant Churches, every single one of whom had quit.

Why had these quit? If I were able to talk with each of them individually, I should doubtless hear many excuses. But I dare to say the most of them, were they to give the real reason, would give that that lay back of the desertion of John Mark. They simply have not devotion enough to the Cause of Christ and His Kingdom to be willing to pay the price. They are not willing to bear the burden and to face their responsibilities. They are unwilling to meet that test of discipleship laid down by the Master Himself: "If any man will come after me, let him deny himself and take up his cross daily and follow me." The Bishop of London was entirely correct when he said some years ago that our modern Christianity is terribly lacking in the element of heroism. "Were it not for the fact," says he, "that the cross of Jesus

Christ can be made into a lovely ornament to wear about our necks instead of an ugly instrument of torture upon which we are to die to self and to the world, we would have thrown it away long ago." Mark was afraid of the Cross. And that fear has gripped many of us in pulpit and in pew to this day.

IV

But what says Paul of this man who deserted his post? What is it he is writing about this quitter? Listen! "Take Mark and bring him with thee: for he is profitable unto me for the ministry." Then Mark has come back. The coward of yesterday has become the hero of to-day. That is amazing! That is wonderful! That is a story full of thrilling hope for ourselves. If God could make a weak man into a tower of strength yesterday, if He could make a coward into a hero yesterday, then He can do the same for us to-day.

How do we account for the recovery of Mark?

1. I think it probable that the most effective agency that God used in the re-making of John Mark was the Apostle Paul. Barnabas was a tremendously helpful man, always generous, always determined to think the best. But it is altogether possible that his generosity was hurtful to Mark rather than helpful. It rather humoured his cowardice than rebuked it. Mark had a great tendency to be soft and indolent and weak. He needed somebody to cut him to the quick. He needed a good sharp rebuke. He did not need a sedative to put him more soundly to sleep. He needed to be shaken into wakefulness.

This, by God's help, Paul did for him. When Paul

refused to endanger his enterprise by taking such a weakling with him, when Paul told him frankly and lovingly what he thought of him, Mark began to come to himself. He began to see himself as he really was, to realise how hideously he had sinned. And until he was brought to that realisation, there was no hope for him. Mark needed this seeming harshness on the part of Paul. There are times when the greatest cruelty we can do our friends is to be too gentle and too kind to tell them the truth. Many a man has been saved by having some brave Paul or some brave Nathan to look him squarely in the eye and tell him exactly what is wrong.

2. I am persuaded that Peter had no small part in Mark's recovery. When Mark had been made to realise his sin, and when his head was bowed with shame and his heart was broken, then it was Peter that could speak to him better than any one else. For Peter had had an awful fall himself. Peter had himself been a quitter. He had known what it was to make a terrible and disgraceful failure.

You can almost see this kind old preacher with his hand on the bowed head of John Mark while he is talking to him. "Yes, my son, I know. One time I boasted to my Lord that I was ready to go with Him to prison and to death. And a few hours later a little servant girl asked me if I was a disciple of His. Of course I had been perfectly confident of what my answer would be to that question. I had been absolutely sure a little while before of what I would say under the circumstances. I was going to say: 'Certainly I am His disciple. It is the one thing of which I am most proud. I am prouder of it than I am of my own life. I am so proud of it that I would

gladly die for Him.' But I said nothing of the kind.
My heart failed within me. Panic seized me and I
lied and said that I had never known Him. But, you
know, my boy, even then, Christ did not throw me
away; He did not cast me off. He passed by and
looked at me and I saw in that tender look the yearning of a broken heart. And my knees went weak
and my throat choked with sobs, and my eyes filled
with tears, and I went out and wept bitterly. And,
you know, He forgave me. And when He was risen
from the dead, this is what He said: 'Go tell my disciples and Peter.' He took me back and let me go on
in His work, and that is what He will do for you."

And Mark heard and believed and started again.
And the mighty Christ took hold of him, and the man
who yesterday was useless and worse than useless became profitable. He was profitable to Peter. He was
profitable to Paul. And through the long centuries he
has been profitable to an innumerable company. Only
yesterday you were reading a little book. It was the
first Gospel ever written. And as you turned the pages
you had a wonderfully clear glimpse of Christ, and
you thanked God for the book, and then you thanked
God for the author of the book. And when you thanked
God for the author, you were thanking Him for John
Mark. Yes, this useless man, Mark, has become a
blessing and will continue to be a blessing to the end
of the ages.

v

And the fact, my brethren, that Mark came back
is most heartening to me. It gives me hope for myself. It gives me hope for you. For we have all failed

somewhat; we have all been in some measure quitters.
We have all come short of the glory of God. We must
realise that this is true. In an Old Book I read this
sentence, "He shall not fail." And when I read it I
knew the writer was not talking about either you or
myself, for we have both failed. We have not done
our best. We have not realised our largest possibilities.
In some measure we are failures.

What hope is there for us failures? This big hope.
We may start again. The difference between the finally
defeated and the finally successful is not so much in
the fact that one sinned and the other did not. It
is in the fact that one had the courage to begin again
while the other let one great failure overcome him. Just
remember this: that no failure need be final.

> "Each day is a new beginning.
> Each morn is the world made new,
> Oh, ye who are weary of sinning,
> Here's a hope and a chance for you."

If you will dare start again this morning, Jesus Christ
will take you back and remake you by His power.

There is a story of three lieutenants who near the
outbreak of the World War belonged to a British regiment. As the war clouds began to gather one of these
young officers was seized with the sickening fear that
when the test of battle came he would prove a coward
and would be utterly unable to face fire. So firmly
was he gripped by this conviction that he succeeded
through the influence of his father, who was a man high
in political life, in getting himself released from the
army.

Having retired from the service, he went to Ireland
where he was engaged to be married to a charming and

spirited girl. One day as they were standing talking the postman entered and handed him a little neatly-wrapped package. Upon opening it there floated out two tiny white feathers. The girl laughed a ringing laugh and asked for an explanation. And the ex-lieutenant was honest enough to meet the issue squarely. He told her that they were sent by his two friends in the army in token of his cowardice. At once the laughter vanished from the lips of the girl. Instead, two hectic spots burned upon her cheek. And breaking off a little white spray from the plume of her hat, she handed it to him and turned and walked away without a word. The young fellow stood alone under the weight of his shame. Then he squared his jaw, picked up the three white feathers, put them back in the box, wrapped the package, slipped it into his pocket, and hurried back to England where he joined the army under an assumed name.

A few weeks later he found himself, by the chances of war, a part of his old regiment. Then one night there was an excursion into "No Man's Land," and one of his lieutenant friends did not come back. He asked for the privilege of going after him. The officer in charge replied that it would be suicide, but gave him permission to go. He went and came. And when he laid the young officer down on the floor of the trench, the dying man whispered, "Tom, I knew you would come back. I knew you were not a coward." And Tom fumbled in his bosom and brought out a box and gave the dying soldier one white feather, and he clutched it in his chilling hand as he "went West."

Other days passed and there was a charge over the top, and then a stinging pain in head and shoulder. And when the young fellow came to himself he was in a shell hole half on and half under a wounded comrade. His companion was crying piteously for water. He shook his canteen and found it had only enough for one. So he put it to the lips of his companion and let him drain the last drop. Then he looked at him closely and recognised his other lieutenant friend. And as consciousness slipped away, he put into his hands a white feather that when they were found was stained by their common blood.

Then with his painful wounds he was invalided home. One day when he came out from being decorated with the Victoria Cross, among those who greeted him was a beautiful Irish girl who wore the garb of a Red Cross nurse. And as he passed her he handed her a little box stained with the mud and the blood of the trenches. When she reached the secrecy of her room that night and opened it, she found in it one white feather, and she knew that the quitter had come back and the coward had become a hero. Thus it was with Mark. And thus it may be with all the Marks here present. However great a failure you have been, you may yet have written of you this sentence: "He is profitable for the ministry."

THE BELOVED PHYSICIAN—LUKE

II Timothy 4:11

"Only Luke is with me."

I

The text is a strange mingling of songs and sobs. It laughs out loud with irrepressible gladness. It also sighs with a grief that is soaked in tears. There is sunshine in it, bright as the splendours of cloudless noon. There is also darkness in it akin to that of a night without stars. Here is a bit of spring-time, a-riot with colour and fragrance and tuneful with the song of birds. Here also is bleak winter, colourless and cold, with the bitter winds wailing through the skeleton boughs of the trees.

"Only Luke is with me." Whence the tearfulness of this sentence? Why is it grief-filled as the heart of a mother who has lost her first-born? For this reason it tells of absent ones whom the Apostle misses and for whose presence he deeply longs. Some of these are away on errands of service; they are away on missions upon which he has sent them. He misses them, and yet there is joy in their very absence. They are at the post of duty. But there is one whom he misses who is not at the post of duty. Yesterday he was here. To-day he is away. And the Apostle cannot keep back his tears as he writes, "Demas hath forsaken me, having loved this present world." "Only Luke is with me."

But while the old hero weeps as he writes this sentence, his tears flow over a face that is still bright with an inner joy. For even though Demas has gone, even if the love of the world has gripped him, even if in this Vanity Fair called Rome, he has forgotten his high quest and has deserted his old friend, there is still one who is faithful and true. If Demas has proved unreliable, if he has turned his back upon friend and duty and God, there is one who still stands by with unshaken loyalty. There is one who remains steadfast. There is one upon whose fidelity he can count with absolute confidence. The crowd may pass him by in utter forgetfulness, his friends may be ashamed of his chain, but there is one who will never be ashamed. And so, with inner laughter, he writes, "Luke is with me."

II

Who is Luke?

Who is this man upon whom Paul counts with such absolute assurance? Is he one who is bound to the Apostle by close ties of flesh and blood? No, Luke and Paul are no kin. Are they brought together by the bonds of a common nationality? No, Paul is a Jew and Luke is a Gentile. A few years ago they were separated by the very widest of chasms. And yet we find them here bound together by the closest bonds of friendship and of brotherhood. They are brothers because they are worshippers of a common Lord. They have experienced the redeeming love of a common Saviour. They who yesterday were afar off both from each other and from God have been brought near by the blood of Christ.

When did Luke become a Christian? We do not know. How was he converted? Here again we must answer that we do not know. But of this we can speak with absolute assurance. Luke is converted now. That man watching outside Paul's prison cell has a present experience of the saving grace of Jesus Christ. And, mark you, that is the important matter. A very earnest man said to me not long ago that he would not give the snap of his finger for the Christianity of any man who could not tell the day and the hour in which he was converted. It is good to know when you were converted, but it is not necessary. There is something far more important than that. It is this: to know that you are converted now. You may have a very clear memory of how Jesus Christ came into your life a quarter of a century ago, but that is of no avail unless He has a place in your heart to-day. It is well to be able to sing "At the Cross where I first saw the light." But it is far better to be able to sing "Blessed Assurance, Jesus is Mine."

Some of you good mothers have been married almost half a century. Suppose when you get home to-day your husband should tell you how beautiful you were years ago when he led you a blushing bride across the threshold of his home. Suppose he were to grow enthusiastic about how charming you looked before you had divided the roses upon your cheek with daughters that are now mothers, and before you had given your strength to sons that are now fathers. There would be little thrill in all that unless he should pass on to tell you of his feelings toward you now. You would want to hear him say: "Though 'the last feather of the raven's wing has fallen from your hair,' and though there are more wrinkles on your face than there are graves in the cemetery over which we have wept together, still you are more beautiful and far dearer than you were on that distant day when love's morning had its dawn."

And it is the present tense of your Christian experience that is of supreme value. How you were converted, when you were converted, where you were converted, all these questions are interesting, but they are not essential. The only big question is, "Do you know Jesus now?" Can you look into His face this moment and say, "My Lord and my God"? If you can do that, you need never worry yourself about dates. If you can do that, you need never worry yourself about the findings of the critics. A young fellow from our Southland came home from the war to find a big writeup of himself in the paper, telling how and when he was killed at the battle-front. The article was well written and sounded altogether truthful. But the living soldier did not accept the statement of the paper, even though the article was written by one who was evidently both cultured and honest. We know that Luke was a Christian because we see him living the life.

III

Another fact that we know about him is that he was a physician. No doubt he was a practising physician before he was ever converted to Christianity. When Jesus got hold of him He did not call upon him to throw away his old profession and take up one that was altogether new. He called him to the doing of his old task under new motives and in the energy of a new power. It is true that Dr. Luke performed other services that are not peculiar to the medical profession. But it was as a physician that he performed these services. A physician he was at the time of his conversion and a physician he remained to the end of the day.

And Luke's case is not peculiar. The call of God to most of us is not into new fields of service. Of course for some to yield to God is to be called into the ministry. For others to yield is to be called into the foreign field. But for most of us to put ourselves into Christ's hands is to toil at our same task, to work in the way in which we have been working, but to do that in the inspiration of a new power and in the joy of a new fellowship. Dorcas does not throw away her needle when she becomes a Christian. She simply consecrates it to Christ. Luke does not throw away his bandages and his healing medicines. He uses them to the glory of God. The business man does not quit his business. He conducts it as a good steward of Jesus Christ.

God does not want all of us to do the same thing. We cannot all render the same service. But we can all render some service. Dr. Luke cannot preach like Paul, neither can Paul heal like Luke. This kind physician has a task all his own. And it would be hard to find one that is capable of being used more to the glory of God. The physician who goes to his work as God's man carries something to his patients that is better than his skill, however skilful he may be. Blessed the patient that falls into the hands of a physician whose powers have been dedicated to his Lord. There is no end to the service that is rendered by such a man. He is a fellow worker with the Great Physician.

IV

But Dr. Luke did more than practise medicine. He was a writer of great brilliancy and power. Thus he has brought the whole world into his debt. There are sixty-six books in the Bible. Sixty-four of them were written by Jews. Only two of them were written by a Gentile, and the Gentile that wrote these two was Dr. Luke, the Christian Physician. And these two books are about as choice bits of literature as even the Word of God contains. It is to Luke we are indebted for the thrilling story of the conquest of the early Church. It is he that tells of the coming of the Promise of the Father on the day of Pentecost. It is Luke who tells us of Peter's inspired sermon on that day, and of the conversion of the three thousand. It is Luke who lets us into the intimate fellowship of the great saints of that day—Paul, Peter, Barnabas, and others.

Then we are indebted to Luke for the third Gospel. Renan called this Gospel of Luke the most beautiful book ever written. It tells of course the same story as that told by the other evangelists, and yet there are touches that make it far different. Luke was not writing to the Jews, but to the Gentiles. He was writing especially for ourselves. Naturally he does not place his emphasis always where the other evangelists place theirs. He goes beyond them, as others have pointed out, in giving emphasis to at least two important truths.

1. It is Luke who emphasises the universality of Christ's forgiving love. Matthew makes the wise men ask, "Where is He that is born King of the Jews?"

Matthew has the Jews in his eye as he writes. But when Luke writes the story he gives no prominence to the Jewish claim. "And lo, the Angel of the Lord came upon them, and the glory of the Lord shone round about them; and they were sore afraid. And the Angel said unto them, Fear not: for, behold, I bring you good tidings of great joy, which shall be to all people. For unto you is born this day in the city of David a Saviour, which is Christ the Lord." Then Luke proceeds to tell us story after story in which he emphasises the fact that his good tidings are really meant for all the people.

Down in the rich city of Jericho there was a man named Zaccheus. This man was a publican. He had sold himself to a foreign power. He wore the livery of Rome, and, therefore, he was more despised than if he had worn the garb of a slave. This man was rich, but he was an outcast. He was rich, but he was hated and shunned, and every door to decency was shut in his face. But one day Jesus Christ came that way and invited Himself to be a guest in the home of this despised grafter. And Jesus Christ said to him: "To-day is salvation come to thy house." Luke is the only one that tells us this story.

Then one night there is a feast in the house of a certain Pharisee. Jesus is a guest. During the meal there is a disturbance. A berouged woman of the street steals in from out the dark. She falls down at the feet of Jesus and washes them with her tears. Then she undoes the cascade of her hair and wipes those feet with the hairs of her head. And Simon, the Pharisee, shudders with horror because the Master allows Himself to be touched by this soiled rag of womanhood. But Jesus declares that her sins that are many are forgiven because she loves much. We owe that precious bit to Luke.

But the finest story ever written has not yet been mentioned. It begins like this: "A certain man had two sons, and the younger of them said to his father, Give me the portion of goods that falleth to me. And he divided unto them his living. And not many days after the younger son gathered all together and took his journey into a far country, and there wasted his substance in riotous living." It is needless to tell the whole story. It is about the most familiar in the literature of the world. And the reason it is so familiar is because, above all other stories, it reveals the compassionate and tender heart of our Heavenly Father. It tells us how eternally eager He is to give heaven's best even to those who have wasted their substance in riotous living. Luke makes most plain to us the universality of the forgiving love of God.

2. It is Luke also who emphasises the perils of prosperity. Come all you who would be rich and read and re-read the Gospel of Luke. Do you remember that story that Jesus told of the rich farmer? Do you recall the man who was so pressed by the work of barn building that he had no time for soul building? Do you recall him who was so busy piling up treasure for the few days in which he might live that he utterly forgot to make any provision for the eternity in which he must live? Do you recall that shrewd man who one day tumbled into his abundant crops and got drowned just as you have seen a bee get drowned in its own honey? Did you ever sit down and let the Rich Fool tell you what a perilous something is prosperity? It is Luke who has preserved for us this startling story.

It is Luke also who tells us of another very pros-

perous man called Dives. No charge is made against
this man. He is simply shown to us for a typical
day in his life. He is dressing well and trying to
get rid of some of his money by giving banquets. There
is a beggar at his gate, but he does not see him. He
is too busy trying to amuse himself. Therefore, he
neither helps this beggar nor does he drive him away.
He simply lets him alone. Then one day death comes
for this rich man, and he leaves his palace dreaming
of the bosom of Abraham only to hang his daintily san-
dalled foot in the rags of the old beggar at his gate
and fall flat into hell. Truly Luke forces us to see
how right was the Master when He said, "How hardly
shall they that have riches enter into the Kingdom
of God."

Ɛ

What kind of a man was Luke?
1. We would like much to know. But Luke was not
good at having his picture made. He took absolutely
no pains to leave us a life-size picture of himself.
In fact he kept his own face hidden as much as possible. But he revealed this much in spite of himself:
that he was a scholar. Luke was one of the best
trained men of his time. He was a man of wide reading and accurate information. He was capable of
mental fellowship with St. Paul, and St. Paul was
one of the intellectual giants of all time. It is true
that Luke does not tell us what university he attended,
nor what degrees he had. He is too modest for that.
But no thoughtful man can read his books without
realising that he is reading from a painstaking and
well-trained scholar.

2. Another fact that Luke cannot conceal about himself is his beautiful modesty. He lets us into the secret not by what he says, but by what he fails to say. When he wrote his Gospel, for instance, it was necessary for him to interview many notable people. The Virgin Mother was doubtless among these. But he does not tell us so. In fact he never mentions his own name in all the story. And when he wrote The Acts, though he himself was a part of some of the stirring stories that he tells, yet here again his name is never mentioned. There is no use to ask Luke's left hand what his right hand is doing. You will not get the least information. He sees to it that such matters are kept secret. How beautifully Christ-like he is in his modesty! He does the work, but he does not see fit to tell us who did it. He paints the picture, but he does not put his own name in the corner when the job is finished. He presents us with two of the most beautiful and helpful books ever written. But when we look over on the flyleaf we see that he forgot to autograph them. When we turn the pages, though we look carefully, we fail to find any calling card. A modest and scholarly man was Luke.

3. Luke was lov.ble. Paul calls him the Beloved Physician. And is it not a great privilege to be loved? Why is it that we love some folks? Answer: Some folks are so lovable. There are some people that we cannot resist. We may hear things about them that we do not like. We may come to them with pre-conceived notions and with unfair prejudices, but their presence strikes the death blow to all these enemies of love. Our hearts capitulate and we yield to them in spite of ourselves. Luke was like that. He took the heart of Paul captive, and the heart of many another.

What ammunition did he use? Can you not guess? He used love. There is no conqueror of hearts like that. It is the weapon that God Himself uses for the conquest of you and me. "We love because He first loved us." If you want to be lovable—and that is a prize to be coveted—if you want to be as attractive as a garden caressed by the springtime, if you want to be as sweet and winsome as the music of the mocking bird, then let love into your life. Folks can resist logic; they can resist the best arguments, but they melt like snow at the sun's kiss under the mighty influence of love.

4. Luke was steadfast. He was modest and loving and lovable, but that did not keep him from having the heart of a lion. The touch of his hand was as soft as the touch of a mother, but he was not soft in his moral fibre. He was a man of the hardiest courage. It is a tremendous help in fighting a hard fight to have the companionship of comrades. It is exceedingly encouraging when we are facing danger to know that brave hearts are standing by our side. Luke needed this encouragement, but it was not absolutely essential. "Dr. Luke, Paul has lost his popularity. The crowds have turned from him." "Then," said Luke, "I will do without the crowds. By the grace of God I am able to stand alone."

And Paul, with an appreciation that sets his burdened heart to singing, takes his pen and writes, "Only Luke is with me." What a fine virtue is that of steadfastness. How God needs men and women in the Church that can be relied upon. Every church has a few of this kind. The pastor soon learns them. When the prayer meeting comes, they are there. When the revival comes, they are there. When the day is ugly and stormy and few find their way to God's house, they are among them. They are dependable. They are steadfast. They are those to whom God will be able to say by and by: "You have been faithful." When I see Luke watching alone outside the prison cell of Paul, my heart fairly bows the knee within me in honour of him. Thank God for Luke.

"Only Luke is with me." And the man who writes this pathetic sentence is in disgrace and in prison. But Luke does not choose his friends because of their popularity nor because of their success in the eyes of the world. He may be counted on in the days of prosperity. He may be counted on no less in the days of adversity. A great, brave, loyal soul is he. He is modest, lovable, steadfast. Thus Paul could write of him, "Only Luke is with me." And it is my conviction that if Paul were writing a letter to us to-day from "Life's Other Side," he could say this same word, "Luke is with me." Luke was with him in the battle, he stood by him in death, and these friends have found each other about the Round Table of the King. May God give us something of the winsomeness and the steadfastness of Luke, the Beloved Physician.

VI

LUKEWARM—THE LAODICEAN
CHURCHMEN

Revelation 3 : 15-16

"I know thy works that thou art neither cold
nor hot: I would that thou wert cold or hot.
So then because thou art lukewarm, and neither
cold nor hot, I will spew thee out of my mouth."

I

This letter sent by our risen Lord through the
Apostle John to the Church at Laodicea is one of the
most arresting utterances that ever fell from His lips.
We cannot read it intelligently without being stirred.
It tends to lay a strong hand upon us and shake us
into wide wakefulness. It startles us, if we hear it
thoughtfully, like fire bells ringing in the dead of
night.

There is an emotion ascribed to our Lord in this
letter that, so far as I know, is not ascribed to Him
anywhere else in the Word of God. There are times
when Christ is represented as being grieved. There are
times when He is represented as being angry. But
here He is represented as being disgusted. He is not
slightly disgusted, but disgusted to the point of utter
nausea. "So then because thou art lukewarm, and
neither cold nor hot, I will spew thee out of my mouth."
Literally, "I am about to vomit you up."
68

II

Who are those with whom are Lord is so thoroughly
displeased? They are not some daring and outbreaking sinners. So far as we are able to find out, Jesus
Christ never showed the slightest disgust for the very
greatest of sinners. There were many beyond the
pale of decency and respectability, but there was not
one beyond His sympathy and His tender compassion. No sin was black enough to fling its victim beyond the reach of His interest and of His forgiving
love.

That was an awful sin that Peter committed on
the night of Christ's arrest. Before the test came he
had solemnly declared that he was ready to go with
his Master both to prison and to death. But he did
not make good his boast. Confronted by a servant girl
who inquires of his loyalty to Jesus Christ, he refuses
to confess that there has ever been any friendship
between them. Worse still, he swears that he has never
met Jesus at all. And this he did, mark you, when
his Master stood alone and was most sorely in need
of a friend. But what response did Jesus make to
this contemptible and cowardly denial? With what
eyes did He look upon Peter after this?

There was no disgust when He looked upon this
disciple whose knees had gone weak and whose heart
had utterly failed in the presence of danger. He did
not scorn Peter. There was sorrow, there was compassion more tender than ever looked out of the eyes
of a mother, but there was no scorn. That is the
reason this look broke Peter's heart. That is the
reason he went out and wept bitterly. That is the
reason Christ was able to send him this glad word

after His resurrection: "Go tell my disciples and Peter."

One day the Pharisees threw an ugly piece of human wreckage at the Master's feet. She was a woman of blasted character. She had walked to that hour through the stench and filth of a moral swamp. She belonged to that class that in all ages has been the victim of man's keenest scorn and disgust. But Christ was not disgusted with her. He looked upon her with a tenderness that gave her hope. He spoke to her with an encouragement that turned her wavering steps toward the heights. He prophesied for her the dawning of a bright to-morrow. "Neither do I condemn thee. Go and sin no more."

The object of Christ's contempt, then, is not some reckless and aggressive sinner. Strange to say, the object of his contempt is a church. It is a group of religious people who have formed an organisation presumably for the purpose of fighting under His banner and spreading His Kingdom. They are people who call themselves Christians. Not only so, but they pride themselves upon being a very superior grade of Christians. And yet for this group Christ has no word of commendation. He has nothing better to say to them than "I am about to spew thee out of my mouth."

III

Why was Christ disgusted with this church at Laodicea? He has nothing to say against their organisation or against their doctrine. His objection is just this: "Thou art lukewarm." The typical member of the church at Laodicea was neither cold nor hot. He was half-hearted; he was limp, flabby. He had no earnestness, no zeal, no glow, no go. He was not aggressive. He was a straddler, a sitter on the fence, lukewarm.

IV

Why is Christ so antagonistic to lukewarmness? Why does He hate it more than positive and aggressive sin? For it is evident that He does so hate it. Here are His words: "I would that thou wert cold or hot." Of course our Lord wants us to be out and out for Him. He wants us to be enthusiastic in His service. But He declares that if we are not going to be positively hot, then He desires that we be positively cold. If we are not going to be genuinely for Him, He desires that we be genuinely against Him. There is nothing that He so loathes, that He so hates, as lukewarmness.

1. He hates it because he cannot help hating it. Lukewarmness, half-heartedness, is in itself offensive both to God and man. How would you like to see a football game played between two teams neither of which had enough interest in the game to care to win? Who cares to play a game with an antagonist that is limp and half-hearted?

Who wants such an individual for a friend? Who cares for such an associate in the social circle? Did you ever shake hands with one that was so limp that there would not have been any hand-shake unless you had done it all? Is there any tang in Hamlet's conversation with Polonius when the old gentleman is ready to agree that the cloud looks like a camel or a mouse, or anything else that Hamlet may suggest?

Addison may not have deserved the ugly wound that Pope inflicted upon him, but he will never recover

from it.   Pope has made us feel that the object of his
satire is not the type of man we would want as our
friend.

> ". . . but were there One whose fires
> True genius kindles, and fair Fame inspires;
> Blest with each talent and each art to please,
> And born to write, converse, and live with ease:
> Should such a man, too fond of rule alone,
> Bear, like the Turk, no brother near the throne.
> View him with scornful, yet with jealous eyes,
> And hate for arts that caus'd himself to rise;
> Damn with faint praise, assent with civil leer;
> And without sneering, teach the rest to sneer;
> Willing to wound, and yet afraid to strike,
> Just hint a fault, and hesitate dislike;
> Alike reserv'd to blame, or to commend,
> A tim'rous foe, and a suspicious friend;
>
> .   .   .   .
>
> Who but must laugh, if such a man there be?
> Who would not weep, if Atticus were he?"

2. Not only does Christ hate lukewarmness because
it is hateful in itself, but because it robs its victim of
all possibility of progress.   This is true because lukewarmness is a child of self-satisfaction.   That is evident
from the letter before us.   The members of this church
were well satisfied, they were content with themselves.
They said: "We are rich and increased in goods, and
have need of nothing."   They had all the knowledge
of God and all the spiritual power and all the usefulness that they cared to have.   They were sure that
they had arrived.

Now such self-satisfaction means death to earnestness. No enthusiasm is possible for such an individual. Not only does this mean death to earnestness, but it means arrested development. It means death to progress. For if you know as much as you want to know, you will not likely learn any more. If you are as good as you want to be, you will not get any better. If you are as high up the hill as you care to be, you will not climb any higher. If you are winning the world to Christ as rapidly as you want to win it, you will certainly not enlarge your efforts.

Christ never pronounced a blessing on the self-satisfied. He did pronounce one on him who hungers and thirsts after righteousness. He declared that such should be filled. If you are fully content to be what you are, if you have no conscious need, then you make it impossible for Christ to bless you and lead you into a richer spiritual life.

That is what our Lord meant when He told about those two men that went to church one day. One of them was a respectable man and the other was an outcast. One of them was honest and the other was a grafter. Yet on a certain Sabbath morning both of these men went to church. One of them, the decent, respectable man, entered the church as if it were his own. He went well up to the front and prayed after this fashion: "God, I thank thee that I am not as other men, extortioners, unjust, adulterers. I fast twice in the week. I give tithes of all I possess." There was no aspiration after a larger goodness in his prayer. He was well pleased with himself. Therefore, he went home as he came. There was no song in his soul and no light in his face.

But the other man, the publican, came to God's

house goaded on by a great need. He felt that his burden was too heavy for him to bear. He felt his sin as an ugly offence against God, and as a gnawing agony to his own soul. Every man might be ahead of him in goodness, but no man passed him in point of being in need. And so this poor, broken man slipped into God's house. He did not go well up to the front, but stood afar off and smote upon his breast and prayed: "God, be merciful to me a sinner." And what was the result? "He went down to his house justified." The peace that passeth all understanding had come into his heart. This was made possible because he came before God with the burning thirst of a man conscious of his need.

3. Not only does Jesus hate lukewarmness because it is hateful, and because it is a foe to all progress, He hates it because it kills our possibilities of usefulness. The battles for the spread of the Kingdom of Christ are all won by those who are in earnest. Lukewarm water never wrecked an engine, neither did it ever move one. It is the soul on fire that fires other souls. It is the whole-hearted man that moves mountains of difficulty. When impossibilities see an earnest man coming, they take to their heels. When such a man gets on his knees to pray "the Angels open the windows."

> "Somebody said that it couldn't be done,
> But he with a chuckle replied,
> That maybe it couldn't, but he would be one
> Who wouldn't say so till he'd tried.
> So he buckled right in with a trace of a grin
> On his face. If he worried, he hid it,
> He started to sing as he tackled the thing
> That couldn't be done, and he did it.

"Somebody scoffed: 'Oh, you'll never do that,
At least no one has ever done it.'
But he took off his coat and he took off his hat,
And the first thing he knew he'd begun it,
With the lift of his chin and a bit of a grin,
If any doubt rose he forbid it;
He started to sing as he tackled the thing
That couldn't be done, and he did it.

"There are thousands to tell you it cannot be done,
There are thousands to prophesy failure;
There are thousands to point out, one by one,
The dangers that wait to assail you,
But buckle right in with a bit of a grin,
Just take off your coat and go to it,
Just start in to sing as you tackle the thing
That cannot be done, and you'll do it."

Less than two centuries ago an undersized man came
out of a service in Alger's Gate Street, London. Had
you asked this man about the service, he would have
told you that it was a good service. He might have
gone on to tell you that he felt his heart strangely
warmed, and that he did trust Christ and Christ alone
for salvation; and that an assurance was given unto
him that God had forgiven his sins. And when you
had heard the story, you might have doubted; you might
have passed down the street saying: "He felt his heart
strangely warmed. I wonder if anything will come
of it. Doubtless he will forget all about it by to-
morrow."

But he did not forget. Instead of forgetting, this
man with his hot heart pounding in his bosom mounted
his horse the next day and started on a long journey.
He rode literally through the century. And as he

rode, account for it as you may, the icicles fell from the eves of the houses and the winter-stripped trees put on their verdant foliage, and the birds sang and the flowers bloomed and the human heart stood up in the glad consciousness that God had come. And civilisation moved into a new day because this man got his heart on fire.

V

Is there a cure for lukewarmness? Can the listless life be made earnest? Can our dead enthusiasm be revived? Can the half-hearted man become whole-hearted? He can. Thank God, he can. Christ is as clear in pointing out the remedy as He is in administering His rebuke. Hear Him! "Be zealous, therefore, and repent." "Behold, I stand at the door and knock. If any man will hear my voice and open the door, I will come in to him and sup with him and he with me."

Christ is the cure for lukewarmness. His presence makes half-heartedness an impossibility. "The zeal for God's house burned him up." His passion for man sent Him to the cross. His enthusiastic love for others made Him glad to die. And this earnest Christ and lukewarmness cannot home in the same heart. If Christ comes in, then this disgusting foe of our progress and of our usefulness must go out.

Will you accept this remedy? "Behold, I stand at the door and knock." Notice the tense. It is not "Behold, I have stood at the door and knocked." That would of course be true. Christ has knocked at the door of some of our hearts for years. He knocked through all yesterday. He has been knocking through the hours of this blessed Sabbath. But His knocking

is not all in the past, neither is it a great expectation
for the future.   It is a blessed fact of to-day, of this
present moment.   "Behold, I am now standing at the
door and knocking."   If you will open the door and
let Jesus in, your lukewarmness will vanish as win-
tertime vanishes at the kiss of spring.

VII

THE BUSINESS WOMAN—LYDIA

Acts 16 : 14

"And a certain woman named Lydia, a seller of purple, of the city of Thyatira, which worshipped God, heard us: whose heart the Lord opened, that she attended unto the things which were spoken of Paul."

I

Lydia is one of the choicest characters of the New Testament. She grips us with her winsome womanliness. This is true in spite of the fact that she was a business woman. She had a home, but her task was not primarily that of a home-maker. If she was ever married, she has become a widow when we make her acquaintance. She toils not in the home, but upon the big world stage. She is engaged in commerce. She is a live and an alert woman of business.

Because Lydia was in business, her story sounds very modern. It smacks of to-day rather than of a far-off yesterday. She was in a small minority then, but were she living to-day she would find herself a part of a vast multitude, for roadways lead directly from a woman's door to-day into all the vocations into which man has entered. And the number of women engaged in business other than home-making is increasing daily.

And we are not disposed to find fault with this

situation. There was a time when about the only honorable vocation open to women was that of wife-hood and motherhood. But now, thanks to the power of Christ's Gospel, she has come upon a better day. She has found a larger liberty. She has entered upon a larger independence. Once she almost had to marry in order to have a home. To-day this is not neces-sary. She is thoroughly capable of earning her own way. Hence she does not have to marry unless she so desires.

Not only was Lydia a business woman, but she had made a thorough-going success in business. The record seems to indicate that Lydia was rich. If she had not made a fortune, at least she had succeeded in wisely managing a fortune that had been left to her by an-other, and this often requires quite as much wisdom and quite as much sagacity as the making of one. She was therefore a woman of keenness and courage. She had real ability. She was perfectly capable of match-ing wits with her male rivals. And so her sisters have proven themselves in our day. The modern woman has demonstrated the fact over and over again that she is capable of taking her place in the business world alongside of men.

But while Lydia had entered the business world and had won, while she had either made a fortune or had kept one, her struggle and her success had not spoiled her. She had not become mannish. She had not been coarsened by her battle with the world. She had not been swept from her moorings. Though wealthy and successful, she was still religious. We read in the text that she was a worshipper of God.

The modern business woman has not always kept her faith. The liberty that she enjoys has its dangers.

The woman of to-day is not so well protected as her sister of yesterday. The girl who works is oftentimes subjected to temptations of which our mothers knew little. The atmosphere of the business office is not always wholesome. Many a girl has to do her work in an environment the very coarseness of which tends to take the fine edge off her modesty. And we cannot deny that many have yielded to the lure of this vulgar atmosphere. We cannot close our eyes to the fact that there are many girls who not only work largely as men work, but sin as men sin. They have become cheap in thought and vulgar in conduct. Sometimes they have degenerated into cigarette smoking and liquor-sipping creatures who are a disgrace to their sex. I must confess, however, that this is not the case so often with the business girl as it is with the society girl who has no business.

But while some business women have been unable to stand the strain, there are vast multitudes that have been able. There are multitudes who have kept both their modesty and their religion. I was once pastor of a church almost half of whose membership was made up of business women. And never have I seen any church better attended in proportion to its membership. Nor have I seen any church whose finances were so easy. There is no bigger asset that the Church of Jesus Christ has to-day than the business woman.

II

How did Lydia come to be a Christian? For, while she was a religious woman when we first met her, she had no knowledge of Christ. She was a follower of the religion of the Jews.

THE BUSINESS WOMAN—LYDIA 81

1. She was faithful to the opportunities she had. She did not have access to a Christian church. There was not a single Christian in Philippi. She did not even have access to a Jewish Synagogue. There was not one in her city. But there was an insignificant prayer meeting held every Sabbath Day out on a river bank some miles from the city. It was doubtless a rather tame and uninteresting affair. There was probably not much spiritual life in it. Yet Lydia went. She had the habit of attending these prayer meetings. Her opportunities were meagre, but she religiously embraced such opportunities as were within her reach.

It is evident that this business woman made a business of her religion. That is fine. She was not alert and alive six days in the week and then dead on the seventh. She was not all interest and enthusiasm in the market place and listless in the place of prayer. She was not clear-eyed in the presence of a chance to buy and sell purple, and bat-eyed when facing an opportunity to buy "wine and milk without money and without price." She brought to her religious duties the same earnestness, the same clear-eyed intelligence that she brought to her commercial enterprises. Hence, though in some measure a child of the light, she was as wise in her generation as the children of the world.

Since Lydia made a business of her religion, we find her rising with week-day promptness on this Sabbath morning to take her way out to the place of prayer. She did not know that anything marvellous was going to happen that day. She did not know that an event was going to take place that morning that would make her name remembered when the Empire of the Cæsars had vanished for centuries. She did not know that anything would take place out of the ordinary. But, because she thought it was her duty, and because she needed heart help, she went to this prayer meeting that was held by the riverside under the open sky. She was living up to the best she knew. She was using all the light that God had granted her. This made it possible for Him to lead her into the fulness of the light.

The first step, therefore, in Lydia's finding of Christ was her fidelity to the light she already had. The next step came through the ministry of a certain preacher named Paul. God ever works through human instrumentality. He sends His message through human lips. He walks upon his errands of mercy upon human feet. He reaches forth to lift through human hands. For this high task He uses men of every type. He uses educated and uneducated; He uses cultured and uncultured. He uses old and young. He uses the magnetic and the attractive. He uses those who are wanting magnetism. But at least this quality they must have. They must be men ready and willing to obey.

Paul was such a man. When he set out on his missionary journey he had no thought of attending this prayer meeting and speaking to Lydia. He tried to go into Asia, but God shut the door in his face. Then he turned to Bithynia. Again God shut the door in his face. Then there came the call of the man of Macedonia, and immediately, Luke tells us, Paul responded. He set out accompanied by Luke and Timothy and Silas. This army he led from Asia into Europe to claim that important continent for Christ. And no more important army ever crossed any sea or marched into any field.

Why did Paul go to Philippi? Answer: He went

there to help. A man of Macedonia was calling for
help. He did not find that man in the city. Therefore, he set out to the prayer meeting to find him.
Why did Lydia attend this prayer meeting? She was
seeking help. Why was Paul going to attend it? He
was seeking to give help. He was not in search of
fame, though he became famous. He was not in search
of wealth. His one big task was helping. It is for
this reason that he came to the prayer meeting by the
riverside.

Had Paul seen only with the eyes of flesh, he must
have been terribly disappointed in the congregation
that was waiting for him in this prayer meeting. It
was not a large audience. It was a mere handful.
And we love crowds. Every preacher loves a crowd.
There is that in a small audience that tends to depress
us and take the heart out of us. There is that in a
large audience that inspires and creates enthusiasm
and generates hope. But here was only a pitiful little handful, possibly not more than half a dozen.

Not only was this audience depressing in that it was
so small, it was also depressing in that it was made up
entirely of women. There was not a man present.
All the men had gone to the gladiatorial contest, or
to business, or somewhere else. They had not the
slightest interest in this memorable service. That,
however, does not argue the worthlessness of the service.
It rather argues the stupidity and blindness and wickedness of the men. The fact that there are far more
men in the penitentiary than women does not prove
that the penitentiary is an altogether desirable place.
No more does the absence of men from this service prove
its worthlessness.

What did Paul do in the presence of this insignificant audience? He might have said: "I am too busy establishing churches and conquering the world to waste my energy here. I will go where I can appeal to the multitudes." But Paul was wise enough to be faithful to the seemingly small opportunity. He was not seeking a place to deliver an oration. He was not seeking for an opportunity to win applause. He was seeking for an opportunity to help. Therefore, he sat down among these women and talked. He did the simple thing that the least gifted and the most timid of us can do. He spoke face to face and heart to heart about the things that were fundamental in his own life.

And as he spoke there was one auditor, one clear-eyed, intelligent woman who listened with peculiar interest. Her rapt attention drew the very best from Paul. He spoke out of the depths of his great heart, and as he spoke a wonderful event took place. It was the greatest event that ever took place in Macedonia. Alexander the Great had marched across its fields, but he had accomplished nothing that is to be compared with what took place in this service. A battle was fought near this spot that decided the history of the civilised world, but even this is insignificant in comparison with the event that took place when Paul spoke to Lydia. For the Lord opened Lydia's heart and she believed. And that was the beginning of Christianity in Europe.

III

Now look at the outcome of this conversion.

1. Lydia brought to Christ all her enthusiasm, all her earnestness, all her fine intelligence and tact. She

was as zealous for Him as she had ever been for herself. Therefore we are not surprised that she won her household to the Lord. She won her children, if she had any. She won her slaves. She won her employés. She at once began to preach the Gospel in her own home and to those associated with her in business, and she won every one of them to her Master.

2. She changed her house into a church. There was no church building in Philippi. The saints were at that time too few in number and too poor to build one. Therefore, this consecrated woman opened her house as a place of worship. It was evidently a roomy place. Lydia might have used it for low forms of social entertainment. With this big house at her disposal she might have shone in the society of that day. But she preferred to dedicate her home with her other possessions to the service of Christ.

3. She also opened her home to give hospitality to Paul and his friends. No man was ever more independent than Paul. He was the farthest possible from being a sponge. He made it a matter of conscience to pay his own way. But Lydia would not let him off. She was bent on being of service. She was determined to give. She had a passion for helping. Therefore, she earnestly urged those saints to make her home their own. Luke says, "She compelled us." Thus Paul and his friends found a home in her house. And thus they were made the freer for the doing of the work to which God had called them.

4. This church that held its services in Lydia's house became one of the most helpful churches that Paul ever founded. We feel safe in saying that no other church was more possessed of the missionary spirit This church shared in a peculiar way Paul's passion

for world conquest. Nor was there any other church
so bent on serving the Apostle himself. It was this
church that "sent once and again" unto Paul's necessity while he was at Thessalonica. It was this church
that remembered him so helpfully while he was a
prisoner at Rome. And the moving spirit in all this
good work, we feel safe in saying, was none other than
this business woman, Lydia.

5. Lydia, as we have already pointed out, was the
first convert to Christ in Europe. Therefore, all that
Christianity has done in that great continent had its
inception here. This is the fountain. This is the
source of the river. That river has since spread over
Europe. Not only so, but it has spread over America.
It has even flowed into many a foreign land and into
the islands of the sea. All the rich blessings of our
present Christian civilisation had their beginning here.
Therefore, the ultimate outcome of this one conversion
was nothing less than the re-making of the world.

IV

There are certainly plain and important lessons here
that we all need to remember.

1. There is a lesson for the Christian worker. From
this story we learn not to despise the day of small
things. It seemed a very trifling service looked at
through the eyes of blindness. But to the seeing eye
it was one of vast and eternal importance. That seemed
like a poor service that an ignorant Methodist layman
conducted when he spoke pointedly to a young fellow
named Spurgeon. But when he won Spurgeon to
Christ, he won a multitude. It seemed of trifling importance when a certain layman spoke to an ignorant

shoe salesman in Boston; but when he won D. L. Moody to Christ, he pushed two continents up closer to God.

Therefore, let us not despise the day of small things. You never know when the seemingly insignificant is going to become the supremely great. Sunday School teacher, you can never tell just what sowing of yours is going to result in an abundant harvest. That hour of patient instruction given to a handful of restless children may prove to have been the beginning of a moral revolution. That lesson that in faithfulness you taught your class of boys may yet mean the dawning of a new day for America or for some distant land that sits in darkness. We cannot know the importance of our smallest efforts. We will never know until we look back upon them from some watchtower in the Eternal City.

2. There is a precious lesson for the seeker after God. Are the services in your church a bit dead? Are the sermons of the preacher or teacher rather mean deliverances? Keep in the path of duty. Keep your face turned toward the light. For it is true to-day, as it was true then, that "if any man is willing to do His will, he shall know."

VIII

THE MAKING OF A MINISTER—PAUL

The Acts 26:16

"But rise, and stand upon thy feet; for I
have appeared unto thee for this purpose, to
make thee a minister and a witness both of
these things which thou hast seen, and of those
things in the which I will appear unto thee."

I

This is a court scene. The place is the city of
Cesarea, and the time is about A. D. 60. A great con-
course of people has come together in the hall of hearing. There are present the leading citizens of the city
and the ranking officers of the Roman army. King
Agrippa is on the judgment seat. His sister, Bernice,
is at his side, as outwardly fair as she is inwardly
rotten. Paul, the prisoner at the bar, is brought in.
Then Festus opens the proceedings with these words:

"King Agrippa, and all men which are here present with us, ye see this man, about whom all the multitude of the Jews have dealt with me, both at Jerusalem
and also here, crying that he ought not to live any
longer. But when I found that he had committed
nothing worthy of death, and that he himself hath
appealed to Augustus, I have determined to send
him. . . . Wherefore I have brought him forth before
you, and specially before thee, O King Agrippa, that,
after examination had, I might have somewhat to write.

For it seemeth to me unreasonable to send a prisoner and not withal to signify the crimes laid against him."

"Then Agrippa said unto Paul, Thou art permitted to speak for thyself. Then Paul stretched forth the hand and answered for himself." And in this defence Paul accounts for the marvellous change that has been wrought within him. He tells how, more than a quarter of a century ago, life for him had taken on a new purpose. The commission that he had from the Chief Priest had been thrown away and the commission of Jesus Christ had been accepted in its stead. At that time he was changed from a persecutor into a preacher, from a menace into a minister.

II

How was this marvellous change wrought?

Paul is absolutely sure of the answer to that question. It was not wrought by the might of man. It was not brought about by the learning of schools. The worker of this mighty revolution was Jesus Christ. "I heard a voice speaking unto me saying, Saul, Saul, why persecutest thou me? And I said, Who art thou Lord? And He said, I am Jesus, whom thou persecutest. But rise and stand upon thy feet, for I have appeared unto thee for this purpose, to make thee a minister." It was Christ, therefore, that made Paul a minister. And every true minister is so made.

But how did Christ accomplish this high task? Answer: He gave Paul a vision of Himself. Little did Paul dream that day when he set out from Jerusalem to Damascus on his mission of persecution that this wonderful experience would come to him. This, we may say, in spite of the fact that he did not find his self-chosen task of destroying the Church pleasant. He was finding it hard to "kick against the goads." But in spite of this he was keeping up the fight. He was even then nearing the city where he purposed to further redden his hands with Christian blood. Suddenly there was a flash and a fall, and a voice speaking to him. And when he arose to his feet, he was no longer a menace to the Church, but a good minister of Jesus Christ.

III

Now what did this experience do for Paul? How did it fit him for the work of the ministry?

1. It was this vision that made it possible for Christ to give him a new nature. Out on the highway that day Paul was reborn. Out in the glare of that noonday sun he became a new creation. He was lifted upon his feet and made erect by the power of Christ. He became a partaker of the Divine Nature. He passed out of death into life. He was completely transformed. Henceforth he could say in all sincerity and truthfulness: "For to me to live is Christ."

Now since this vision resulted in the remaking of Paul, since it brought him into a personal and saving knowledge of Jesus Christ, it gave him the first and supreme essential for an effective ministry. Certainly nothing could have come to him to take the place of this experience. Without it he would never have preached a single sermon, nor founded a single church, nor won a single soul. And there is absolutely nothing still that will take the place of a like equipment for him who would be a minister. No amount of learning, no amount of eloquence, no amount of personal magnetism can serve as a substitute for the new birth.

The first and fundamental and supreme equipment for the Christian minister is that he experience for himself this mighty transformation that came to Paul that day on the way from Jerusalem to Damascus.

But, mark you, it is not necessary that we enter into this experience in the same way in which Paul entered it. There does not have to be for us a blazing light that flings us prostrate into the dust. Christ may dawn upon us like a sunrise. Or our hearts may open gradually to His incoming as a rosebud opens to full-blown beauty at the kiss of the morning. The conversion of Lydia was far different from that of Paul. She saw no blazing glory. She heard no voice. Yet she was as truly born from above as was the great apostle. The method is not of supreme importance. The fact is the only essential. But every one who aspires to be a true minister of our Lord, whether he serves in pulpit or in pew, must have this absolutely necessary equipment—a personal, saving knowledge of Jesus Christ.

2. This experience gave Paul a compelling motive. Paul had been zealous before his conversion, but his zeal had been for a creed rather than for a person. But the motive power of Paul's life after this experience was not simply a creed, though Paul had a creed. It was love and loyalty to a Person. Had you asked Paul the secret of his ceaseless toil, had you questioned him regarding those daring missionary journeys, he would have answered simply: "The love of Christ constraineth me." What a giver he was! How constantly he was spending and being spent! He ceased not to warn men night and day with tears. His life was a daily dying. What is the secret of this self-giving? Had you asked him the question, this

would have been the answer: "He loved me and gave himself for me."

And this, my brethren, is an essential equipment for every minister. It does not take any great motive to send men on enterprises that cost nothing. It does not take any great motive to enlist us in campaigns that have in them no sweat and no blood. But for those who live lives of constant self-giving, there must be a mighty motive. You may visit the slums with no higher motive than curiosity. But if you live in them in order to redeem them, there must be a motive far more compelling. "Except a corn of wheat fall into the ground and die, it abideth alone." But it takes a motive of mighty potency to make us willing to thus die.

"Why did you become a missionary?" a friend asked Judson one day. "I never thought of that," Mr. Judson replied. But when he had considered the matter for a little while, this was his answer: "I became a missionary because I thought Jesus Christ would be glad to have me become one." He simply wanted to please God. And the reason he wanted to please Him was because he loved Him. There is no other motive so compelling as this. There is none other that will enable us so gladly to give ourselves in sacrificial service morning, noon and night till we reach the goal post at the end of the race.

Not only did this experience bring to Paul love to Christ, it also brought him love to men. After this vision Paul seems to put his arms round the whole world. His heart became a veritable house of many mansions. There were abiding places in it for all sorts and conditions of men. There he gave hospitality to a runaway slave. There he entertained a demon-possessed girl who followed him through the streets of Philippi. There he received as guests soldiers and sailors, Jews and Gentiles, ignorant and educated, bond and free. He loved his friends. He loved those who were indifferent. He was willing to spend and be spent for them, though the more he loved them the less he was loved in return. He loved those whose faces he had never seen. He loved his enemies. He did not even refuse hospitality to scornful Agrippa. "King Agrippa, believest thou the prophets? I know that thou believest." And King Agrippa is disposed to sneer: "With a little thou wouldst persuade me to be a Christian?" And how tender is Paul's answer! "I would to God that not only thou, but all these that hear me this day, were both almost and altogether such as I am, except these bonds." That is love speaking. Paul is saying: "I would not bind you as I have been bound. But, oh, how gladly, were it in my power, would I give you my liberating and satisfying vision of the Lord Jesus Christ."

3. This experience also gave Paul his message. Here is where Paul found his gospel. He tells the Galatians very plainly that he did not receive his message from man, but that he received it through the revelation of God. One day he wrote a letter to the church at Rome. In this letter is this majestic sentence: "I am not ashamed of the Gospel of Christ, because it is the power of God unto salvation to every one that believeth." How had this conviction come to him? It had come through a personal experience. He believed that the Gospel was the power of God unto salvation because he had tested it and found it true. There was a time when he was not saved. Today he is saved. The change has been wrought through

Jesus Christ. Therefore he has a message. Therefore he can call the Gospel my gospel.

We are not to understand, of course, that this one experience brought Paul all his knowledge of Jesus Christ. Hear again the word of Christ to him: "Rise and stand upon thy feet; for I have appeared unto thee for this purpose, to make thee a minister and a witness both of these things which thou hast seen, and of those things in the which I will appear unto thee." His experience of Christ was a fact of history. It was a memory of the past. But it was far more than a memory. It was also a present fact! He was to witness to what happened yesterday. He was also to witness to what was happening now and would be a witness to what would happen to-morrow. He had a growing experience. His gospel was a growing gospel. His intimacy with Christ was an ever-increasing intimacy.

But Paul's knowledge of Christ as a personal saviour had its beginning here. Ever after this experience he could say: "I know." And men are waiting to-day with pathetic heart-hunger for the preacher who can speak with authority. They are waiting for the minister who has in his voice a note of absolute certainty. There is no other preaching so gripping, so arresting, so fascinating as that of the preacher who has a sure word. There is no other man who helps us so much as the one that comes into the pulpit to tell what he has found true in his own personal experience. He may lack education, he may lack ability, he may lack polish, but if he has assurance, he will not be lacking in usefulness. Let him be able to say, "Here is the road that I took and it led me unto the heights. Here is the rock to which I clung in the storm, and I found it to be the Rock of Ages," and the hearts of the saints will be comforted, and the careless crowd will be won to a vital faith.

This accounts for the effective preaching of that outcast woman that met Jesus at the well. Had you seen her as she hurried into the city you might have asked her purpose. Suppose she had shouted at you as she hurried on, "I am going into Sychar to preach Jesus." How astonished you would have been! When you had recovered from the shock enough to speak, you might have shouted after her: "You going to preach, you who are nothing more than a filthy piece of human driftwood! You going to preach, and to a crowd that knows the story of your soiled and ragged life!" And you might even have laughed in scorn. But in spite of all her defects, and they seemed sufficient to make her mission utterly hopeless, we read this: "Many believed because of the saying of the woman."

Why did this woman win? It was not because of her unclean past. She won in spite of that. She won because she could speak with assurance. And, my brethren, if we are to preach effectively, we must see to it each for himself that the Gospel becomes "my gospel." We must know something of the saving power of Jesus Christ in our own personal lives. Having experienced this, then let us tell a doubting, questioning, troubled world what we ourselves have tested and found true. Let us be silent about our uncertainties and speak of our certainties. Let us be silent for a while about the things of which we are not sure and tell the things of which we are sure. Let us leave off the discussion of what we do not know and tell of what we do know. Men are hungry for a sure word, and when they hear it they will not hear in vain.

IV

But how was this vision that came to Paul able to work this great change in his life?

We sometimes feel that there was a bit of compulsion in it. We feel that if only such a vision should come to us, we too would be entirely re-made. But this vision in itself did not re-make Paul. What, then, was the secret of its transforming power? It was this: Paul responded to it. Here is his joyful declaration: "Whereupon, O King Agrippa, I was not disobedient unto the heavenly vision."

Paul might have disobeyed. Millions have done so. He might have turned from this vision to utter moral blindness. That has been the history of multitudes. You can treat the truth in such a fashion as to make it untrue to you. You can so rebel against the light as to turn it into darkness. You can refuse to see till you lose your capacity to see. The secret of the transforming power of this vision was that Paul then and there became obedient. "Who art thou, Lord?" he cries while prostrate in the dust. As yet he is uncertain about many things, but of this at least he is sure: the One who has appeared unto him is henceforth his Lord. He puts himself absolutely at His disposal. He surrenders to Him unconditionally. Henceforth he stands ready to give up all things to which Jesus objects. Henceforth he stands ready to undertake all tasks to which He calls. But for that act of personal surrender, Paul, the gospel minister and missionary, would never have existed.

And the conditions are not different for ourselves. All visions are of no avail, all knowledge about Christ comes to naught unless we ourselves are obedient. We must enthrone Jesus Christ as our Lord. We must give ourselves in unconditional surrender to Him. If we do this He will accept us. If we do this He will use us. Some He will send into the pulpit, some He will send into the uttermost parts of the earth. Every one He will use somewhere. For He delights to give "to every man his work." Only let us come to Him! Only let us fling ourselves in utter abandon before Him, and He will speak to us the word He spoke to Paul: "Rise and stand upon thy feet; for I have appeared unto thee for this purpose, to make thee a minister and a witness both of these things which thou hast seen, and of those things in the which I will appear unto thee."

IX

A NOBLE BOAST—PAUL

I Corinthians 1: 22-23

"The Jews require a sign, and the Greeks seek after wisdom; but we preach Christ crucified, unto the Jews a stumbling block and unto the Greeks foolishness, but unto them which are called, both Jews and Greeks, Christ the power of God, and the wisdom of God."

We call your special attention to a part of the twenty-third verse: "We preach Christ crucified." This is an autobiographical touch. Paul is speaking out of his own experience. And it will be well worth our while to listen to him, for he is truly great. I doubt if any other single individual has ever influenced the human race as he has influenced it. During his own lifetime he touched and produced moral revolutions in two continents. Even his enemies said of him that he had turned the world upside down. More than eighteen centuries have passed since he lived. Civilisations that flourished then are now no more. Thrones have toppled down and crowns have rotted in heaps. But this man's influence instead of diminishing has only increased with the years. To-day if he were here he might say once again: "I press toward the mark for the prize." For his days of greatest power are yet ahead.

I

What is his secret? What did he to influence the world so mightily? What did he to enrich the moral life of the world?

It is said that Napoleon lowered the stature of the manhood of France by one inch. But here is a Christ-conquered Jew who has marvellously increased the moral stature of the race. How did he do it? When he accounts for himself here in this text he does so by saying: "We preach." His work was the work of the ministry. His highest claim for himself was that of being a preacher of the Gospel of Christ.

"We preach." And, mark you, the word "preach" as here used does not carry the idea of theorising or of wordy discussion. "We preach" means we proclaim, we deliver a message not our own, but one that was delivered to us. We preach, we enunciate, we assert, we declare. Paul was evidently a positive preacher. He was emphatic. He did not deal in mere doubts and interrogations. He did not come to peddle out proba-bilities. He spoke to men the revelations that had come to himself. That he called preaching. He had a right so to call it, and I think I have a right to say that nothing else is, in the true sense, preaching.

II

No doubt there were times when Paul was tempted to do something other than preach. There was great demand among his hearers for something else.

1. The Jews were constantly demanding signs. That is, they wanted physical and visible demonstrations of the truth. They wanted to witness miracles, wonders.

This eagerness for signs is with us still. It expresses itself to-day in our love for ritualism. As we lose a sense of the invisible Christ we seek to atone for the loss by outward show and splendour. When they have taken away our Lord, we try to content our souls with creeds and candles and crucifixes. Then the passion of the sign seeker shows itself in another way. We find it in the greediness for physical cures such as those claimed by the Christian Scientist. We want an eye and ear demonstration of the fact of immortality, such as the Spiritualist is constantly seeking and oftentimes fooling himself into believing that he has found.

But the tragedy of all this sign seeking is that there is in it no saving power. It does not conquer sin. It does not make us holy. It does not transform us into the image of Christ. "A wicked and adulterous generation seeketh after a sign." And after all their seeking and maybe finding, they remained wicked and adulterous. Paul knew this. Hence he refused to turn aside from the work of preaching to that of the giving or working of signs.

2. Paul was no doubt tempted at times to satisfy the hunger of the Greek after wisdom. The Greek loved elaborate philosophies. He was fond of rhetoric and oratory. He revelled in eloquence and happy epigrams. He admired cleverness. He was a worshipper of intellect. He prostrated himself before genius. And whenever a congregation begins to seek first in its minister mere human wisdom, whenever you come to hear a man simply because he is clever, you are not on your way to salvation. This Paul knew. So he refused to be diverted even by worldly wisdom from his high task of preaching.

III

What was the theme of Paul's preaching?

He did not give himself up to a discussion of the themes of the forum or of the market place. He did not give over his hour of opportunity to commenting on the latest scandal or crime that had been committed in Corinth. "We preach Christ." His was the gospel of a Person. He was a man of vast powers, but he believed that here was a theme worthy of his most intense efforts, worthy of all the powers of his gigantic intellect.

"We preach Christ." Note the word. He does not say, "We preach about Christ." Anybody can do that. A preacher who has lost his vision, whose heart has grown cold, into whose voice the metallic has crept, can talk about Christ. A dead Sunday School teacher can preach about Him. Even a backslidden and lifeless church member can preach about Christ. In fact the rankest atheist might do the same. Many of them do. It is almost fashionable for folks who do not accept Christ to speak flatteringly about Him. But Paul does not claim simply to talk about Christ. What he says is: "We preach Christ."

Now there is only one man who can do that and that is the man who knows Christ, the man who has opened the door of his heart for the incoming of Christ. That is the man who can say: "I am crucified with Christ; nevertheless I live, and yet not I, but Christ liveth in me." When Paul opened his lips Christ spoke through them. That was the secret of his power. That is the secret of the power of every really effective preacher. I shall bless and help you to-day only as Christ has right-of-way in my own heart. If He speaks through my own blundering lips, then even I shall have "a mouth and a wisdom that the world cannot gainsay nor resist."

Not only does Paul preach Christ, but Christ crucified. This does not mean that every sermon that Paul preached dealt with the crucifixion of Jesus. It does mean that every sermon that he preached had as its fountain a suffering and dying Saviour. Had he merely preached Christ as a great teacher or as the world's ideal man, he would have given very little offence. Neither would he have wrought any great revolutions. Neither would there have been anything wonderfully new or revolutionary in his message. But the theme of his preaching was this: "Christ crucified."

IV

Why did Paul cling to this theme through all the stormy and stressful days of his ministry?

He did not do so because the theme was universally popular. It was not. One night he saw a vision of a man of Macedonia who was stretching out eager hands and calling for help. But when he hurried to the rescue he met no flattering reception. He had only been in the city of Philippi a very few days when he found himself with torn garments and a bleeding body in the inner precincts of a Roman prison. Released from there he went to Thessalonica, where lewd fellows of the baser sort again raised the mob against him. Thence he fled to Berea, thence to Athens and now he is in Corinth. Everywhere he has gone his message has aroused scorn and hatred and opposition.

Arrived in Corinth there seems no doubt that he

was for a while sorely tempted to keep silent. Preaching seemed so futile. Its whole result, he felt tempted to believe, was to awaken the scorn and anger and contempt and hatred of the people. "I was with you in weakness and in fear and much trembling." And it required a special vision from the Lord to set him preaching again. They had called him a babbler over in Athens. But God said to him now: "Babble on and hold not your peace, for I have much people in this city." And so he took up his task of preaching Christ crucified, but it was not at the call of popularity.

Neither did Paul preach Christ crucified because it was all that he knew. Paul was a scholar. He was a man of profound intellect. He was familiar with Greek culture and Greek thought. He knew quite well that he had it in his power to win these contemptuous Greeks. He knew he could bring them to his feet in profound admiration. On Mars' Hill he had talked the vernacular of Greek philosophers as if he had been born and bred in Athens. But the results had been disappointing. So he refused to cater further to this love of wisdom. It cost him a battle, for he was human. But here is his declaration of independence: "I determined not to know anything among you save Christ and Him crucified."

Paul persistently preached Christ crucified for the following reasons: Because he was fully persuaded that it was this message and this alone that was sufficient adequately to meet the needs of our lost and ruined race. He believed this because it is through Christ crucified and through Him alone that we can come to really know God, His nature and His thought of ourselves.

1. Christ crucified is a revelation of the holiness of God. The Jews had conceived of God as holy before Christ died. Isaiah had seen angels veil their faces in His presence and cry, "Holy, holy, holy is the Lord of hosts." But even this is not the deepest revelation of the holiness of God. The deepest revelation of His holiness is God suffering and dying in the person of Jesus Christ to redeem man from the curse of sin.

2. Through Christ crucified we come to understand God's hatred of sin. Sin is such a trivial matter to many of us. We say, "It will all come out in the wash." Or, "It will not matter a hundred years from now." How we are suffering to-day from a cheap idea of sin! What we need for the correction of this terrible and tragic ignorance is a vision of Christ crucified. If it seems a small matter to you to sin, it is because you know nothing of Him who sweat bloody sweat under the trees of Gethsemane. You have never seen Him of the thorn-crowned brow. You have never come into vital touch with Him who cried on the cross: "My God! My God! Why hast thou forsaken me?" Christ crucified is God's eternal heartache because of your sin and mine.

3. Through Christ crucified God reveals to us his estimate of man. What does God think of the moral condition of man? I am not asking how modern scholars think of him. I am not asking what we ourselves think. We may think of ourselves as very decent and respectable. We may think of ourselves as rich and increased in goods and in need of nothing. But God's thought of man is different. He says we are wretched and miserable and poor and blind and naked. He says: "There is no difference: for all sinned and come short

of the glory of God." You cannot understand the cross except in the light of the lostness of man.

But just as firm as is God's conviction of the lostness of man, just so firm is His faith in his salvability. He dares to speak to the most hopeless of us this amazing word: "Be ye perfect even as your Father which is in heaven is perfect." He believes that the worst man in Jericho is a possible son of Abraham. He believes that the fluctuating son of Jona can become a rock of Christ-like character. He believes that even a dying robber can be made into a saint fit to companion Himself in Paradise. Therefore, just as clearly as the cross reveals God's belief in the lostness of man, just so clearly does it reveal His faith in man's perfectability.

Some one tells this story: Over in Scotland a few years ago a charming young girl discovered that a trestle had been washed away on a certain line of railroad. She hurried down the track to meet the oncoming express. She met it in a narrow defile. She flagged the train, but lost her life. At one end of that train there was a deep, yawning chasm. At the other end there was the mangled body of the girl. Now the only adequate explanation of this mangled body at the rear of the train is the yawning chasm in front. And the only intelligible explanation of the cross of Jesus Christ is the terrible chasm into which man's sin has plunged him and the possibility of his being rescued from that doom.

4. In Christ crucified we see love bringing a remedy for man's sin. Paul had no doubt of the lostness of man. Just as little did he doubt the power of Christ crucified to remake man. He was not ashamed of

the Gospel because it was the power of God unto salvation.   This he knew as a matter of personal experience.
This he knew in the deepest recesses of his own soul.
He declared with the profoundest conviction that Christ
crucified was the power of God, because he had experienced that power in his own life.   So satisfying
was that experience that we hear him shout: "God
forbid that I should glory, save in the cross of our
Lord Jesus crucified; whereby the world has been
crucified unto me and I unto the world."

                              V

Brethren, all our needs are met in Him.   No wonder Paul clung to this gospel.   He knew it to be fully
adequate to his own needs and to the needs of the
whole world.   It is said that some years ago an engi-
neer was driving an excursion train up a grade some
miles west of Altoona, Pennsylvania.   He looked up
the track and saw four freight cars loaded with stone
that had broken loose from the engine and were coming at a terrific rate down the grate.   He ordered the
fireman to go back and stand on the platform of the
baggage car and uncouple the cars from his engine
and let them drift down the grade, while he should
go alone to meet the oncoming cars.   He met them
and they were ditched.   When they dragged his mangled body from under the heap of scrap iron that had
once been an engine, he said: "What! nobody hurt?
Thank God, I turned the trick."

We are not here to give you any elaborate theory
of the atonement.   But this we assert: Christ has gone
alone to meet our enemy and He has met him and
His victory is complete and overwhelming.   So that

we can confidently say: "He was wounded for our transgressions; He was bruised for our iniquities; the chastisement of our peace was upon Him, and with His stripes we are healed."

What will you do with this salvation that is offered to you in Jesus Christ? Those who heard of it from the lips of St. Paul did not all accept it. To some it was only a stumbling block. To others it was mere foolishness. They went on seeking for signs. They went on worshipping at the shrine of wisdom. But those who did accept, those who believed the message found it true. They found that Christ crucified was indeed the power of God. And so may you this day. Therefore, with joy I take these brave words upon my lips: "But we preach Christ crucified, unto the Jews a stumbling block, and unto the Greeks foolishness; but unto them which are called, both Jews and Greeks, Christ the power of God and the wisdom of God."

X

THE WASTE BASKET—PAUL

Philippians 3 : 13-14

"This one thing I do, forgetting those things
which are behind, and reaching forth unto
those things which are before, I press toward
the mark for the prize."

Whatever you may think of my message you will
at least agree that I have a great text. It is a text that
lets us into the secret of one of the most majestic and
useful lives that was ever lived on this planet. Paul,
though poor, made many rich in the far-off day in which
he lived. And he has been at the big business of dis-
tributing spiritual legacies all through the centuries.
How many multi-millionaires here and in heaven owe
their success under God to him! And how did it all
come about? A bit of the secret is in the text: "This
one thing I do, forgetting those things which are behind, and reaching forth unto those things which are
before, I press toward the mark for the prize."

1. From this text we learn that Paul was a special-
ist. Paul was not bent upon a dozen different enterprises. He was not even engaged in two. He was giving all his time, all his attention, all his vast abilities
to one single task. "This one thing I do." And,
mark you, life becomes mighty only as all its energies
are concentrated upon the doing of one thing. Recently I saw a mountainside being removed by hy-

draulic pressure. When that water fell from the clouds
it had a greater height to give it power. Yet even
then so softly did it fall that it would not have hurt
the tender face of a baby. But there was that same
water with sufficient force to move mountains. Why?
It was concentrated. It could say, "This one thing I
do."

2. Not only was Paul a man of one single purpose, but that purpose was one that was altogether
worthy. If Paul staked everything upon one single
adventure, it was an adventure that was genuinely
worth while. "This one thing I do." What was
that one thing? To what end was he striving?
To what end was he battling every hour and every
day and every year of his eventful and fruitful life?
This is his answer: "That I may lay hold of that for
which I was laid hold of by Jesus Christ." And Paul
is back again to that marvellous experience that came
to him on the way from Jerusalem to Damascus. That
day Christ arrested him. He laid hold of him. And
this Christ did for a definite purpose. Christ arrested
Paul that day for Paul's salvation. That day he became a new creation in Christ Jesus.

But Christ meant more in this arresting of Paul
than his own salvation. "Rise and stand upon thy
feet: for I have appeared unto thee for this purpose,
to make thee a minister and a witness both of these
things which thou hast seen and of those things in the
which I will appear unto thee." Christ not only purposed the remaking of Paul. He purposed the making
of Paul into a minister. He saved him that he might
become His witness. He transformed him in order
that through him He might bring this saving and
transforming Gospel to others. Day by day he sought

to bring himself more fully to conform to the will of God. Day by day he gave himself to spend and be spent in the service of others.

3. Not only did Paul set himself to one high purpose, but he went about the achieving of that purpose in a most wise and intelligent fashion. He made the best possible use of his waste basket. He knew what things to throw away and what things to keep. We all have our waste baskets. Now and then it is necessary to go through the desk where letters and papers of various kinds accumulate and sort out what is worth keeping and throw the rest into the waste basket. Unless we clean things up now and then, the desk becomes so littered that it is next to impossible for us to do our work. There are a great many things that need to be thrown away. There are also many things that need to be kept. Happy is the man who knows how to use his waste basket wisely.

I

Watch Paul use his. "Forgetting those things which are behind." This does not mean that Paul forgot everything that was behind. He did not blot out his past altogether and leave it a perfect blank. That would have been at once an impossibility and a colossal misfortune. There were some things that Paul kept. There were some things of yesterday that he did not dare throw away. There are some things that you dare not throw away.

1. If in searching through the desk of last year you come across any unpaid bills, do not tear them up and throw them in the waste basket. That is what some do. But that is not Paul's way. It is not the

way of righteousness and fairness. Last year you got
hard put to it financially. You asked your friend for
a loan. He granted it. That is behind you now, but
do not forget it. Do not forget that bill that you owe
the grocery man just because you have eaten the gro-
ceries. Do not forget the pledge that you made to the
Church just because you made it last year. Do not
forget the vow that you made to God, the pledge of
a new service and of a new loyalty. It is exceedingly
easy to forget these things. But they must not be
forgotten. To forget them is to deal a death blow to
our honesty.

2. Do not forget the wrongs that you inflicted last
year, which wrongs you might right if you desired.
Do not forget the apology that you ought to make.
Do not forget the wound you made that it is your duty
to heal. For God not only expects us to stop doing
the wrong; He expects us to right the wrong so far as
it is in our power. You will never find peace so long
as you cling to that which is not rightfully yours.
You will never enter into the joy of your Lord so
long as you refuse to make right that injustice that was
wrought by your hands.

A few years ago Gypsy Smith was holding a meeting in Chicago. A very wealthy old bachelor who was
a member of a prominent church attended the services.
Gypsy Smith preached a sermon on restitution. That
sermon brought home to the conscience of this wealthy
bachelor a great sin committed in the hot-blooded days
of his youth. A woman had been wronged by him.
She slept now in a distant grave. But there were two
children, a boy and a girl. They had been put in an
orphans' asylum. That wealthy bachelor went for these
children and found that the girl had died. But the

boy he brought to his palatial home in the city. As they sat together the first night he said to the lad: "Son, do you think you could ever love your father, though he did your mother a great wrong?" And the boy said, "I do not know." "Do you think you could ever be happy here in the city?" Again he said, "I do not know." Then the man said, "Would you like to see your father?" The boy looked wistful for a moment and then said that he would. Then the man said, "Put your arms around my neck and call me father." And that man testified that he found Jesus Christ through the clinging arms of his son. Do not forget your un-righted wrong. God has not forgotten and you must not.

3. Paul is not asking us to forget the kindnesses that have been shown us during the year past. Do not forget the flowers that were sent to you when your heart was heavy. Do not forget the sympathy that helped to dry your tears when you were in the midst of great grief. Do not forget the encouraging word that was spoken by a friend when you were weak and faltering and ready to fall. Do not forget the hand that steadied you when your feet were about to stagger out of the path. If somebody has been a blessing to you, it is well to carry the memory of that fact with you into the new year. That was Paul's way. "The Lord give mercy unto the house of Onesiphorus, for he often refreshed me and was not ashamed of my chain."

4. Do not forget the mercy of God that came to you last year. Paul was the last one who would have urged upon us that we forget the blessings that are behind us. Again and again he was going back to that great event when his soul had its birthday. He was

always thanking because he was thinking so constantly of past mercies. And if we would not fling away real treasure, let us carry the memory of God's mercies with us into the year that is ahead.

II

But there are some things that we can afford to throw away. There are some things, in fact, that we must throw into the waste basket or we shall be seriously hampered. We must part with these things or the chances are we shall make no progress at all.

1. I would advise that you throw away whatever wrongs you may have suffered last year. Why keep them? They do not help you in the least. Did somebody write you a love letter? Keep that. Did somebody write you a word of appreciation? File it away and some day when the rain is on the roof get it out and read it. It will help you. But why keep the other kind? I went into the office the other day to find the most bitter and scathing letter that I have ever read. Do you know what I did with it? I tore it up very quickly and put it into the waste basket. Why keep it? I would not mind keeping a butterfly, but why pet a snake? It is worth while to cultivate roses. But why give your time to the cultivation of nettles?

Has somebody injured you, deceived you, cheated you, done you a great wrong? Forget it. For if you remember it the memory of it will harden into hate. Hate will be changed into cynicism. You will become bitter, antagonistic, disillusioned. Of course you may get even with the one who wronged you. You may succeed in getting revenge. But while you make him suffer, you yourself will suffer the pangs of hell. You remember Silent Kate in "The Light in the Clearing." Silent Kate was grievously, horribly, hideously wronged. A man whom she loved wrecked her life and threw her away. Kate gave the rest of her years to an effort for revenge. She won. She saw the son of her enemy die on the scaffold. She saw the enemy himself die of a broken heart. But her triumph was only the bitterest disaster. Her success had in it the sting of a million fiery serpents. Therefore if you love happiness, if you yearn for the sunshine, if you covet a bit of springtime in your soul, throw away hate. Cast out all your grudges. You can find peace in no other way. "Forgive us our sins as we forgive those who sin against us." Christ cannot forgive you unless you forgive others. He cannot because His forgiveness means not simply the remission of a penalty, but it means a new heart. But He cannot give you a new heart when you cling tenaciously to the old.

2. As you enter into to-morrow you can afford to throw away the record of your past failures and blunders and mistakes. You made a terrible failure last year. You made a mistake that you feel will cast a shadow over all your to-morrows. What are you doing about it? I can tell you what not to do. Do not keep your eyes fixed upon it. Do not be guilty of the tragic blunder of trying to break through the door of the past and live it over again. You cannot do that. Do not allow it so to unnerve you and discourage you as to keep you from doing anything with the present.

A few weeks ago a mother came to see me. She was one of the most broken-hearted women I ever met. Her boy had gone wrong. He had committed a crime.

She felt that his going wrong was due in large measure to herself. She realised that she had failed. But
instead of turning her back upon her failure and setting herself to do the best with to-morrow, she declared that she would never try again. She declared
in her bitterness that never again would she pray.
Never again would she open God's Word. Never again
would she enter God's house. She allowed her yesterday to utterly rob her of her to-day and of her to-
morrow.

But Paul's word to her, Paul's word to you, is to
forget the tragic mistake and failure of yesterday.
To always be gazing upon it will make it no less a mistake. It will only palsy your hand and take the courage out of your soul. That was a terrible failure that
the disciples made when they went into Gethsemane
to watch with Jesus. They failed to watch. They
went to sleep. They slept till the Son of Man was
betrayed into the hands of sinners. But what said
Jesus to them even after this horrible failure? He
said: "Rise up; let us be going." If yesterday was
a failure, there is but one thing to do with it. Forget it. Tear it up as you would a worthless piece of
scrap paper and throw it into the waste basket.

3. Then there is your old sin. Yesterday you sinned.
What are you going to do about that grim fact? Maybe
all last year you spent in sin. What is to be done with
all the scarlet stains that are upon your soul? What
is to be done with all the foul pages written into your
life's story? What is to be done with sin, the sin
of last year, the sin of the years past? The answer to
this question may startle you. Forget it. Turn your
back upon it through faith in Christ. For God Himself forgets it. "He will forgive your transgressions

and remember them no more." If you are trusting in Jesus this morning He has forgotten that you ever sinned. Every sin that you have ever committed He has blotted out of the book of His remembrance. And what God forgets you have a right to forget.

4. Paul forgot himself. As we enter into the New Year it would be well for us to forget ourselves. Is not the biggest tragedy of our lives just this: that we are self-centred rather than God-centred? We live within our own wills instead of within His will. Is it not true that this has been the source of our wrongdoing, of our heartache, of our failure, of our loss of opportunities? But if we are trusting Christ today, the old life of self is to be forgotten. "For ye are dead, and your life is hid with Christ in God." So as we pass out of the old into the new, let us forget self. Victory will come in no other way.

III

And why does Paul forget the things that are behind? Why does he urge us to forget? For the simple reason that he knows we will never run forward when our eyes are turned backward. If you are constantly looking in the past, looking at past sins and failures, you will never go forward. Men walk in the direction in which they look. And if you have the backward look this morning, you also have the backward step. It is only as we turn our eyes to the future, to the things that are before that we will make progress. The backward look means loss. It means we shall stand death-smitten and petrified, as did Lot's wife when she looked back at the burning city.

IV

But you say, "That is all well enough. But how can I forget?" Yes, that is the question—How? And let me tell you frankly that you will not forget by simply trying to do so. You will never succeed in this great undertaking by simply saying, "Now, go to. I am going to forget." I remember a man I met years ago who was resolved to forget. He said he had to. But he could not. He went on remembering and remembering in spite of himself. He tried to dodge memory, but he could not. He tried to out-run it, but he found it impossible. At last he went stark mad because he could not forget.

How can I forget the things that are behind? There is only one way and that is by becoming absorbed in the things that are before. Do you remember that first love affair of yours? or can you remember back that far? You felt that it was going to be fatal. You were sure that you would marry. But she went away and you forgot her. How did it come about? You became interested in somebody else. You forgot one by remembering another. That is the way Paul forgot his yesterday. He became absorbed in the things of to-day and to-morrow.

How did Silas Marner lose his love for gold? Not by having his gold stolen. He loved it just as well after it was gone, possibly even better, than he did before. But one night when he came home he saw something on the hearth that scintillated and sparkled in the flare of the fire somewhat as his gold used to do. Eagerly he rushed forward with the hope that his gold had come back. But as he gripped this sparkling something with his miserly fingers, he found that it was not gold, but the silken tresses of a little lost child. Eppie slipped into his heart and filled it so full of tender, new, human love that he forgot his love for gold.

Do you remember the Jackal in "The Tale of Two Cities"? What an unlovely and self-centred and repellent personality was Sydney Carton! But one day he forgot himself. And in that noble forgetfulness he slipped into a prison cell. He took another man's place at the guillotine. And those who saw him die said his face was the most peaceful face upon which they had ever looked. How did he manage to forget himself? By remembering somebody else. He lost his self-love in the love of another. And so we are to forget self by giving our heart's love to Christ and to our brethren for Christ's sake.

V

"Forgetting the things which are behind and reaching forth unto those things which are before"—that is the only way we can become emancipated from the past. That is the only way we can achieve our present and our future. We must become absorbed in the things that are before. And what are some of those things? I know there is much that is lovely that lies behind us. But what are some of the things that are ahead of us this morning that still make life worth living, that make the hilltops ahead golden with blessed possibilities?

1. Jesus Christ is still ahead of us. You rejected Him last year maybe. But you have not run past Him yet. He was in yesterday, but, thank God, He is in

to-day and will be in to-morrow. "He is the same yesterday, to-day and forever." But though Christ was in yesterday, you cannot find Him there. But you can find Him in to-day and you can walk with Him to-morrow. Christ is ahead. So you have Him to look forward to as you turn your back upon the past. And He says to you just what He said to His disciples who failed Him as you failed Him: "Rise up; let us be going."

2. Eternity is ahead of you. Many here are no longer in the springtime of life. Our hair is growing grey. Our strength is failing and we say, "Few and evil have been the days of the years of my pilgrimage." Some of us have spent the best part of our lives in sin. There may be some who have spent all their lives up to this hour in sin. What have I to say to you? Just this: Eternity is yet ahead of you. "Yes, but I have wasted so much. I can never be the same again." I know. But though you have wasted many a precious day, there is yet as much time ahead of you as there is ahead of God Himself. If God can only wake you up and get you started, blessedness undreamed of is yet possible for you. You have a whole eternity yet on your hands. And what a wonderful man you may become among the tall sons of the morning if you will only begin! If you have only one more minute to live in this world, still I say, eternity is ahead of you. Lay hold of this heartening fact and you will start even yet to press toward the mark for the prize.

3. If you will dare to begin, perfection is ahead of you. However warped and bent and broken and unsightly you are at this moment, however stained and tarnished, however eaten and disfigured by the leprosy of sin, yet perfection is ahead of you if you will only

claim it. For that is His own promise. "We know not what we shall be, but we know that when He shall appear we shall be like Him; for we shall see Him as He is."

4. Home is ahead of us. Where is your home? If you mean the home of your childhood, it exists only in the yesterday. In the drawer of my desk I have a photograph. It is the picture of the home of my childhood. It is about all that is left of it, except an old ruin and many a precious memory. It can never be what it once was. That I know beyond a peradventure. Childhood's home is in the past. It has slipped out beyond my reach. There is absolutely no road that leads to the old front gate and the front porch where Mother used to wait when we came home from school.

Yet, though that is gone, our real home is ahead. "Let not your heart be troubled. Ye believe in God, believe also in me. In my father's house are many mansions. If it were not so I would have told you. I go to prepare a place for you; and if I go and prepare a place for you, I will come again and receive you unto myself, that where I am there ye may be also." Thank God that blessed experience is not behind us. It is in this home that we shall find our finest friendships. It is in this home that we shall lock arms with those whom we "have loved long since and lost awhile." Therefore, let us say with Paul this last Sunday of the old year, "This one thing I do, forgetting those things which are behind, and reaching forth unto those things which are before, I press toward the mark for the prize."

XI

THE GIVER—PETER

Acts 3:6

"Silver and gold have I none, but such as I have give I thee."

I

These are the words of Simon Peter. He is speaking to a certain beggar who has asked him for alms. In reply to this beggar's appeal Peter said: "I have neither silver nor gold, nevertheless I give." These last two words, "I give," have an autobiographical flavour. They give in some measure an epitome of Peter's life. In them he tells the task at which he toils morning, noon and night. In them he tells what it means to him to live and what it has meant ever since his meeting with Jesus. What is Peter's work? It is giving. He can sum up his whole biography since he became a follower of Christ in these two short words, "I give."

Now the story we have before us is a good illustration of this fact. Peter's encounter with the beggar is a picture of a typical day in his life. Not that Peter did the same things every day. Not that he was every day made the agent through whom God worked miracles. But Peter was actuated always by the same passion. He was dominated always by the same spirit.

121

His passion was not that of getting, it was not that of winning fame or fortune, it was not that of achieving greatness in the eyes of men. The one white hot passion of his life was that of giving. His ambition was to be able to say, "I give."

Look at the story. It is the prayer meeting hour. At least that is the hour that had struck for Peter and his friend John. That hour has not struck for some of us yet. The prayer meeting hour is one that never comes in the calendar of most folks. It is an hour that is not to be found even in the calendar of most church members. Do you happen to know a more lifeless service than the ordinary prayer meeting? Do you know of any service that is more trying to the pastor, that is often more pathetic in its grave-like chill and deadness? How often have I heard some discouraged saint thank God that where two or three were gathered together there was He in the midst? But there was no thrill in the prayer because the one who uttered it was not half so much moved by the joyful sense of the Divine presence as by an oppressing sense of the human absence.

When the hour came for the prayer meeting Peter turned his feet toward the house of God. There are those who possess his wisdom still. When other church members have gone to the show or have gone to sleep or have gone to the dance, these find their way to the place of prayer. Thank God for the large number in our own church who have this as their custom. We have one of the best attended prayer meetings in America. But in all frankness I am not giving the credit for this to some of you who hear me. I am not giving the credit for this to some of the officials of the church. You have never made the slightest contribution toward making the prayer meeting a success. If everybody had treated it as you have, it would be so dead that it would make a funeral vault look like a street carnival.

Peter went to prayer meeting. And this he did in spite of the fact that he was a very busy man. In all probability he had been much engaged in religious work during the morning hours of this very day. Possibly he had preached and had seen thousands of souls brought into the Kingdom. But in spite of the fact that he was busy, in spite of the fact that God had used him to preach to great multitudes, in spite of the fact that He had honoured him by allowing him to win great numbers to Jesus Christ, yet he was not too busy to attend prayer meeting.

Not only did this busy man go to prayer meeting, but he went in spite of the fact that the meeting to which he went was doubtless a rather tame and uninteresting affair. But Peter is not going simply for what he can get. He is going for what he can give. "Peter, it is a dry desert of a service into which you are going." And he replies: "I ought to be there, for my Master has said that if we believe on Him, out of our inner lives shall flow rivers of living water. Maybe I can help turn the desert into a garden." "It is a dead service," I tell him. But he answers: "If it is dead, it is all the more necessary that I go. Maybe I can bring some life into it. The more impoverished a service is, the more necessary it becomes that I go. If there were all the light and warmth and joy and power in it that there ought to be, then my presence would not be so needful, but since so much is wanting, my presence is absolutely necessary."

Now it was while Peter was on his way to this service

that he came face to face with his great opportunity. Since he was eager to give he was seeking an opportunity to give. Since he was eager to help his eyes were wide open for a chance to help. And it is ever true here as elsewhere that "he that seeketh findeth." Peter's opportunity came in the person of a beggar. This beggar did not mean opportunity to every one. To some he meant only a pest, a nuisance, a parasite. But to Peter he meant an opportunity to give.

This beggar did not ask for much. He would have been well satisfied with a penny. Peter would have been glad enough to have given him a penny if he had only had one. But when this apostle searched his pockets he found that he did not have a cent. So he turns to this beggar and tells him frankly that he has not a penny in the world. "Silver and gold have I none." And having said this, we expect to see him hurry on into the temple, telling John meantime how glad he would have been to have given him something if he had only had as much money as some Crœsus of their acquaintance. But Peter did not do this. Instead, he said: "I have neither silver nor gold, but what I have, I give."

II

What did Peter give?

He did not give money. He had none. He did not give this man a position. He had no position at his disposal. He did not give him an education. That was beyond Peter's power. He gave him simply what he had, not what he expected to have to-morrow, nor what he had yesterday, but that which was a possession of his at that moment. "What I have I give."

Now, since Peter gave what he had and only that, we cannot but realise that the very poorest of us may do as well as he. This great apostle could do nothing bigger nor better than give what he had. But the very least of all can do that well. Every man can be a giver. We may be failures financially. We may be physical failures. We may spend our best years in the sick roof fisticuffing with death. We may not be greatly gifted intellectually. We may have but few educational advantages. We may be devoid of all musical talent. But in spite of all difficulties, in spite of all weaknesses, we can give. Every man can be a giver if he wants to be.

And giving is a privilege. It is blessed to receive; it is good to watch the parched earth receive the rain after a long drought. It is good to watch the dew-drenched world receive the sun's kiss when night is gone. It is good to see a man open his hands and heart to receive God's gifts. But, according to Christ, "it is more blessed to give than to receive." It is more blessed because it is more Godlike. Giving is the task at which God works from eternity to eternity. The very heart of the Gospel is this: "God so loved the world that He gave." And when we are at our best we also long to give. "Not to taste sweet things, but to do true and noble things and to vindicate ourselves under God's heaven as God-made men and women, is that for which every son of Adam dimly longs."

Now, because every man may give, it is every man's duty to give. To refuse to give is to refuse to live. There are two seas with which we are familiar in the Bible story. One of these seas looked out one morning and saw a delightful visitor coming. It was the River Jordan. And when it came singing and shimmering and laughing, the little sea of Galilee was glad. It opened wide its arms and took the gracious river to its heart and kissed it on the lips and said, "Precious gift, you are too good to keep."

"The dry fields burn and the mills are to turn,
  And a myriad flowers mortally yearn."

And so it passed the river on to others.

And there was another sea and it looked out and saw this same river coming. And it too was glad. It also gave the river welcome. But once it had taken it into its arms it held it fast and said: "It's mine, all mine. I will not give a drop for the watering of the rose's petal or for the moistening of the lips of a fevered child." And that day this sea put on its shroud. And that day it slipped into its coffin. And that day the laws of nature, which are the laws of God, said above that sea, "Earth to earth; ashes to ashes; dust to dust." And we know this sea to-day by the name of the Dead Sea. For "he that saveth his life shall lose it." To give is to live. To refuse to give is to die. Peter found life instead of death by being able to say: "I give."

III

What did Peter possess? Since he was unable to give money to this beggar, what then was his contribution?

1. He gave him hope. There was little of high expectation in this beggar's heart before he met Peter. The utmost for which he hoped was to be able to continue to beg enough to keep soul and body together

for a few more weary years. A beggar he was to-day, a beggar he expected to remain to the end of the chapter. He had no thought of serving, no thought of giving. He never dreamed of being a helper. The weary road that stretched away before his feet was the dull, drab, unromantic road of the parasite. But Peter made him hope. Peter kindled in his heart the expectation of the dawn of a better to-morrow.

It is a great privilege to be a hope bringer. There are those in every congregation who seem especially gifted of God for this high task. They know how to make a sobbing heart sing. They know how to make clouded skies bright. And we need such desperately, for their opposites are always with us. I have known those who were more skilled in going through your pockets than the Artful Dodger. They could leave you thoroughly discouraged after a five minutes' conversation. Sometimes to even meet them on the street was to be depressed. But this man's expectation rose from the dead in the presence of this apostle. Peter gave him hope.

2. Peter gave him faith. He gave him faith in man. This beggar came somehow to believe in Peter. He was brought also to a new faith in himself. He began to believe that he might be and do something in the world. He was led to a new and uplifting faith in Christ. Peter preached to him, and he preached in such a fashion as to give him a daring and vigorous faith.

3. Peter gave him love. Scores of people had put money into the beggar's hands, but they had despised him while they served him. They had scorned while they helped him. He would have thrown their money back into their faces but for the fact that hunger made

him refrain. He had possibly felt many times like the beggar in Lowell's poem. The Knight threw him a bit of gold, but there was no love in the gift. So:

> "The beggar left the coin in the dust.
> Better to me the poor man's crust
> Though he turn me empty from his door."

This beggar was sure of Peter's love. It was a love that expressed itself. That is what love is always seeking to do. Peter stretched a helping hand to him: "And he took him by the right hand and lifted him up." He gave him the handclasp of a brother. It seems a very simple gift, and yet there is none that is more needed to-day and always.

IV

What was the outcome of Peter's giving?

1. This beggar was re-made. The man who had never before stood upon his own feet was able to stand erect. The man who was physically infirm became physically strong. The man who was morally weak became morally strong. So this apostle, in spite of his empty pockets and his depleted bank account, was still able to give gifts so rich and priceless that the one privileged to receive them was utterly transformed.

2. Peter's gifts not only resulted in the re-making of this beggar, but they passed on to the enriching of other lives. When Peter reached the prayer meeting that day, he brought somebody besides himself. There was a man with him who had never been to prayer meeting before. He had been to the door, but he had never managed to get in. There was a new face at the prayer

meeting. There was a new man, and he was not carried there. He went there "walking and leaping and praising God." And many at that prayer service were blessed by his presence. And I dare to believe that he will be a blessing to you and to me at this very service.

v

It is evident, therefore, that all God needs to bring about victory is for us to give what we have. It is true here, it is true everywhere. Here is a man named Moses. God wants to send him on a difficult mission. Moses is timid. He hesitates. "What is that in thy hand?" God asks. "It is a rod," is the answer. "Only a crooked stick." "Throw it down. Dedicate it to me," God says. Moses throws it down. It becomes a serpent. He picks it up again. It is a rod once more. It is the very same that it was before, with this difference. It is one that has been dedicated to God. Armed with this rod Moses invades the great Kingdom of Egypt and succeeds in the emancipation of his people.

There was a lad once who was used of Christ for the feeding of thousands of people. Yet this boy had only five loaves and two fish. How then was he able to accomplish such a great and impossible task? He did not do so by saying what he would do if he had a corner on the wheat market. He did not do so by eating the lunch that he had and saying how sorry he was that he did not have enough to feed the multitude. He accomplished this great task by simply giving Jesus what he had. He might have used the exact language of Peter—"What I have I give."

The most famous contribution of all history was

made by a certain poor widow. It was a contribution so large that it has made her immortal. We count her as one of heaven's multimillionaires. Many who were rich gave much that day, but this widow gave more than all. How came it that one so poor could give so much? Again, her secret is that of Peter. With only two mites in her hand she dared to approach her Lord and say, "What I have I give."

There is a certain character in the Bible to whom the world has given the name "Good." We can never forget this man. He is remembered not because he was the shrewd Samaritan or the brilliant Samaritan or the rich Samaritan. We remember him because he was the "Good Samaritan." And how did he earn this magnificent name? He did not do so by boasting of what he would do for a certain wounded man if he had only had medical training. We call him good because when he came face to face with a great need he gave what he had. He was not a physician, but he bound up a man's wounds the best he could. He had no ambulance, but he used a blundering donkey. He gave what he had and the wounded man was saved. He gave what he had and the world has crowned him. And better still, God has crowned him.

"What I have I give." If everybody would do that, the world would be won before sunset. And, mark you, it will never be won in any other way. God needs the gifts of the brilliant and talented. He needs the gifts of the man of genius. But just as genuinely does he need the gifts of those of us who are ordinary. God tunes the voice of the mocking bird to sing all the songs in the birds' hymn book. But He does not expect this mocker to be the only singer in His feathered choir.

He is quite as much interested in the songs of the least gifted and the least tuneful. The world has been greatly blessed by the gifts of the conspicuous workers. But its greatest blessings have come through the faithful gifts of the hidden and the obscure.

I was on a battlefield some months ago. Here and there I stopped before monuments to read the names of those who "had paid the last sad measure of devotion." In the course of my ramble I came to a monument that bore no name. Inscribed upon it instead were these words: "To the Unknown Dead." It was erected in memory of those who gave their all, but forgot to sign their names. When the subscription list was passed they made their offering. It was this: "One life." And when we said: "Name, please," all they answered was, "Never mind, write it down 'A friend who loved the cause.'" They had no great gifts of genius, but what they had they gave. They were so busy giving in fact that they forgot to leave their names.

> "Common as the wayside grasses,
>   Ordinary as the soil,
>   By the score he daily passes,
>   Going to and from his toil.
>   Stranger he to wealth and fame—
>   He is only What's-His-Name.
>
> "Cheerful 'neath the load he's bearing,
>   For he always bears a load;
>   Patiently forever faring
>   On his ordinary road;
>   All his days are much the same—
>   Uncomplaining What's-His-Name.

"Not for him is glittering glory,
Not for him the places high;
Week by week the same old story—
Try and fail and fail and try,
Life for him is dull and tame—
Poor, old, plodding What's-His-Name.

"Though to some one else the guerdon,
Though but few his worth may know;
On his shoulders rests the burden
Of our progress won so slow.
Red the road by which we came
With the blood of What's-His-Name."

Oh, my brethren, our task is simple. It is as simple as that at which Simon Peter worked. We are to be able to write our autobiographies with one sentence: "I give." If we can do that we write ourselves as kinsfolk to God Himself. The most blessed word we read about Him is this: "I give." And nothing better can we write or read about ourselves. Our task is giving, and what we are to give is not the wealth of another; we are to give what we have. Our pockets may be as empty as those of the apostle Peter, but that does not mean that we must be useless. We can still say: "Silver and gold have I none, but what I have I give."

XII

DOUBTING CASTLE—JOHN THE BAPTIST

Matthew 11:3

"Art thou he that should come, or do we look for another?"

This question was asked by John the Baptist. He did not ask it in the atmosphere of the class room. He did not ask it while he was enjoying the privilege of his work in the out-of-doors. He did not ask it with the applause of his cheering followers ringing in his ears. He did not ask it amidst the luxuries of a palace. He asked it while he was occupying a prison cell. He asked it amidst the stenchful gloom of a dungeon where the sunlight was a stranger, and where no physical comforts ever came.

I

Why did John ask this question?

He did not ask it for purposes of argument or speculation. He did not ask it because he had become impatient with the slowness of Jesus and wanted to compel Him to show His hand. He did not ask it to satisfy his own wavering disciples. He asked it to satisfy himself. John's faith has gone into eclipse. There was a man preaching out in the open that he had declared to be the promised Messiah. But now he

133

is in the grip of a chilling fear that he has made a mistake. His former certainty has given place to uncertainty. Therefore, he asks this question: "Art thou he that should come, or do we look for another?"

You remember in Bunyan's immortal allegory how his pilgrims wandered out of the way and went to sleep on strange soil. The next morning they were waked to find themselves in the grip of Giant Despair. This grim giant led them roughly away and thrust them into a dark and stenchful dungeon. The name of this fearful dungeon was "Doubting Castle." Now it was in this same dungeon that John the Baptist found himself. That was the reason he asked this question. And, mark you, he is not the only one of God's saints that has been imprisoned there. You have possibly passed not a few days of darkness and nights of wretchedness in this same grim castle. The floors of this gloomy prison are damp with the tears of some of the choicest sons and daughters of God. Its walls yet echo with the voice of their prayers. Elijah has been here. And so has Thomas. And so have countless others. It is a trying experience that few escape.

II

What was the cause of John's doubt?

His uncertainty did not grow out of the fact that he had never become acquainted with Jesus. That may be the secret of the doubt of some of us. Maybe you have never really met the Lord. Maybe you have never in true heart earnestness said to Him, "My Lord and my God." Maybe you have never been able to sing: "Blessed assurance, Jesus is mine." But this was not the case with John. He knew Jesus. John had baptised Him. He had been privileged to see the Spirit of God come in bodily form as a dove upon Him. And the message had already come to John that upon whom he should see the Spirit descending and remaining, the same was He that should baptise with the Holy Ghost. He had heard the voice of God saying: "This is my beloved Son, in whom I am well pleased."

Not only had John come to know Jesus for himself, but he had borne witness to Jesus. He had pointed his own disciples to Him. He had preached in one sentence a sermon that is the sum of all saving sermons: "Behold the Lamb of God which taketh away the sin of the world." John had seen in this man that he was now doubting the One of whom the Prophet spoke, "He was wounded for our transgressions, He was bruised for our iniquities: the chastisement of our peace was upon Him; and with His stripes we are healed. All we like sheep have gone astray; we have turned every one to his own way; and the Lord hath laid on Him the iniquity of us all." Therefore, John was not doubting for lack of personal knowledge of Jesus.

Neither was he doubting because he had fallen into sin. Sin is a most frequent cause of doubt. There is nothing that more surely saps our faith than conscious sin. You can sin against your deepest convictions till they cease to be convictions. You can outrage your conscience till it loses its voice of warning. The only way to continue to believe your beliefs is by putting them into practice. But John had put his into practice. It would be hard to find one who had done so more courageously.

Look at this picture. John has begun preaching in the wilderness. So arresting is his message, so compelling is his earnest personality that he empties the cities round about and crowds the wilderness with the eager throngs. He speaks fearlessly to the hearts and consciences of men. He urges upon them the necessity of repentance. And men of all classes are moved by him. Men of all classes accept his baptism. Therefore, his fame so spreads that he is invited to preach at the court of Herod.

Here he is put to a very sharp test. It is evident that Herod admires him. He is much impressed by him. But he rebukes Herod's sin. He does not tell him that it is not expedient for him to live the corrupt life he is living. He tells him that it is not lawful. He makes him smart. He makes him tremble. For this courageous stand Herod's harlot has John put in prison. But he goes to his prison cell with the consciousness that he has done his duty as God has given him to see his duty. So John's doubt was not born of his unfaithfulness.

1. John was idle. Idleness is exceedingly hard to endure. A graduate of Princeton University wrote some time ago: "I am dying of nothing to do." His father had left him a fortune. Work was unnecessary. Since work was unnecessary, he refused to work. Therefore, he found himself dying by the inch. Unable to endure the torture, he put a pistol to his temple and blew his brains out. He might have saved himself by going to work, but he preferred the easier path of suicide.

Multitudes die from the same cause in the Church every year. For, mark you, no man is strong enough to be a Christian and be deliberately idle. Such a thing is an utter impossibility. This is true, because idleness is in itself a sin. "To him that knoweth to do good and doeth it not, to him it is sin." Then idleness persisted in leads inevitably to positive sin. Nature abhors a vacuum. If a man will not fill his hands with positive good, then sooner or later he will fill them with positive evil. There is only one sure method of victory over sin and that is to roll against it an overcoming tide of good.

But John was not willingly idle. He was idle because he could not help himself. His idleness was enforced. Yet even this form of idleness is hard to endure. That is the reason that knights of the sick room find it very hard to keep a sunny and vigorous faith. That is the reason that old bodies who are no longer able to work find it so easy to look backward to a golden age instead of forward. The good days were the days when they were on the firing line. Now the grace of God is sufficient to keep one sunny even in the midst of enforced idleness, but much grace is needed. John did not avail himself of that needed grace. Hence his faith went into eclipse.

2. John misunderstood Jesus.

(1) John was perplexed by the work Jesus was doing in the world. He had expected the Messiah to perform tasks that were altogether different from the ones that Jesus was performing. The Christ that he had preached was one who had a fan in His hand. He was to thoroughly cleanse the threshing floors. The wheat He was to gather into garners and the chaff He was to burn with unquenchable fire. Every tree that did not bear good fruit He was to cut down. He was to rescue His oppressed people and enable them to put their feet upon the neck of their oppressor.

His conception of Christ's work, therefore, was physical rather than spiritual. He thought the King-

dom of God was to come with observation. He believed
that Christ's conquests were to be outward and political
rather than inward and moral. He looked for a victory such as only physical weapons could achieve. His
expectations did not rise to the height of those who
realise that the supreme victory is that wrought by
those weapons that are not carnal.

There are those to-day who are depressed and discouraged and in doubt for this same reason. Such
people often claim that Christianity has failed. But
in making such complaint they indicate their failure to
realise Christ's method of work and also His purpose
in the world. Christ is not here to win a victory
through physical force. He is here to make the appeal
of love to the hearts of men. If men yield to that
appeal, He wins. If they refuse that appeal, He
loses so far as they are concerned. Christ's Kingdom
cannot come only in but one way, and that is through
the yielding of our hearts to the appeal of the divine
love.

(2) Then John was perplexed by the dealing of
Christ with himself. John was suffering. Not only
so, but he was suffering unjustly. If he had been unfaithful to Jesus, it would have been far easier for him
to have understood the hard ordeal through which he
was passing. But he had not been unfaithful. He had
not played the coward. He had not shirked. He had
not turned his back upon his Master. He had marched
breast forward. He had been unflinchingly loyal when
loyalty cost him everything.

Now the One to whom he had been loyal was at
liberty in the big outer world. He was out there
preaching to the poor. He was opening blind eyes.
He was cleansing lepers. He was even raising the

dead. Evidently He had power. He had power beyond the human. Why then did He not exercise that power in his own behalf? Why did He not pay him for his loyalty and for his faithfulness by breaking down his prison door and working for his physical deliverance? Many have been perplexed by this same problem. Men have somehow felt all through the centuries that God ought to pay them wages for being loyal. But this is not His method. The Devil pays wages. God never does. "The wages of sin is death, but the gift of God is eternal life, through Jesus Christ, our Lord."

Some weeks ago I received a letter that read a bit like this: "A little more than a year ago my business partner left me and went into the bootlegging business. He urged me to join him, but I refused because I could not get the consent of my conscience to engage in such an evil enterprise. He laughed at my scruples and went his way. Since then I have not prospered. But my friend has grown rich. He lives now on Massachusetts Avenue. He has two or three high-powered cars and plenty of servants. What I want to know is if it pays to do right?"

And what could I answer this man? What would you have answered? There was but one answer to give and that was a very definite affirmative. Certainly it pays to do right. Certainly it pays to be loyal to God and to your conscience. That does not mean, however, that it pays in dollars and cents. There is no place in the Bible where you are promised so much per day for being a saint. Other things being equal, the genuine Christian has the better chance at material prosperity. But when he does prosper, his prosperity is a by-product. God does not promise financial or political or social success to any man for being righteous. Christ is not in the world primarily to make men successful. He is not here to make men rich. He is not here to give men an easy time. He is not here chiefly to exempt men from pain and from hardship and from conflict and from struggle. He is here that we might have life, and that we might have it in abundance. And He spares no pains on the part of Himself or of ourselves in order to reach this end.

For this reason all prison doors are not opened, even for God's saints. For this reason all fiery furnaces are not abolished. For this reason all tears are not dried. There are pains that come to us that we must endure to the end. There are thorns that pierce us that must continue to pierce us till the very last hour of the twilight. There are agonies that torture us that will keep up their torture even till the coming of night. This is true not because our Lord does not love us. It is true because He does love us. He loves us so well that He is willing to allow us to suffer in order to bring us to a fuller and larger life. John did not realise this. Therefore, his own personal agony made him doubt.

III

What did John do with his doubt?

1. He defied it. He did not allow it to turn his feet from the plain path of duty. He did not allow it to swerve him an inch from the road of righteousness. Frederick W. Robertson was like him in this respect. He, too, was tortured by doubt. But through it all, with the realisation that right is ever right, he clung to the right as God had given him to see it. He lived up to the truth insofar as it was revealed.

Hear again this question: "Art thou He that should come, or do we look for another?" "It may be," says John, "that I have been deceived. It may be that thou art not the Coming One. Even if I have been mistaken, of this I am sure, that God is going to make good His promise. If thou art not the Coming One, then there is another. Therefore, I will not turn my back toward the eastern horizon. I will face the East in the expectation that the Sun of Righteousness will yet rise with healing in his beams. I will mount my watchtower and keep a constant lookout till the promised Messiah does come."

2. John carried his doubt to Jesus. He did not consult the enemies of Jesus as some do. He went to Jesus Himself. And, mark you, that is every man's privilege. We do not need any go-between here. We do not need a priest. We do not need the Virgin Mary. We do not need the saints. We have, every one of us, the privilege of a personal appeal to Jesus Christ Himself.

And what said Jesus thus appealed to? Did He reply that He had no patience with a doubter? Did He show any anger at Nathanael as he doubted if any good thing could come out of Nazareth? Was He angry with Peter when he sank under the weight of his doubts? Was He angry with the two disciples who walked that Easter Sunday from Jerusalem to Emmaus? Was He angry with Thomas when Thomas so brutally said that he would not believe unless he put his fingers in the print of the nails and thrust his hand into His side?

No, He was not angry. When they came to Him in sincerity wanting to know He replied to them. He gave them certainty for uncertainty. He gave them faith instead of fear. And so He replied to John. He said to the two who interviewed Him on behalf of their master: "Go tell John the things that you see and hear; how that the lepers are cleansed and the lame walk and the blind receive their sight and the dead are raised up and the poor have the Gospel preached to them." And though we are not told what John said when these messengers returned, yet I have a conviction that he was entirely satisfied.

And to you who are troubled and perplexed, I bring this message: Jesus Christ is able to meet your need. He is able to dispel your doubts. He is able to bring you into a place of blessed certainty. His grace is suf ficient for you. Appeal to Him. "Come boldly unto the throne of grace." Do this and you will go away from His house to-day with the conviction that He satisfies the longing soul. You will go away singing: "I will bless the Lord at all times. His praise shall continually be in my month. For I sought the Lord and He heard me and delivered me from all my fears."

XIII

LOVE IS DEAD—THE LEPER

Mark 1:40

"If .thou wilt, thou canst make me clean."

I

This is a very pathetic prayer. It is deeply marked with heartache, disillusionment and bitter disappointment. It is soaked in despairful tears. "If thou wilt, thou canst make me clean." "I believe that thou hast the power, but I hardly think that thou wouldst care to exercise it in my behalf. Thou hast the necessary ability, but I am in doubt about thy love." "If thou wilt, thou canst make me clean."

What is the matter with this poor fellow? He has lost faith in love. He still believes in power, but for him love is dead. There have been glad days in his past, doubtless, when he believed in love. There were yesterdays that were tender and bright and beautiful because the light of love illuminated them. But they have all dropped into the sunset. Black night is upon him now because he believes that love is dead.

II

It is easy to imagine how he came into this sad state. He was not a deliberate cynic. He had not made up his mind to believe in the complete selfishness of every

143

one in an effort to excuse his own selfishness. There
are those who are guilty of such conduct, you know.
But such was not the case with this man. He had come
to this sad state because of his terrible suffering. His
faith in the fact of love had been pounded out of him
by hard-fisted pain. He had suffered long and alone
and hopelessly.

1. He was a victim of physical disease. He was a
leper. He had a malady that was most loathsome and
horrible. It was a disease that made him ghastly in
the eyes of every beholder. It was a dogged sickness
that was eating him up piecemeal. The man who died
of it had to see himself drop into his grave by the inch.
Suffering thus, it is not to be wondered at that, if he
had had no other pain, he lived in the torture of a per-
petual nightmare.

2. He was unfriended and alone. His physical suffering was the least of his agonies. When his leprosy
stole upon him, more fearful than the ghastly death
that he saw in the distance was the thought of separation from all that he loved. For his malady made its
victim unclean. It drove him from the fellowship of
his kind. It scourged him from the haunts of men.
His lips might ache for the kiss of wife and child, but
they must ache in vain. And the home to which he
was sent was not one where every comfort was provided. It was a cave or an open grave. To such an
abode this man had gone. Here he had lived un-
visited and uncared for till he felt himself utterly forgotten. Here he had suffered, despised, neglected and
alone.

3. He was seemingly forsaken of the Lord. Not
only had he been separated from his fellows, but he
felt himself utterly separated from God. He had been

taught to believe that the fact that this ghastly disease
had come upon him was a mark of the Divine displeasure. The fact that he had thus suffered showed
that he was under the frown of God. That is why he
had been thrown out among the filth and rubbish of the
tombs. He was a creature so inwardly and outwardly
rotten as to be unfit for the fellowship either of God or
of man. Naturally he had come under such suffering
to be sceptical about the very existence of love. He did
not believe there was a man on earth or a God in
heaven who really cared for him.

III

But one day strange rumours came to him. Most
amazing stories were told about a young Rabbi who
was doing works out in the big world that were beyond
the human. Some had declared that he had healed
the sick, that he had shown skill to open the eyes of
the blind and let the morning in. In these stories he
at first took only mild interest. They did not concern
him personally in the least. Why should they? He
was as one already dead. He was no longer a part of
that world of which these stories were told. That
world had forgotten him, had broken his heart and
thrown him utterly away.

Then one day a traveller passed his way whose step
was made quick by irrepressible joy. His face was
wonderfully sunny, and he seemed bent on telling his
story to any one who was willing to listen. And when
this leper cried, "Unclean! unclean!" at his approach,
he did not flee away. On the contrary, he came close
enough to speak to him. And a wonderful story he
had to tell! "Yesterday I was blind," he cries joy-

fully, "but I met Jesus of Nazareth and He cured me. You just ought to go to Him. He can cure any disease."

And there was such a ring of sincerity in the testimony that the leper found it impossible to doubt. "I think this physician could cure me," he said to himself, "if he only cared to do so. I believe that he is able to cure me, and maybe he would want to do so if he only knew how wretched I am. Maybe he could be led to care if he could only see how this awful leprosy is gnawing the flesh from my body. Oh, if he knew how long are my nights; if he knew how bitter are my days; if he knew how dead weary I become of this long fisticuff with death, surely he would help me. I believe I will try him. Anything is better than sitting here and seeing yourself slip into the grave by the inch."

Thus this unhappy wretch decides that he will at least make an effort. He makes up his mind to do something. Others may stay in their tombs and wish they were sound and well, but he knows that wishing will not get him anywhere. It is well to wish that you were a better man; it is well to wish that you were clean, but all that comes to naked nothing unless you act. It is not enough to sit idle and wish. You have got to do something. This man decided that he would not let this only chance of salvation pass by while he sat in idleness. If he had to die, he would at least die after giving himself this one possible chance.

So he came to Jesus. I know he came without a full orbed faith. He was beset by many a doubt. He was exceedingly uncertain of his reception. He was hampered by his disease. He was hampered by his fear of the crowd. He knew that the people about

Jesus would not welcome him. He was dogged and hounded by a hundred fears. But in spite of his meagre faith and in spite of all his difficulties, he did come. And that, mark you, is more than many of us have done. We have heard the Gospel from our infancy. The Bible has been an open book in our homes. We have heard sermons enough to save the world. We have looked wistfully toward the heights and have at times longed to be better. But in spite of our chances, we have never yet come to Jesus. In spite of all our good impulses, we have never come to fling ourselves down at His feet. This man came to Jesus.

IV

Not only did he come, but he prayed. Listen again to his pathetic plea! "Lord, if thou wilt, thou canst make me clean." It is a very humble prayer. The story says that he threw himself down at the feet of Jesus. People can pray standing; they can pray in any position in the world, and they can take the most humble attitudes, and yet fail to pray. But I somehow feel that the kneeling position is the most natural, especially when we are really humble in our hearts. When you get heart hungry, when you feel that your situation is desperate, when you feel that your need is compelling beyond all words, it becomes quite natural for you to get down on your knees. The leper was humble in his attitude. He was so because he was truly humble in his heart.

Listen to him! He makes no claim for himself whatsoever. He comes with no parading of any fancied soundness there might be in him. He tells the Lord frankly that he is unclean. When he said, "Thou

canst make me clean," that was a confession that he
was not clean. And that was the first step also toward
getting clean. If you are all that you ought to be,
then you have no need of Jesus. If you are white and
unspotted, then there is no place for you at the foot of
the cross. "They that are whole need not a physician,
but they that are sick." It was to seek and to save
those that are lost that Jesus came. If you are not
ready to confess your sin, then you are not ready to
find salvation.

This man has no plea to make except the plea of his
own deep need. "Thou canst make me clean." That
is a confession that the task is beyond himself. He
cannot cure himself; he is wise enough to know that.
So are you, if you are a man of any moral earnestness
at all. If you have ever made any serious effort to
live right, you have at least come to this discovery:
that you are powerless to resist evil in your own
strength. No man is in himself equal to the task of
conquering sin in his own life. Every man who with
any degree of earnestness undertakes it must come at
last to that heart-breaking cry of St. Paul, "Oh,
wretched man that I am, who shall deliver me." This
man knows that he needs help. "Lord, I am unclean.
Lord, I must remain unclean to the end of eternity
except I am cleansed by thee. I cannot cleanse myself.
Man cannot cleanse me. 'Not all Neptune's ocean can
sweeten' this rotting body. There is no chance for me
except at thy hands. 'And now, Lord, what wait I
for, my hope is in thee. If thou wilt, thou canst make
me clean.' "

You can see that this leper believed in the power of
Christ. He believed in His might. He was sure that
Jesus was able to cure him, even if he was not sure of

His willingness. Have you got that far along, you
who were cradled in the arms of a Christian mother?
Do you believe that the Son of God is able to make
you absolutely free? Or have you let the Devil convince you that it is impossible for you to ever be delivered from sin? Are you yielding complacently to-
day to your own selfishness, to your own lust, to your
own evil habits because you have concluded that you
can do nothing else? Do you believe that there is a
sin from which Christ cannot save you, or do you believe what the word teaches: "He is able to save unto
the uttermost them that come unto God by Him"?
This man believed in the power of Christ.

But here his faith broke down. Though he believed
in the power of Christ, he doubted His love. "If thou
wilt, thou canst." It is as if he said: "Jesus, Master,
I am not sure that you will care to heal me. I fear it
does not matter to you whether I go or come, rise or
sink, live and laugh and love, or suffer and sob and rot.
I am certain of your power, but I am uncertain of
your love."

v

Now, do not be too hard on this man. It is not always easy for us to-day with all our light to believe in
the love of God. It is no trouble to believe in His
power. We see evidence of that everywhere. We
read of His might in the majesty of the templed hills,
in the rugged mountain heights, in the vast ocean and
in the shimmering stars. It is not hard to believe
that our God is a mighty God. But when we turn to
these same things for the tokens of His love, we do not
always find them. The mountain hurls her stones and

her avalanches to the destruction of human life. The tempests swoop down upon the defenceless and they are swept away. The ocean shakes itself in its rage and swallows the crippled ship as ruthlessly as any sea monster. Wherein do we find the proof of the love of God? The mountains say: "It is not in us." The skies say: "It is not in us." Nowhere, in fact, in nature do we find sure proof of the healing, cleansing, forgiving love of God.

So we find it hard at times to believe in the love of God. And yet how much better chance we have than this man had. He did not know that the man who stood before him was going to the cross for him in a few more months. He did not know that that brow bent above him was soon to be crowned with thorns for his sake. He had never heard that message pulsating with deathless hopes for the last and the lowest and the least of us: "For God so loved the world that He gave His only begotten Son, that whosoever believeth in Him should not perish but have everlasting life." This fact is most familiar to us. And yet, even we at times doubt the love of God. Therefore, it is not to be wondered at that this battered and tossed and bruised piece of human wreckage did not find it easy to believe in Christ's love for him.

But if there was some doubt in his prayer, it was deeply honest and genuinely sincere. He did not claim a faith that he did not possess. He did not come with an avowal of trust upon his lips when utter doubt was in his heart. He was downright honest and frank in that pathetic prayer of his. And it is my conviction that our prayer life would be enriched greatly if we would cultivate the habit of absolute sincerity in dealing with Christ. "He looketh on the heart," remem-

ber. There is no use in claiming a faith that we do
not possess. There is no use in professing submission
when our hearts are in hot rebellion. Let us dare to be
honest with Him and frank with Him, as was this man,
who told Him just what was in his heart.

VI

And what was the result?

1. Christ had compassion on him. He did not repel
him. He did not drive him away because he did not
have a perfectly well-rounded faith. He did not and
never does. He ever makes good the promise, "Him
that cometh unto me I will in no wise cast out." This
man came blunderingly, hampered with doubt. But
this big, blessed fact remains: He did come. And
when he prayed his humble, sincere prayer, "If thou
wilt, thou canst make me clean," Jesus did not repel
him. He had compassion on him."

Notice the word. "He had compassion on him." It
is something finer than pity. You can pity people
without loving them, but you cannot have compassion
unless there is love in your heart. "He had compassion on him." He entered into sympathy with him.
He got down under his load with him. He smarted
through his wounds and suffered in his broken heart
and wept through his tears. "He had compassion on
him."

2. Christ touched him. That was the outcome of
his compassion. Compassion is an active something.
You can pity folks and do nothing. It is altogether
possible that the priest and the Levite pitied that poor,
wounded fellow whom they found dying by the road-
side, but the Good Samaritan had compassion on him.

And, having compassion, he went to him and bound up his wounds and took him to an inn and took care of him. Christ had compassion on this leper, and, having compassion, He touched him.

That touch was the spontaneous act of love. The leper recognised that fact instantly. He no longer doubted love, no longer thought love dead. He knew it was alive and active. Love was putting its helping hand upon him. It was touching him. And it was this touch that woke up the dead love in his own heart. When Jesus put his hands upon him, his own dead love stirred, opened its eyes and smiled, and came into vigorous and joyous life.

3. Christ healed him. It was no trouble now for this leper to believe that Jesus cared. The touch convinced him. There was nothing in the world of which he was so sure. Such a touch always makes us sure. It is an indication that the one who so touches has identified himself with us, is getting under our load. It brings conviction that he is going to help us so far as is in his power, because he loves us. It was that touch that made it possible for Jesus to cure this leper. I do not believe the cure would have been possible without it, because the leper would not have sufficiently believed in Jesus to open his heart to Him.

And there is no exception to the rule. When Jesus wanted to save the world, there was no cheaper way for Him to do so than by identifying Himself with that world. "Forasmuch then as the children are partakers of flesh and blood He also Himself took part of the same." Before Jesus could save us and lift us out of our ruin utter and complete back again to God, He must needs bridge the wide chasm that separates man

and God and identify Himself with us. And there is
no cheaper method for you and me. We must identify
ourselves with those whom we would help.

Years ago a young man offered himself for membership in a certain church. The preacher asked him
about his conversion, and he said he owed his conversion
to Henry Drummond. The preacher next asked him
what Mr. Drummond said to him. "He said nothing,"
was the reply, "he simply put his hand on my shoulder
and looked at me." But there was that in the touch
that broke his heart and brought him to Christ, because
it was a touch of real sympathy born of real love. It
was a brother's touch. And there is nothing that this
old world needs to-day so much as the touch of a
brother. It will be saved, it will be won to Christ, it
will be softened and mellowed and wooed in no other
way.

> "When a man ain't got a cent
>   And is feelin' kinder blue,
> And the clouds hang low and heavy,
>   And won't let the sunshine through,
> It is a great thing, O my brethren,
>   For a fellow just to lay
> His hand upon your shoulder
>   In a friendly sort o' way.
>
> "It makes a man feel curious,
>   And it makes the teardrops start,
> And you sorter feel a flutter
>   In the region of the heart,
> And you can't look up and meet his eye,
>   And you don't know what to say,
> When his hand is on your shoulder
>   In a friendly sort o' way.

"Oh, the world's a curious compound,
    With its honey and its gall,
    With its cares and bitter crosses,
    But a good world after all;
    And a good God must have made it,
    Leastwise that is what I say
    When his hand is on my shoulder
    In a friendly sort o' way."

4. Christ cured him immediately. "Jesus stretched forth His hand and touched him and said, I will, be thou clean. And as soon as He had spoken, immediately the leprosy departed from him and he was cleansed." "I am willing," said Jesus, and the man was cured. He was cured at once. He did not have to wait. He did not have to go mourning for days and weeks and months and years. He was cured immediately. Thank God for immediate salvation. Thank God for One who is able instantly to loose us from our sins and wash us and make us whiter than snow. I preach to you to-night on immediate salvation. This salvation you may have now, at this very moment, this very instant. You do not have to even wait until the sermon is ended. You can be saved by the power of God right now.

"I am willing," said Jesus to this man who was uncertain about His willingness. He had been willing all along to cure him and make him whole, but the trouble was that the man was not willing. Do you think that the Lord is willing to save you? Do you think that the reason that you are away from Christ to-night is that He does not want you? Is your Godlessness due to the unwillingness of Christ to save you, or to your own unwillingness to be saved? Oh, you know where the fault is. It is not with Him, it is with you.

Yonder stands Jesus sobbing over the city that He loved. "How often," He said, "would I have gathered thy children as a hen gathers her brood under her wing, and ye would not." That is, "I was willing to save, I was willing to shelter you, I was willing to give you a place in my loving care, but you did not want it." And God cannot save any man against his will. But the fact that Jerusalem was lost, and the fact that any man is lost, is not the fault of the unwillingness of Christ, but of the unwillingness of the one who refuses His salvation.

Will you be saved to-night? Jesus is willing. He is willing to work an immediate deliverance. He is willing to receive you and make you every whit whole. But His willingness will go for nothing, His love will go for nothing, His cross will go for nothing so far as you are concerned, unless you are willing. It all hinges there. It is a question of your own willingness and of that only. He has declared His willingness times innumerable. He has declared it in the pathetic language of the cross. And now He waits for you. Believe me, there is nothing that will keep you from His cleansing except your own unwillingness to come and be cleansed. Will you let Him speak this word to your heart? "I will. Be thou clean."

XIV

A BEAUTIFUL WORK—MARY OF BETHANY

Mark 14: 6

"She hath wrought a beautiful work on me."

I

This was the verdict of Jesus. Judas did not agree with Him. He had not the slightest admiration for Mary's deed. He did not think that it was beautiful in the least. He rather regarded it as an ugly bit of extravagance. He looked upon it as a foolish piece of waste. To him it was so much money absolutely thrown away. It was the sum of three hundred pence squandered for naked nothing. Judas felt somewhat as if Mary had taken this sum out of his own pocket. Therefore, her deed did not excite his admiration.

But Christ said that it was beautiful. Of course we accept the verdict of Jesus rather than the verdict of Judas.

1. We accept the verdict of Jesus because Jesus has the seeing eye. He sees things clearly and sees them whole. Judas, on the other hand, looked on everything with warped vision. His selfishness had poisoned his sight. He was not possessed of the single eye. Therefore, the very light that was within him was darkness. But Jesus had the single eye of love. Therefore, we know that a work that He calls beautiful is beautiful indeed.

2. We feel safe also in accepting this verdict of Jesus because He has lived from eternity to eternity in the realm of perfect beauty. There is no ugliness where He abides. Every face is winsome. Every soul is transfigured. Every song is perfect in its melody. Every flower is fair and unfading. No landscape is marred. In this abode of perfect beauty Christ has lived from everlasting. Therefore, He is naturally skilled in His judgment of what is beautiful.

3. We may accept the verdict of Jesus because He is the creator of beauty. There is nothing beautiful in heaven or on earth that was not fashioned by His fingers. His might kindled every sun. He gave the gleam to every star. He clothes the lily with a glory surpassing that of Solomon. He paints the wing of the butterfly. He crimsons the East with dawn. He makes the death of the day as winsome as its birth by the glory of His sunsets. Therefore, since He is the creator of all that is beautiful, He can speak with authority on the subject of beauty.

II

What was there beautiful about this deed?

1. It was beautiful in its motive. When Mary anointed her Lord she was not simply seeking a place in the limelight. She was not selfishly struggling to have herself remembered. She was not trying to win the applause of the crowd. What she did was done because of her keen devotion to her Lord. This work that she wrought was born of the highest possible motive, the motive of love to Jesus Christ Himself.

Now it is almost trite to say that no deed can ever be beautiful that is born of a mean and ignoble and selfish motive. The music that selfishness makes is only "a sounding brass and a clanging cymbal." The flowers that selfishness sends are only nettles and night-shade and obnoxious weeds. The jewels that selfishness gives are only so much paltry glass. Every deed, however seemingly fair it may be, becomes unsightly and ugly when we realise that it was born of a mean and impure motive.

Take the kiss of Judas, for instance. Suppose Judas had kissed Jesus because he loved Him. Suppose he had kissed Him in token of the fact that he was deter-mined to be loyal to Him. Suppose that when the soldiers and the mob came to arrest Jesus, Judas had stepped bravely forward and had said: "Jesus, Master, the world may forsake you, the world may turn against you and crucify you, but I want you to know that you have my loyalty and my love now and evermore. And in token of my devotion to you, I bestow upon you this kiss." Had Judas' motive been pure, he would have been regarded as about the sweetest saint of sacred story. But as it is he is the most hated. This is the case not because the deed he did was ugly in it-self. It is true because it was done from an ugly motive.

Now, while no gift is truly beautiful that is done through a wrong motive, it is equally true that the very smallest deed becomes beautiful when it is done from a noble motive. Some months ago I sat talking to a mother. Suddenly a little laddie of about three sum-mers came upon the scene and broke into the conver-sation. He had been out playing in the yard. His little apron was soiled and his face was soiled. His fist was also soiled. But he held that little dirty fist up to his mother and said: "Mother, I brought you a bouquet." I could not see any bouquet, but when he opened his hand there lay in his palm one little withered dog fennel blossom.

Could any gift be smaller or meaner than that? Who wants a dog fennel blossom? How natural it would have been for this mother to have pushed the little fellow aside and said: "Take that ugly thing and throw it out the window." But the mother did not look at the flower. She looked at the motive. Therefore, she gathered the little lad in her arms, kissed his face and kissed his soiled hand. As she kissed him this dog fennel blossom bloomed into a Marshal Neil rose. Yea, it became a veritable flower garden under the transfiguring power of love.

2. This deed was beautiful in its recklessness. There was a mad abandon about it. Mary might have anointed Jesus with a mere fraction of what was in that alabaster box. But with a lack of prudence and business sagacity, that was absolutely insane in the eyes of Judas, she lavished the whole of it upon her Lord. And Christ praised her for so doing. He was ever ready to eulogise the reckless giver, but never did He have a word of praise for the prudent and careful giver who was constantly counting the cost. This deed was beautiful in its lovely recklessness.

3. This deed was beautiful in its uniqueness. It was so thoroughly original. It was so winsomely individual. Mary could not make the contribution to this feast that her sister Martha made. Martha served. She waited on the table. She was good at that. But Mary was not. Her hands seemed to have no skill for such tasks. But because she could not make Martha's contribution, she did not refuse to make any at all.

Mary was a lover, you remember. And love is always eager to give. Since love is eager, it is inventive. It may do the conventional thing. It may do the ordinary and commonplace thing. But of this you may be sure, it will do something. It will find some mode of expression. You can no more hide love in the heart of an individual and expect that individual to stay still than you can hide springtime away in a garden and expect that garden not to express itself in terms of colour and perfume. Mary could not do what Martha could. Therefore, she did the beautifully unique deed that was within her reach.

4. This deed was beautiful in its timeliness. Many a work that would have been beautiful has lost all its beauty by being wrought too late. Many a gift that would have been worthful has lost most of its worth by being behind time. For instance, Nicodemus gave Jesus one hundred pounds of myrrh and aloes. But Jesus was dead then. This disciple, like many another, was too late.

But Mary was on time. "She came," Jesus says, "aforetime." With the fine intuition of love she looked down the way and saw death coming to her Lord, and she said: "I will beat death to Him." And so she did. She anointed Him while He was yet alive. And when death came and touched His brow, her deed made even death's frozen fingers to smell of perfume.

A few years ago I went to take an offering of flowers to a faded old grandmother. She was past eighty years of age. But she had told me weeks before about her birthday. And so I went in remembrance of that event and carried her a small offering of flowers. And her old face lighted up as she received the gift as it might have lighted if she had been sixteen and I had been her lover. And she smiled upon me through tears that she took no pains to conceal, and this is what she said: "Oh, I am so glad that you did not wait till I was dead to bring them." Mary's deed was beautiful in its timeliness.

III

What was the outcome of this beautiful work.

1. Incidentally this deed made the name of Mary immortal. Not that she was seeking this immortality. Had she performed this deed in order to be remembered, she would have doubtless been forgotten. The world is not diligent in preserving the names of those who are merely hungry for the limelight. This boon of an abiding place in the memory of Christ and of man came to her as a kind of by-product of her deed of devotion. She was not seeking to be remembered any more than we are to seek for that end for ourselves. She was seeking to serve, and in so seeking she won everlasting fame.

Now to be remembered is no mean privilege. None of us desires to be forgotten.

> "Who to dumb forgetfulness a prey,
>   This pleasing, anxious being ere resigned,
>   Left the warm precincts of a cheerful day,
>   Nor cast one longing, lingering look behind."

Those of you who have visited South Cheyenne Canyon in Colorado will doubtless remember seeing a loose heap of stones upon a mountain top overlooking this lovely canyon. This is the spot where Helen Hunt Jackson was first buried. Her body has since been removed. She left this request to those who should visit the spot: They were to lay two stones upon her grave and take one away with them. Thus she sought to build an ever-growing monument. Thus she sought to keep alive her memory.

Now there was possibly much of mere selfish ambition in this. But we shrink from being forgotten even when we are utterly unselfish. One of the last words that our Lord left us is "Do this in remembrance of me." He yearns to be remembered. He does this not because he is vain and ambitious, but because He is unselfish and loving. There is no greater pain that can come to loving hearts than the pain of being forgotten by those that they love. Every lover is eager for an abiding place in the memory and the heart of the beloved.

For this reason it must have brought much joy to the heart of Mary when her Master told her that she should never be forgotten. Of course He himself remembered her. He remembered her during those tragic and trying last days. He remembered her amidst the betrayal of Judas and the denial of Peter. I think He remembered her, and strengthened His heart by that memory, amidst the conflict of Gethsemane and the agony of Calvary. And He remembers her still, now that He is seated at the right hand of the throne of the Majesty on high.

Not only does Christ remember her, but He sees to it that we do not forget. He has linked her name to His own by chains that cannot be broken. "Wheresoever this Gospel shall be preached throughout the whole world, this also that this woman has done shall be spoken of as a memorial of her." The memory of Mary of Bethany will last as long as the Gospel lasts. When the world has forgotten her, then it will have forgotten the story of Him who "was wounded for our transgressions and bruised for our iniquities."

2. This deed that Mary did helped Jesus. It warmed His heart. It served to strengthen Him for the terrible ordeal that was ahead of Him. I am aware of the fact that Judas said that the ointment was wasted. But Judas was mistaken. The trouble with Judas is that he did not have any scales that were capable of weighing such precious jewels as this. His scales might serve to weigh pig iron and fertiliser. They might serve very well the purposes of a junk dealer. But in the shop of one who deals in rare and priceless gems they would be entirely out of place. For nothing was of value to Judas unless it could be used to put bread into somebody's mouth or garments upon his body. He had absolutely no conception of a value that was not reckoned in terms of the material.

But we all know that there are many things that seem useless to men of the type of Judas that are exceedingly useful. There are many things that seem to such men unpractical that are after all exceedingly practical. What, for instance, is the value of a handshake? Ask Judas and he will tell you that it is worth absolutely nothing. It is so much wasted energy. And yet we know that there are times when such a seemingly useless something is worth far more than gold. Certainly that is the opinion of the man who, upon being asked how he was rescued from the slavery of drink, replied: "I was rescued through the handclasp of a friend."

What is the value of a smile? Here again the verdict of Judas would not be trustworthy. Judas might stop to salvage a wrecked piece of machinery, but he would throw such priceless things as smiles upon the scrap pile. But here again he would show his blindness. God has used as simple a thing as a smile to make a hopeless heart sing. He has used a smile for the re-making of a shattered and broken life. Therefore, there are times when smiles are of more value than precious jewels.

What is the good of a mother's kiss? Is there any healing power in it? Ask Judas and he will answer with an emphatic "No." He may tell you that kissing spreads disease. He will certainly assert that it has no power to heal our hurts. But those of us who remember our mothers know better. Just the other day a little fellow that belonged to a home where I was visiting fell and hurt himself. With face wet with tears, he hastened to his mother. This mother gathered him into her arms and said: "Yes, yes, tell mother where you are hurt." And the little fellow touched the bruised place upon his forehead. Then the mother kissed that place, and what do you suppose happened? The child's tears were dried, the pain was healed, and he went gladly again about his play.

We are not, therefore, to be taken in by the plausible criticism of Judas. "Why was this waste of the ointment made?" he questions. It might have been sold for three hundred pence and given to the poor. How businesslike that sounds! A very practical man is Judas, so he himself thought. So also thought his fellow disciples. For they agreed with him, you remember. But there are practical ways of helping that appeal neither to the palate nor to any other bodily comfort. There is a way to help that appeals to the heart. That was the way that Mary chose. And I dare to believe that in doing this deed that looked so utterly worthless in the eyes of Judas she rendered to Jesus the most helpful service that she could possibly have rendered.

3. This beautiful deed helped others. John tells us that the house was filled with the odour of the ointment. But it was impossible to confine this sweet fragrance within the narrow bounds of that one house. It floated out through the windows and spread and spread until it has gone literally round the world. It has been wafted across all oceans and into all lands. This sweet perfume is with us this morning as we worship together in the peace of God's house. Even now, though separated from this scene by seas and continents and centuries, our atmosphere is a bit sweeter because of Mary's winsome deed.

Now, what is the message that the fragrance of this deed brings to us to-day? It tells us that we may serve as Mary served. What did Mary? She did her best. She gave her all to Christ for love's sake. Our Master said of her, "She hath done what she could." That much you can do. That much I can do. And that is enough. If we do this, then one day we shall be privileged to share the reward of her of whom the Master said: "She hath wrought a beautiful work on me."

XV

THE DRUDGE—THE ELDER SON

Luke 15 : 25-32

"Now his elder son was in the field: and as he came and drew nigh to the house, he heard music and dancing. And he called one of the servants and asked what these things meant. And he said unto him, Thy brother is come; and thy father hath killed the fatted calf, because he hath received him safe and sound. And he was angry, and would not go in; therefore came his father out and entreated him. And he answering said to his father, Lo, these many years do I serve thee, neither transgressed I at any time thy commandments; and yet thou never gavest me a kid, that I might make merry with my friends: But as soon as this thy son was come, which hath devoured thy living with harlots, thou hast killed for him the fatted calf. And he said unto him, Son, thou art ever with me and all that I have is thine. It was meet that we should make merry, and be glad: for this thy brother was dead, and is alive again; and was lost, and is found."

This is a story of the boy that did not go away from home. He does not care to claim kin with his prodigal brother, but he is close kin to him none the less. They are brothers not simply because they are sons of the same father. They are brothers in character. They are both self-seekers. They are both concerned, at least at the beginning of the story, with pleasing themselves, with gaining their own ends rather than with pleasing their father. Of the two, the one that stayed at home is the more hopeless because he is less conscious of his need. In fact, he has no sense of need at all. He believes himself an object of genuine congratulation.

I

Look at the story: "Now his elder son was in the field." That is fine so far. That was where he belonged. He was out where the yellow wheat waved in billows. He was out where the barley rustled and spilled out its perfume. He was out where the blue sky bent above him and the sun kissed a healthful tan upon his cheeks. He was out where he could breathe an atmosphere that was sweet and pure. He was where he could avail himself of the strong moral support of a wholesome environment. He was in the place of all others where he had the best chance to keep clean. He was in the field.

Not only so, but he had actually appropriated many of the benefits of his fine environment. He had kept clean. His garments might have a bit of the odour of new-mown hay upon them, but they were certainly not rank with the stench of the hog pen. He had never visited the Far Country. He had never sowed any wild oats. He had not marred and scarred himself by long years of dissipation. He had remained thoroughly decent. And all this is very commendable.

In addition, he was a worker. "Now his elder son was in the field." That speaks of toil. There is sweat in the word. There is the stern strain of effort. This man is no idler. He is no parasite. He is an earnest and strenuous worker. His prodigal brother does not

work with him. He has gone into the Far Country.
He is wasting his substance with riotous living. But
no waster is this elder brother. He is a toiler. And
for this also we cannot but commend him.

II

And yet our Lord has not one good word to say about
this elder son. What is the matter with him? Why
does not Christ commend him? Was it wrong for him
to be in the field? No, that is where he ought to have
been. Was it wrong for him to work? No, work was
his duty. Christ longs for every one to be a worker.
He commands His disciples to pray the Lord of the
harvest to thrust forth labourers into His harvest. The
trouble with this elder son is not that he was in the
field. It is not that he was a clean and decent worker.
He is condemned rather because of the spirit in which
he did his work.

Dr. Hubbard has aptly called this elder son a drudge.
He is that most pathetic of all drudges—a religious
drudge. What is drudgery? A mean task? No, drudgery is not the task, it is the spirit in which we perform
the task. One man can make drudgery out of the singing of an anthem, while another can make poetry out
of the scrubbing of a floor. To do your work in the
spirit of loveless slavery is drudgery, however sublime
the task may be at which you toil. On the other hand,
if you work in the spirit of love, that work is shot
through with abiding beauty, however ugly and menial
your task may be in itself.

Here are two nurses that work in the same hospital.
To one of them the task is purely professional. She
watches, she gives medicine, she cools the fevered face.

She is capable, efficient, earnest, but all she sees is the pay check at the end of the week. She is a drudge. But the other: She too watches, toils, gives out her strength. Possibly she is no more efficient than her sister. But as she goes in and out among these sons and daughters of pain, this song is in her heart:

> "Oh, how could I serve in the wards
> If the Hope of the World were a lie.
> How could I endure the sights
> And the loathsome smell of disease
> But that He said: 'Ye do it for me
> When ye do it for these!'"

And to this latter the task is no longer drudgery. It is flooded with the radiant light that beams from the very face of Christ.

Who is this man pegging away day after day on old shoes? He is a cobbler. He is a drudging shoemaker. His name is Carey. No, a cobbler he is, but not a drudge. He is pegging shoes under the light of the Sun of Righteousness. The song of his hammer is the song that the angels sang above the star-lit heights of Bethlehem. The vision that he sees reaches far beyond the meagre sum he is to receive for his work. The mending of those worn shoes is a means to a glorious end. By his toil the feet of some that sit in darkness are to be shod with the preparation of the Gospel of peace. And here again what might have been drudgery is transformed into poetry by a beautiful motive.

But no such motive transfigured the work of this elder son. There was no love in his task. He did not care for this prodigal brother. Since he did not love his wandering brother, he was equally destitute of love for his father. For "if we love not our brother whom we have seen, how can we love God whom we have not seen ?" The measure of our love to God is what we are willing to do for men. Our devotion to the Unseen is read in our faithful and loyal devotion to those whom we see. It is impossible to love God and at the same time fail to love our brother.

III

Having no love for his brother, there was no pain at seeing him go away. He took the sin and the riotous living of the prodigal very little to heart. The fact that he was in the Far Country starving among swine did not worry this elder brother in the least. He never spent a sleepless night or a sleepless hour over the wrong doing of himself or of any one else. He did not care that men sinned. His father cared. His father grieved and broke his heart. But though his father might have wet his pillow with midnight tears, it mattered nothing to his loveless elder son.

Since this elder son did not share his father's grief over the loss of the prodigal, neither did he share his father's watchfulness for him. He had no part in his eager longing for his return. His father's face was ever toward the Far Country. He was always looking, always loving, always yearning. When at last the prodigal came home, "while he was yet a great way off his father saw him and ran and fell on his neck and kissed him." But this elder son did not see the returning wanderer. He refused to even meet him when he got home.

Not only did he fail to grieve over the wandering of the prodigal, not only did he fail to watch yearningly for his return, but when he came his coming brought

the elder brother no joy. "As he came and drew nigh
to the house, he heard music and dancing. And he
called one of the servants and asked what these things
meant. The servant said: Thy brother is come; and
thy father hath killed the fatted calf, because he hath
received him safe and sound. And he was angry and
would not go in." This marvellous event not only failed
to bring him joy, it brought him positive pain. It made
him angry.

Why was he angry? Not because his prodigal brother
had done him any harm. His anger was born of his
envy. This elder brother was envious. Therefore,
there was no joy in this occasion for him. All the music
was discord because it was not played in his honour
alone. The feast was altogether unpalatable because it
was not prepared solely for himself. He was possessed
of that hideous demon of envy, therefore any honour
done to another was a galling dishonour to himself.

Envy is an old sin. It committed the first crime that
was ever committed. The first murderous club that
was ever wielded was held by its devilish hand. It was
envy that murdered Abel. It was envy that sold Joseph
into slavery. It was envy that hurled the dart at David.
It was envy that plaited the crown of thorns for the
brow of our Lord. It was envy that nailed Him to the
cross. "He knew that for envy they had delivered Him
up."

What is envy? It is not to be confused with jealousy.
Jealousy, as another has pointed out, is a child of love.
When love is cheated of its dues, it has a right to be
jealous. There are times, I confess, when jealousy becomes "the green-eyed monster that makes the meat it
feeds upon." But oftentimes its meat is made for it.
When that is the case, jealousy is neither base nor ig-

noble. God is capable of jealousy. And the same may be said of all who really love.

Envy, on the other hand, is the child of hate. It has no connection with love whatsoever. We never envy those whom we truly love. "Love envieth not." Envy is that fiendish spirit that makes one feel uncomfortable when the ability, or attainment, or character of another is praised. It is a hellish serpent that stings us when we hear of the prosperity of a rival. I know a beautiful woman who seems to take it as almost a positive insult when some other woman's beauty is complimented. That is envy. It is a sin that few confess, but of which many are guilty. Ugly, cruel and devilish as it is, we hardly rid ourselves of it except by the grace of God.

IV

Notice next the experience of this drudge. He had remained at home. He had never gone into the Far Country. Therefore, we naturally expect that he will have a wonderful story to tell of blessed fellowship with his Father. We count upon it that he will be able to lead us to wonderful springs of which only those most intimate with his Father have knowledge. We expect him to be wise to bring us into marvellous gardens that the father has made known to him during his long sojourn at home. When he tells his experience, we lean eagerly forward. We feel sure of hearing a testimony at once winsome and inspiring.

But we are disappointed. This is his experience: "Lo, these many years do I serve thee, neither transgressed I at any time thy commandment; and yet thou never gavest me a kid that I might make merry with my friends." How astonishing! How disappointing! Did you ever hear a more pathetic testimony? "I have been serving my Father," says this man, "five years, ten years, twenty years, but it has meant absolutely nothing to me but hard work. There have been no glad surprises along the way. There have been no lovely oases. It has all been desert. Every day has been sunless and dull and drab and grey. I have lived in my Father's house, but I have lived not as a son, but as a slave. I have lived within reach of the Bread of Life, but I have never tasted it. I have lived with the song of the Water of Life sounding in my ears, but I have never stooped to drink."

Poor fellow! How completely he has missed everything that makes sonship beautiful and worth while! How utterly wanting he is in likeness to his Father! How wanting, therefore, in winsomeness! He reminds us of an artificial flower. What is wrong with that handsome rose? It is quite rose-like in its shape and colour. Yet there is something lacking. What? It has no life. It has never mined in the rich loam of the garden for the gold of real beauty. It has never been christened by the gentle baptism of the rain. It has never drunk from the mystic chalice of the dew. It has never had its cheek touched by the sun's magic brush. It has a form of life without the reality. And so it was with this toiling drudge. He has a form of sonship, but the winsome reality is not his.

And, sad to say, this elder son is not in a class to himself. There are literally hundreds and thousands who, if they spoke the honest truth, would have to confess that their religious lives had been disappointing. They have not found in the Church of Christ what they expected to find. A woman who was a member of my church said some time ago that before she came into the Church she thought it was going to mean so much. And then she sighed and said: "But I have found that it means very little. I am just like I was before I joined."

Why is this the case? Is it because Christ cannot do what He claims to do? Is it because this Word of God is only a cunningly devised fable? Whose fault was it that this elder son had such a lean and mean experience? Whose fault was it that his life had been such a disappointment to himself and such a disappointment to his Father? Our Lord indicates the reason. What said the Father to the son when he complained that he had never given him so much as a kid with which to make merry with his friends? He did not deny the charge. He virtually admits that the son is correct. But the reason he had given him nothing was because he was not willing to receive it.

v

Look at the privileges that might have been his. "Son, thou art ever with me, and all that I have is thine." This son of his might have had continuous fellowship with his Father. That is the experience to which God longs to bring every child of His. He ever yearns to make His promise, "Lo, I am with you alway" an actual experience with every one of us. There is absolutely nothing for which He is so eager as our companionship. He wants to be with us in our joys and in our sorrows. He wants to be with us in life's springtime, and also in life's winter.

And what do we need so much as this divine companionship? How we need Christ in our hours of temptation! I knew a young man who years ago was converted from a life of dissipation. For a while he was an earnest and devout Christian. But in an hour of weakness he fell. He was so ashamed of his fall that he hid himself from his faithful pastor. But that pastor sought him and found him and fought with him for his soul. At last he won him back to loyalty to Christ. Years passed on and that rescued man entered the ministry. One day as he and his one-time pastor were walking together to the church, this reclaimed man told of his constant battle with the sin that had almost wrought his ruin years ago. Then he paid this pastor a great tribute. He said: "You know I feel that I would never be tempted after this fashion if I always had you with me." But his friend replied: "I am not what you need. What you need is Jesus. You can have Him with you always, even to the end."

"Son, thou art ever with me." How we need Jesus in our hours of sorrow! How we need Him when hearts are broken and our hopes shattered! He can bring light to us when all is utter darkness. He can companion us and understand us and comfort us when all human help fails. You may recall that old story of Florence Nightingale, "the Angel of the Crimea": A wounded soldier had to undergo a severe operation. His heart would not permit his taking an anæsthetic. So the doctor informed him that he had better not operate since the pain would be so great that he could not endure it. But the soldier replied that he could endure it under one condition. "I can bear the pain if you will get the Angel of the Crimea to hold my hand during the operation." And this fine saint of God took the rough soldier's hand in her own and held it and caressed it as his mother might. And the knife cut through the tender flesh, and the saw cut through the bone, and the soldier never flinched. When the operation was over the doctor said in amazement, "I do not see how you stood it." But he answered: "I could not do otherwise. My hand was in the hand of the Angel of the Crimea." So in these painful experiences of life that cut into our very hearts, it is our privilege to have our hands, not in some weak human hand, but in the hand of the mighty Christ.

Not only was it the privilege of this elder son to have had the constant fellowship of his Father, but he might have possessed all his Father's wealth. Listen! "All that I have is thine." And that same word our Lord is speaking to our poverty-stricken hearts. "All things are yours." And is there anything more tragic than just this: That we are spiritually poor when we might be rich; that we are weak when we might be strong; that we are defeated and overcome when we might be conquerors? "All that I have is thine." Infinitely more eager than we are to receive is He to give.

It is said that when Helen Keller, that deaf, dumb and blind genius, was a baby, her mother used to bend over her as she lay in the cradle and drop her hot tears down upon her. And she would speak after this fashion: "Oh, Helen, how your mother loves you! And how she longs to tell you of her love! But she cannot make you understand. Your eyes are closed and your ears are stopped." It was the heartache of this mother that she longed to reveal herself; that she longed to give herself unreservedly to her child, and yet could not make her understand.

So this father was feeling toward his elder son. So God feels toward His children always. He is bending very wistfully above you and me to-day. And He is saying: "Oh, child of my heart, how I love you! And how I long to give you of my very best! How I long to enrich you with all spiritual gifts! How I long to bring you to your highest possibilities! 'All things are yours.' 'Son, thou art ever with me, and all that I have is thine.' " Let us claim what the heavenly Father so longs to give. Heaven's best may be ours. "He that spared not His own Son, but delivered Him up for us all, how shall He not with Him also freely give us all things." And thus receiving, life's drudgery will be changed into winsome poetry.

XVI

THE DYING FIRE—TIMOTHY

II Timothy 1:16

"Stir up the gift that is within thee."

I

The word here translated "stir up" really means re-kindle. "My dear Timothy," wrote Paul. "Knowing as I do the trying circumstances in which you are placed, I realise that you are in great danger of losing your zeal. I realise how greatly you are tempted to allow the fires of your enthusiasm to go out. Therefore, I write you this word, Rekindle the gift of God that is within you. Look well to your fire lest it burn low and utterly die."

You can see that Paul is not accusing Timothy of having put out his own fire. He did not say, "Stop throwing water on the fire of your zeal." In order for a fire to go out it is not necessary always that it be put out. When you light the fire in the furnace all you have to do to lose that fire and let winter invade your home is simply to let it alone. And all that is necessary in order for you to waste your gifts, to let all that God has invested in you go for nothing, is simply to let those gifts alone.

Paul is not accusing Timothy of misusing his gifts. He is not afraid that he is taking the talents that God has given him and turning them to base and ignoble

178

uses. Some people waste their substance with riotous living. Others waste theirs with quite respectable and quite decent living. In the Far Country by the swine trough is not the only place where men squander their abilities. They are often squandered no less by people who occupy pews in churches. They are squandered by those who are well-wishers of the Church and of all the forces that make for the world's upbuilding, but who do nothing but wish.

Nor is Paul urging Timothy to acquire new gifts. He is not urging him to use gifts that he does not possess. He simply presses home upon him the sane and practical duty of using what he actually has. "Stir up the gift that is within thee." It is not necessary for you to sing with the voice of another or to preach with the power of another. Your whole duty is to minister with your own hands, walk on errands of mercy upon your own feet, speak, as God has given you power, through your own lips. Use the gift that God has committed to you. That is your duty and your whole duty. And that is all that is necessary for the bringing in of the Kingdom of God.

If we were only as willing to use our own gifts as we fancy we should be to use the gifts of others, what a different Church we should have and what a different world this would be! We know quite well what it is to wish that we were as gifted as certain other individuals. If we were only as rich as a certain man we know, how much we would give! If we could only sing like a friend of ours, how constantly we would use our powers to the glory of God! But God's question to us is His question to Moses: "What is that in thy hand?" He is not concerned with what we do with the gifts of another. He is only concerned with what we do with our own. If He can get what we ourselves actually possess, if He can bring us by any persuasion to the full dedication of our own powers to Him, then His purpose in our lives has been realised.

II

To whom is Paul writing this urgent appeal?

1. He is writing to a Christian. He is not writing to a heathen. He is not writing to one who utterly ignores Christ and His Church. He is writing to a young man of whose conversion he has no doubt. In fact it was Paul's privilege to lead this young man into a knowledge of Jesus Christ. Timothy was his son in the Gospel and Paul loved him with the passionate devotion of a mother. It is with deep joy that he calls to remembrance the unfeigned faith that is in Timothy. He does not doubt in the least this young man's loyalty to Christ. And yet he finds it necessary to urge upon him the necessity of rekindling his fire.

2. Not only is Paul writing to a Christian, but he is writing to a Christian minister. He had been called, Paul reminds him, with a holy calling. He had known by experience the glad thrill of being a herald of the unsearchable riches of Christ. Timothy was a preacher. He was engaged in the highest of all tasks. He was occupied with the most fascinating of all labours. And yet even to this man Paul writes this urgent word: "Stir up the gift that is within thee."

III

Why did Timothy need this exhortation from Paul?

1. He needed it because he was in a hard situation.

There is never a time when Christian work is altogether easy. Let us face the fact at once that the carrying on of Christ's work in the world always has meant and always will mean struggle and conflict. It is hard to stand for Christ to-day if you stand for Him truly. It was exceedingly hard in the day in which Timothy lived. Christians were very few. To go forth as a disciple of Jesus Christ was to be in a small minority. But there was far more involved than this. It was to be scorned, to be hated, to be persecuted, to be imprisoned, oftentimes to be put to death. Thus Timothy, separated from his father in the Gospel, needed this heartening message lest, under the pressure of difficulties, he should allow his gifts to go to waste.

2. He needed this message because of his extreme youth. Timothy had never succeeded in growing up. He never could get to the place where he was impressive to look at. He was not so fortunate as some in that direction. People could easily ignore him because he seemed such a youth. But Timothy was a preacher. He had, therefore, of necessity to take some part of leadership. But how hard it was when people were always saying, as we would say to-day, "What a kid!" So much was this the case that Paul had to urge upon him not to let his youthfulness impair his usefulness. "Let no man despise thy youth," he writes. Timothy was in danger of simply dropping to the rear of the procession and saying, "Let those who are older carry on the work." God needs the old folks, but He also needs the youth. Therefore, to the young, as well as to the old, He says: "Stir up the gift that is within thee."

3. Then Timothy needed this exhortation because he was timid. Now, there are those who simply laugh at

timidity. But those who have known the agonies of it are not disposed to laugh. There are some people who do not know what it is to be timid. But there are others who are altogether different. They become unnerved at the very thought of appearing before an audience. They turn hot and cold at the mere suggestion of their taking any public part in Christian work. Timothy was such a man. He knew what it was to become quite as confused over the handling of his shaky knees as he did over the handling of his sermon.

On one occasion Paul sends this timid young preacher on a mission to Corinth. The great apostle knows that his son in the Gospel is going to have a hard time. It is easy to read between the lines how Paul's heart fairly bleeds for him. As he sees him off he gives him all the encouragement possible. He reminds him of his constant prayers for him. He reminds him also that he has written a personal letter to the Church at Corinth urging them to receive him kindly. "If Timothy come," he wrote, "see that he be with you without fear." "Be gentle with him," he seems to say. "He is very timid. Hold him up by your prayers and your sympathy. Make it as easy for him as you can. If you are disposed to be too critical of him, I fear you will frighten him out of the ministry altogether."

4. Timothy needed this exhortation because he was physically weak. Timothy was not a man of robust and vigorous body. He was subject to sick spells that left his cheeks pale and his limbs a-tremble and his energies depleted. He had an affliction of the stomach that laid him low again and again. And because it is hard to work when pain is constantly nagging at you, because it is hard to stick to your task when disease is thrusting you again and again with its sword, Paul

thought wise to urge upon Timothy the necessity of stirring up the gift of God that was within him.

Now, far be it from me to speak lightly of the heroic knights of the sick-room. Far be it from me to minimise the pain of those whose every hour is a fisticuff with some tormenting malady. But I would remind you that often we allow a slight sickness to keep us from doing our religious duties, when that same sickness would not interfere with us in the least in a matter of business or in a matter of pleasure. I would remind you further that some of the mightiest victories for God have been won by those whose lives were one long battle with physical disease.

You see that man limping his way to his task like one who has been sore wounded in the battle. He is wounded. He has been thrust through with a thorn. And that thorn no surgeon has been able to remove. It is still there jabbing at him as if in fiendish glee. It is constantly torturing him as if in sheer malice. In consequence of his painful wounds he groans and bleeds in the day and groans and bleeds in the night. But he goes on with his work. Yea, the time comes when his work seems even more effective because of his infirmities. God has spoken to him and said: "My grace is sufficient for thee. My strength is made perfect in weakness." And hear his answer: "Therefore, I take pleasure in infirmities, in reproaches, in necessities, in persecutions, in distresses for Christ's sake: for when I am weak, then am I strong."

As I walked the streets of Edinburgh not long ago, I thought of another weak-bodied hero, Robert Louis Stevenson. Whenever he took his pen to write, sickness sat close beside him. Fever flushed his cheek and made his heart beat fast. And how dry his lips became, and his head, how it ached! But still he worked and still he smiled and still he helped. He never ceased as long as life was in him to stir up his gift. A great courageous soul labouring in a tottering house. How like him this work from his own pen:

> "Under the broad and starry sky
> Dig me a grave and let me lie;
> Glad did I live and gladly die,
> And I laid me down with a will."

IV

What reason does Paul urge upon Timothy for stirring up his gift?

He does not ask him to stir up the gift that is within him because of any great financial return that is coming to him. He does not urge upon him this duty and give as a reason that he will thus be able to fill some great city pulpit. Paul himself had preached in these great cities, but his pulpit had at times been a whipping post and at other times a prison cell. He did not urge this duty upon Timothy because the task was becoming easier and opposition was altogether melting away. He offers absolutely no reason that would appeal to Timothy's personal ambition or cater in the least to his cowardice.

1. There is great need on account of great opposition. "Evil men and seducers," Paul says, "are going to wax worse and worse. There are those already, and their number will increase, that have itching ears, and they will turn away their ears from the truth and give heed unto fables." He declares further that the time will come when many will have only a form of Godli

ness without the power. They will cling to the husk and let the grain go. They will grasp at the shadow and fling away the substance.

"Now, Timothy," Paul writes, "since evil days are ahead of us, since you are quite likely to be called to serve churches many among whose membership will have itching ears, you must be prepared to act accordingly. Since you will quite likely have among your hearers those who have only a form of Godliness without the power, and since these are going to oppose your spiritual preaching and make your task exceedingly difficult, I advise that you give over the ministry and cease toiling at so hopeless an undertaking as the bringing in of the Kingdom." That would have been a natural bit of advice, but it is not what Paul says. He rather tells his young friend that, inasmuch as there are many dangers and much opposition ahead, it is highly important that he stir up the gift of God that is within him.

What effect does opposition have upon you? How do you feel toward a hard and trying and discouraging situation? The church in your neighbourhood—is it full of spiritual power, or is it a chilly and sleepy and icebound affair? Supposing that it is, will you withdraw? You will never cure it that way. Nobody helps by quitting. "Behold, I stand at the door and knock," said Jesus. "If any man will open the door and come out I will sup with him." Did I quote that right? I have quoted it the way many people seem to read it. There are tens and thousands that are letting the churches absolutely alone to-day, giving as their reason that they are so dead, so far behind the times, so useless. But Jesus did not invite us to quit. He said: "If any man will open the door, I will come in." The need of this hour is not for more folks to get out of the Church. It is for more of us to open the door and let Christ into the Church. And the greater the deadness of your church, the greater the need. And the greater the need, the more urgent the call for you to "stir up the gift that is within thee."

2. Paul urges Timothy to stir up his gift for the sake of his personal salvation. In giving himself to his task, in utilising his gift to the utmost, Paul said that Timothy would save himself. Now I do not take it that this is one of the many ways of salvation. If Timothy will not use his gifts he will lose them and lose himself as well. If Jesus Christ emphasised any one fact above all others, it was the fact that to simply keep hands off, to do nothing, is the sin of all sins. Every parable of judgment that He uttered, so far as I have been able to find out, is a parable pronounced because of a service withheld.

3. The final reason that Paul gives Timothy for investing his entire self in his task goes beyond the promise that he will save himself by so doing. The salvation of self may seem to you an unworthy motive. Then, take the next one. He said: "By so doing, you will both save yourself and them that hear you." Timothy had it in his power to be a blessing to the needy churches of his day and to the needy men and women of his day. He had it in his power to be a blessing through all the long centuries. And you have it in your power, by putting your gifts in God's hands, to save not only yourself, but to save other precious lives that are even dearer to you than your own.

V

How did Timothy treat this urgent word from St. Paul? He responded. He stirred up his gift. Paul could still write to him as he had written in earlier days: "He works the work of God, as I also do." Timothy is very timid, is he not? Yes, but he works. Is not Timothy an exceedingly young man? Yes, but he is a worker. Is that Timothy coughing? He is sick, is he not? Quite sick. Pain seems to play with him constantly, yet Timothy works. They laughed at Timothy when he tried to preach. Yes, but he did not quit. Timothy went on working.

Then one day they brought him this letter. As he read it his hands trembled—his thin, weak hands. And his cheeks, usually pale, became flushed. And big tears ran down his face till he could hardly make out the words on the parchment: "Dear Timothy: I have the sadness to inform you that all those in Asia have turned away from me. At present I am in prison in Rome. 'Demas hath forsaken me, having loved this present world.' I had a hearing before Cæsar recently, but at the trial no man stood with me. I was utterly alone. Come to me. Do your best to come before winter."

And what did this sickly, timid, youthful preacher do? He said: "Well, poor Paul. I would like to be with him to help him the best I could, but it is a long journey and I feel so bad. He is in prison too, and if I go I too am likely to get into prison. In my present state of health I think prison life would prove the death of me. I cannot go." No, that is not Timothy's response. He took his fears in his frail hands and strangled them. And when Paul went to the block there were at least two friends with him. One of them

was Luke, the beloved physician, brave, gentle Luke.
And the other was Timothy, timid, shy, retiring, sickly
Timothy.

I wonder what it would have been like to have seen
this meeting between Paul and Timothy. How the
white-haired old man rejoiced over his coming! He
was glad to see him because he was lonesome. But there
was a far deeper gladness than that. It was the joy
he had in Timothy's victory over his own fears. His
heart was singing like the strings of a violin touched
by a master because Timothy was really stirring up
the gift that was within him.

VI

How did Timothy win his fight?

1. He had much human help. Grandmother Lois
was praying for him, no doubt. And beside her in the
secret place was his mother, Eunice. Then there was
the abiding memory of Paul, his father in the faith.
And then maybe some obscure saint whose name is not
known here, but is most familiar in heaven, maybe
this obscure saint helped him. I recall one such that I
had in my congregation the first year of my ministry.
More than once, when the load was heavy and the skies
were black and the young preacher did not see how
he could get through the service, did this sweet saint
of God come to his assistance. To this day I feel the
pressure of his arm about me. To this day I hear the
whisper of his voice: "God bless you," he would say,
"God bless you. I am holding you up to-day. I am
remembering you at the Throne of Grace." And
strength came into my heart as tides come in from the
sea.

2. Above all else Timothy owed his victory to Jesus Christ Himself. In spite of weakness and timidity he dared put himself in the hands of his Lord. For His sake he ventured to stir up his gifts. And as he thus obeyed God a new power came into his life, even the power of the Holy Spirit. "For we are witnesses of these things, and so is also the Holy Spirit whom God has given to those that obey Him." And His coming always makes for a new power and a Christlike courage. "They were all filled with the Holy Spirit, and they spoke the Word of God with boldness." Thus timid Timothy became a blessing to his day and to all future centuries. Thus we too may win if we will for Christ's sake stir up the gift that is within us.

THE END